AF328463

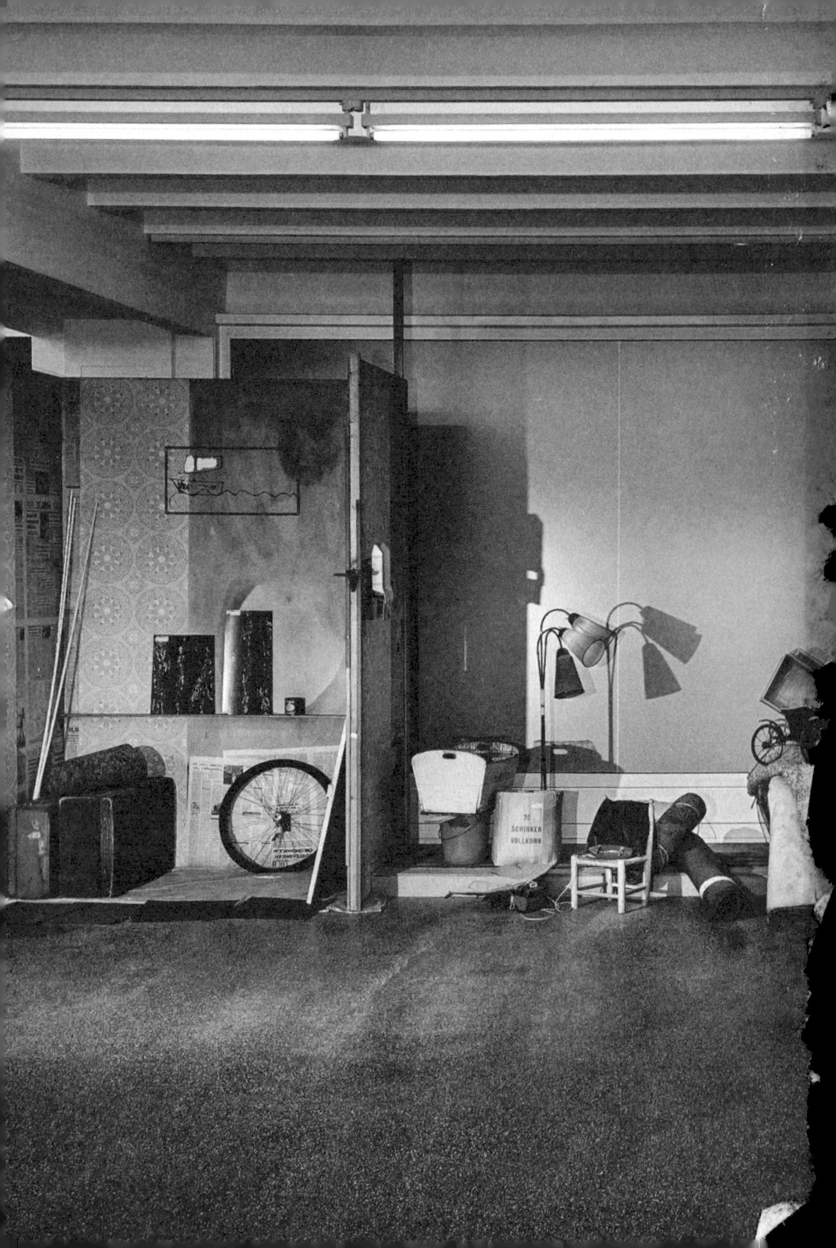

SCHINKEN
VOLLKORN

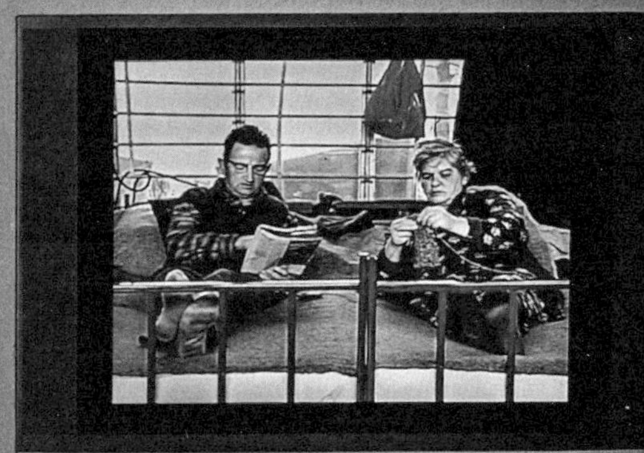

Aytac Eryılmaz, Marion von Osten, Martin Rapp, Kathrin Rhomberg, and Regina Römhild, *Projekt Migration*, 2005–2006, research and exhibition project, installation view Kölnischer Kunstverein, Cologne, photo: © Dietrich Hackenberg/lichtbild

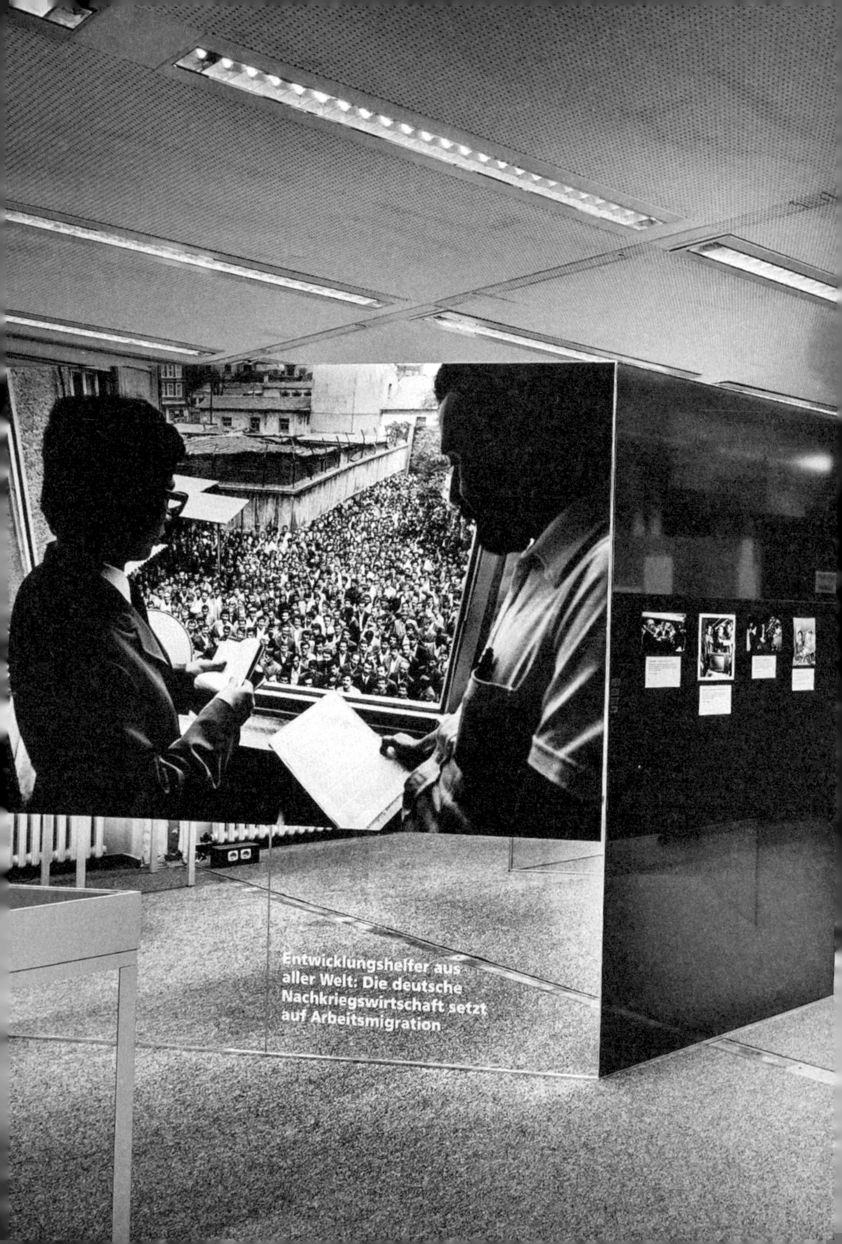

Entwicklungshelfer aus
aller Welt: Die deutsche
Nachkriegswirtschaft setzt
auf Arbeitsmigration

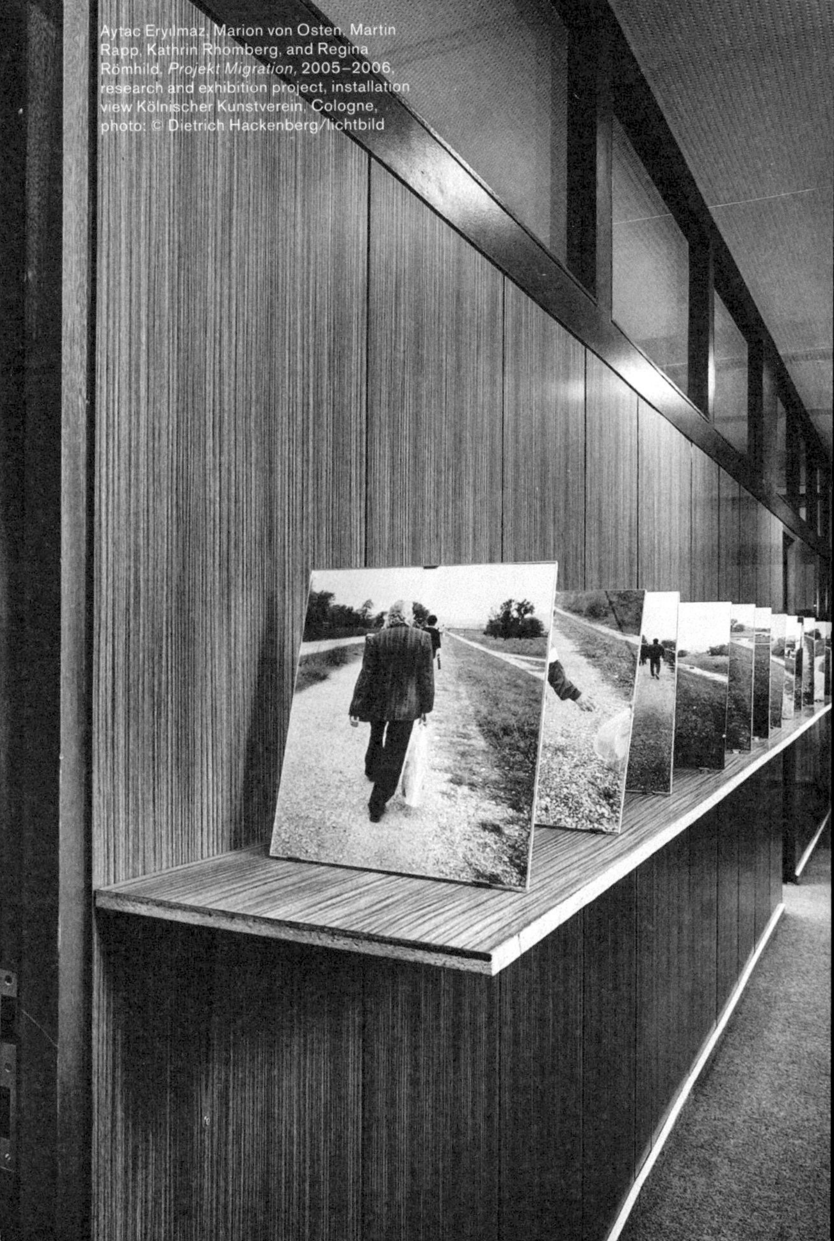

Aytaç Eryılmaz, Marion von Osten, Martin Rapp, Kathrin Rhomberg, and Regina Römhild. *Projekt Migration*, 2005–2006, research and exhibition project, installation view Kölnischer Kunstverein, Cologne, photo: © Dietrich Hackenberg/lichtbild

Marion von Osten: Once We Were Artists (A BAK Critical Reader in Artists' Practice)

Editors: Maria Hlavajova and Tom Holert
Managing Editor: Hidde van Greuningen
Research and Editorial Support: Hidde van Greuningen, Lucy Lopez, and Whitney Stark
Language Editing and Proofing: Aileen Derieg, Cielo Lutino, and Whitney Stark
Editorial Assistants: Emily Rhodes and Julia Steenhuisen
Design: Kummer & Herrman, Utrecht
Lithography and Printing: Lenoirschuring, Amsterdam
Printed in the EU

ISBN (BAK): 978-90-77288-23-8
ISBN (Valiz): 978-94-92095-14-5

Published by:
BAK, basis voor actuele kunst
Postbus 19288
NL–3501 DG Utrecht
T +31 (0)30 2316125
info@bakonline.org
www.bakonline.org

and

Valiz, book and cultural projects
Het Sieraad, Studio K34K36
Postjesweg 1
NL–1057 DT Amsterdam
T +31 (0)20 6764144
info@valiz.nl
www.valiz.nl

2017

Marion von Osten: Once We Were Artists (A BAK Critical Reader in Artists' Practice)

Edited by Maria Hlavajova and Tom Holert

Table of Contents

Maria Hlavajova and Tom Holert in Conversation with Marion von Osten
Once We Were Artists

Dedicated to the extraordinary cultural practice of Marion von Osten, this publication is the second in the *BAK Critical Reader in Artists' Practice* series, which revolves around artistic work that radically shifts perspectives and understandings of the space of art in the contemporary world. As an *artist*, feminist, organizer, curator, friend, collaborator, editor, lecturer, writer, researcher, participant, educator, comrade—in no particular order, the list could go on—von Osten's is a multifaceted practice that is as significant for the field of art and beyond as it is complex to unpack. Although never standing alone and always *in relation*, her cultural work has been key in shaping the practice of art that *is* the public sphere and political space. This reader is an attempt to draft some contours of the manifold trajectories of von Osten's work as they have unfolded over the past three decades through her many projects, and to understand—and learn from—how working from the conditions of the world can be turned into rewriting these very conditions, and become the art of constituting not just new imaginaries, but new realities.

This volume includes an array of challenging reflections on von Osten's practice, and as its co-editor and artistic director of BAK, basis voor actuele kunst in Utrecht, I would like to take this opportunity to thank all the contributors for their exceptional insights. Throughout this process, I have had the immense privilege of working with my co-editor Tom Holert, and I feel particularly moved by and grateful for the depth of knowledge that he is always prepared to share, as well as his thoughtful, patient way of guiding us through the process of making this publication. I would like to thank BAK's team for their commitment to our work, and in particular Lucy Lopez, Hidde van Greuningen, and Whitney Stark for their care and dedication to this book. Most importantly, I want to thank Marion von Osten for her work and unceasing energy in questioning just about everything, making our working together not only assuredly exciting, but steering it toward no less than wanting to change the world together, and embarking on a path of *becoming more* around that very mission. With this in mind, and before delving into the texture of the book, I invite you to read through the conversation below, composed of fragments from many exchanges between Marion, Tom, and me while bringing this volume to life.

Maria Hlavajova

<u>Tom Holert</u>: Let us start from this publication series. Maria approached me, three years ago, to think about artists who could be discussed in the follow-up to the volume about Rabih Mroué,[1] one criterion being that the reader focus on a practice that has not yet been covered thoroughly, mainly because it escapes the conventional parameters of art writing, art publishing, and even theory. I proposed Marion von Osten. I see Marion's as quintessentially such a practice of art; it is as unique as it is persistent in questioning art's extant categories, as well as in its approaches toward art, toward curating, and toward the production of knowledge. I wonder to what extent this opportunity to examine Marion's work in depth corresponds with your own institutional quest, Maria, at and with BAK, which you see as an ongoing process of instituting away from the settled conventions of the art institution. Does this series support this endeavor in *instituting otherwise*, as you call it?

1   Maria Hlavajova and Jill Winder, eds.,
*Rabih Mroué: A BAK Critical Reader in
Artists' Practice* (Utrecht and Rotterdam:
BAK, basis voor actuele kunst and post
editions, 2012).

Maria Hlavajova: I am indeed driven by a question I consider to be one of the largest urgencies of our time, namely: How do we engage in processes of instituting otherwise so as to envision and actuate infrastructures in art that have, maintain, and expand upon a robust stake in the rethinking of, and working through, the fabric of the contemporary? I see this proposition of instituting otherwise in Marion's avowal in the title of this publication; for "once we were artists"—although witty and a tiny bit nostalgic at first sight—is in my view a radical call to reclaim the notion of the artist for our time *differently* than how we got to know it. It is an enthralling statement suggesting that seemingly unmovable fictions—such as that of the (heroic, male) figure of the (modernist) artist—must be reconsidered in the face of present-day challenges and in sync with the political, cultural, economic, environmental, and other recompositionings underway, specifically given their transversal links to gender, class, race, sexuality, ethnicity, religion, and so on. It is under these very conditions that, alongside the notion of the artist, the (art) institution must be recomposed, as much as how we understand and approach (the notion of) the public, the audience. In this respect, it seems of utmost importance to me to inquire into how the "we" in the subjectivities constituted through collective aesthetico-political experiments like those in Marion's practice is brought to life, much like the "we" in "once we were artists." Aimed at undoing the "us/them" divide (whereas "us" would be the artists and other intellectuals and "they," the consumers of these practices), such practices demand that art claims stakes in the public sphere and political space. That it be, or is, not entertainment or spectatorship, but something of vital significance in an era of disenchantment, structural injustice, and precarity: to put it boldly, art as access to political life.

Marion von Osten: These are indeed grand challenges of our times. We need to begin from asking *why* the notion of the artist is in question, or why it should be. Approaching the topic with a feminist understanding, there has been a specific idea of "the artist," which was re-introduced when I was at the art academy in the 1980s: the male genius. Reinforced by a world-view defined by the nuclear family and its gender binaries in which I grew up, becoming an artist was a strange impossibility. I took this impossibility personally and turned it into an urgency. Thinking that the only way to work through it was, well, to work through it, to redefine it.

TH: You are now speaking about the late 1980s?

MvO: The mid-1980s, actually; post-punk in Cold-War West Germany, the era in which the paradigms shaping subcultures were no longer so much a driving force and when the "end of history" was palpable. You did not know where and how to direct your desires. And you were absolutely nobody in society. No future. There was a strange emptiness; a void. It was from here that it has become very important to question the notion of the artist as an antidote to the endless delving in the ideology of impossibility. From a feminist perspective, it has meant opening ways of looking at how one's own work relates to the work of others, and how our work depends on those others— friends, colleagues, institutions; for we cannot work alone. It brought about a new form of practice, one could say, of collaboration as a political act, in which interdependencies were made visible—even if by the seemingly simple act of naming, of acknowledging all involved.

It was in this period, the end of the 1980s, that I had the opportunity to live in New York City as a young artist. This was incredibly empowering. Being able to see Martha Rosler's *If*

You Lived Here…(1989); to see Group Material's exhibition *Group Material: Democracy* (1988–1989), both at the Dia Art Foundation; to see the film *Privilege* (1990) by Yvonne Rainer. And to witness the attention and crucial debates that these projects raised and the importance the art institutions assigned to such critical artistic practice! These were prospective endeavors working with minorities, debating critical issues such as homelessness and democracy and ageism and sexism and racism and elitism. . . a practice of becoming minoritarian in a society in spite—or because—of its global claim to power.

TH: You were invited to New York by The Kitchen, an innovative nonprofit that went from an artist collective to a creative force shaping the cultural field in the United States and beyond, which had a strong orientation toward new media practices. Were you invited because you were involved in video and new media at the time?

MvO: The Kitchen embraced early explorations with new media indeed, but it has always engaged in interdisciplinary art forms. This was an opportunity for me to be close to experimentations in music, performance, documentary, theater, collaborations. It completely changed my perspective on the potentials of art; which resonated strongly with my intuitions. As part of my exodus from the art academy, I started to work with new media, with computers. Nothing seemed further removed from art practice back then: the computer was an absolutely distant and unthinkable "bad object" in art. But our way of engaging computers—together with the artist group MetaAusStelLung— was to simultaneously counter this idea of a technological progress that was to be gradually embraced by the field. This may sound as an absolute paradox, and to some extent it was: in this rift between these developments, it was a Dada approach to the first personal computers.

TH: Was this approach directed against the emerging establishment of computer art, new media art, electronica, the Center for Art and Media in Karlsruhe (ZKM), and the like? The environment that, in a way, became quite dominant at the time for certain parts of the cultural world and was engaged in shaping a techno-savvy, yet at times depoliticized and neo-futurist alternative to a certain mainstream, painting-based idea of contemporary art in the 1980s/early 1990s?

MvO: For sure. And there was another dominant narrative taking shape in the art world at that time, the critique of which influenced the emergence of practices of which I have been part. This was the figure of the artist as a role model for neoliberal subjectivity and subjectification as the contours of neoliberalism took firm shape in the 1980s and early 1990s. When I worked at Shedhalle Zürich,[2] there we engaged with a specifically new form of capitalist critique, and tested it out in exhibitions and other projects, making crossroads with feminist economists, and realizing how seemingly simple questions querying the immediate contexts of our lives became extremely difficult to tackle: What does this term "globalization" want to express? And who has the right to it? What actually is a market? Who gives shape to cognitive capitalism? And how come these make such totalizing claims to our lives and practices? We somehow had to find our own way within these emerging constellations, and develop our own strategies to deal with what has turned out to be a complete takeover of critical ideas and concepts. That's what defined my generation's 1990s: a struggle to work through what was superimposed upon counter-practices; new economic-social realities that we needed to first understand and digest, so that we could determine how to, if at all, move about them.

2   Von Osten was the curator at Shedhalle
Zürich, Zurich between 1996–1998.

Maria Hlavajova and Tom Holert in Conversation with Marion von Osten Once We Were Artists

<u>MH</u>: But isn't this something of equal concern today? This reality of continuous hostile takeover of critical ideas, concepts, and positions by neoliberal ideology?

<u>MvO</u>: With this comparison you run a risk of failing to notice the term "creativity" appearing in our lives and monopolizing, through "creative industries," the conditions of both life and work. Originating outside of our own practices, it has suddenly become somewhat required to comply with this enactment of "creativity," not just for cultural producers, but for all members of society. It has become an "imperative" to seamlessly link life and work together, like artists have always done, to make life productive—much like how we have posited through the project *Be Creative! The Creative Imperative* (2002–2003)[3] that inquired into the shifts from the utopian ideal of self-creation to its becoming a social obligation. The violent imposition of creativity upon all members of society, together with the expansion of flexibilized labor and freelance work, has had far-reaching consequences that we saw were shaping the conditions of precarity across a wide spectrum of society. These concerns galvanized a very active field of feminists, economists, and other practitioners, who invested their artistic and intellectual labor in *fostering* and *intervening into* the emerging societal debate on precarity. Our goal was to create ruptures in this reality with discussions, reading groups, films, exhibitions, books, and so on, involving cultural practitioners across the formerly divisive disciplinary lines. Today, we see this genealogy of transversal practices reflected in major projects in our field, as they rely on collectivities far beyond the narrow understanding of the artist and engage quite diverse actors—like curator Anselm Franke's projects at Haus der Kulturen der Welt in Berlin or FORMER

[3] *Be Creative! The Creative Imperative*, 2002–2003, Museum für Gestaltung, Zurich, conceptualized by Marion von Osten and Peter Spillmann and realized in collaboration with Labor k3000, Zurich.

WEST[4] that you, Maria, carried out transnationally—intervening in the hegemonic concept of culture. We could not have foreseen in the 1990s and early 2000s that counter-practices would come to shape major events, including the biennials and other large-scale international projects.

TH: It seems to me that, although building on the premises and achievements of institutional critique, you have left, in a way, its modes for a new practice of using—and changing—the existing infrastructures of cultural institutions. Acting as a cultural producer in the sense you claim this notion for yourself (a notion that embraces a specific yet evolving set of skills, interests, urgencies, and networks that reaches beyond those of "the artist" or "the curator"), the political economy of the institution became material to be worked upon and transformed in the process of each project. Now that we are zigzagging randomly through the fragments of the past three decades: How would you consider the institutional conditions you met in the 1990s? There was, for example, this moment when Kunst-Werke—now KW Institute for Contemporary Art, Berlin—was becoming a rather visible but still emerging art institution in post-reunification Berlin, and it was at its best in my view when "hijacked," even if for a short while, by a network of (mostly) women cultural producers from different fields, who then organized the *when tekkno turns to sound of poetry* exhibition (1995).[5]

MvO: This was mainly the achievement of art historian and critic Sabeth Buchmann and philosopher Juliane Rebentisch.

4   FORMER WEST, 2008–2016, was a long-term, transnational research, education, publishing, and exhibition project developed and organized by BAK, basis voor actuele kunst, Utrecht. See www.formerwest.org and Maria Hlavajova and Simon Sheikh, eds., *Former West: Art and the Contemporary After 1989* (Cambridge, MA and Utrecht: MIT Press and BAK, basis voor actuele kunst, 2016).
5   *when tekkno turns to sound of poetry: Technologie, Feminismus, Konzept-Kunst & Politik* (Technology, Feminism, Conceptual Art & Politics), 1995, Kunst-Werke, Berlin, initiated by Sabeth Buchmann, Renate Lorenz, and Juliane Rebentisch.

TH: They enabled an already existing and practicing network to materialize in this two-part exhibition, first at Shedhalle Zürich (1994) and then in Berlin at Kunst-Werke a year later. At the time, this was a significant effort of working both with and against the foreseeable future of this institution. Then you moved to Zurich to work at Shedhalle as a curator, where you had this rare opportunity to work with an institution that had a rather hybrid identity—it was neither a *Kunstverein* nor a conventional art center, but an institution in constant flux—due to its history of being part of Zurich's leftist compound Rote Fabrik. It has had a history of radical exhibition practices and a different, strongly feminist, anti-racist, anti-biased profile. This was the much politicized environment that you then entered with a new perspective and energy. I find it interesting because with artist Renate Lorenz and curator Justin Hoffmann[6] you changed it even further for it to become better suited to your interests and for the kinds of projects you had in mind. How did that happen?

MvO: You make me think of a film that was shown in the *Projekt Migration* exhibition (2005–2006)[7] about women occupying a factory—*Pierburg: Ihr Kampf ist unser Kampf* (Pierburg: Their Struggle Is Our Struggle) by Edith Schmidt and David Wittenberg (1974/1975); a still from the film with two super cool migrant women, one smoking a cigarette, is featured on the project's publication cover. Every time I think about the film or this image, I am reminded of a situation, or better, I recognize this situation *bodily*. There is something familiar. This body-space relation, how the women are sitting on the still machines, chatting and exchanging about the next step

6   Lorenz and Hoffmann were curators at Shedhalle Zürich, Zurich between 1994–1997 and 1997–2000, respectively.
7   *Projekt Migration*, 2005–2006, project exhibition at Kölnischer Kunstverein and various locations in Cologne, artistic direction by Marion von Osten and Kathrin Rhomberg.

to take. This reminds me, as I have found later, of Kunst-Werke Berlin in the times of *when tekkno*! An embodied knowledge—what it means to *occupy* a space with your body, to take it over, even if for just a while. It's not just the act of intervening into the program; rather, a spontaneous physical *force* of sorts fills the space. Especially in this project's second installment, Juliane and Sabeth *gave* the exhibition to all the involved artists and cultural producers. We were all present, living in—inhabiting, dwelling in—this environment. It was for sure not the Kunst-Werke of today; it was an artist-run space with another sort of energy, which allowed for this very same sensation that the image of the women migrant workers emanates: that of when the machines stop and momentarily there is an opportunity to fill the space with another possibility—even if fleetingly.

This compares as well with the energy of a new emergence I experienced in New York around Group Material, for example; this strong sense of belonging, a sense of something meaning-ful—in contrast to harsh competition in the art market. This very energy prompted me to apply for the job at Shedhalle—besides, to be sure, this being the way to make ends meet—Shedhalle as a place working at that time with extraordinary artists like Brigitta Kuster and Pauline Boudry, among others. It was a place of and with artistic knowledge; where being an artist meant a particular attitude—an artistic perspective, one could say—in the way one deals with words, with visual and material culture, but also in terms of creating situations or questioning them. It is to be an artist *otherwise*, to concur with Maria's way of putting it.

MH: Thinking through your work in and with existing art institu-tions, it appears as if your projects take place mostly at the moment institutions transition from one working paradigm to another. You seem to intervene, whether as a participating

artist or as a curator or educator, into that vital moment of
another possibility, of the possibility presented by the "in-
between," before the organization stabilizes new routines and
binding protocols and pre-set agendas: not only with *when
tekkno*, as you describe; so was *Projekt Migration* commissioned in the early days of the German Federal Cultural
Foundation, and the *In the Desert of Modernity: Colonial
Planning and After* project (2008–2009)[8] also, in my view,
was part of the process of critical institutional reorientation
of Haus der Kulturen der Welt.

MvO: I am fascinated by the "interim" and the opportunities
it offers; indeed, it is a moment in the life of an institution that
presents this precious opening for different practice. And so it
was as well, now that I am thinking of it, at Shedhalle; I joined
the team of Renate and curator Sylvia Kafhesy to bridge the
curatorial constellations with Justin and artist Ursula Biemann,
and I think that is precisely what allowed us to work together
differently. But it is not to say that this was received by the public without objections; there has always been a lot of criticism
around feminist and critical practices; a price to pay, perhaps,
for putting the extant constellations under pressure through
asking confronting questions—of ourselves and of others.

TH: Where does this mode of questioning—of the persona
of the artist, of the art institution, and the possibility of art in
society—come from? Where do you see the origins of it?

MvO: Modernism. I think we need to ask ourselves if we have
moved beyond it.

8   *In the Desert of Modernity: Colonial
Planning and After*, 2008–2009, exhibition
and conference, Haus der Kulturen der Welt,
Berlin and La Fabrique Culturelle des

Anciens Abattoirs de Casablanca,
Casablanca, curated by Marion von Osten in
collaboration with Tom Avermaete and
Serhat Karakayali.

TH: So if modernism, is there still a kind of progressivism involved?

MH: Then it would mean the future is still possible! But what future?!

MvO: To an extent, yes, there is a progressivism involved. It might sound paradoxical in the context in which we are speaking here. But reconsider the avant-garde mode of thinking: you cannot understand modernist artists without being aware of their efforts to always leave existing practices behind. Counter-practices I have been involved in are still echo-spaces of these histories, as even my question is what would be beyond.

TH: But isn't the idea of futurity or future-orientation that you talk about traceable rather to the second wave feminist art of the early 1970s? I am thinking of the Feminist Art Program at CalArts, California Institute of the Arts in Santa Clarita, and CalArts's 1972 *Womanhouse* as key examples. There, the women artists, under the guidance of Judy Chicago and Miriam Schapiro, were actually turning against the imperatives of both the art market and the modernist art system by, as you described it, inventing a new kind of practice: a collaboration-based developing of self-organized structures and translocal networks. This involved organizing new archives of feminist art—slide registries at the time—to fill the void of art by women in any repository, historical or contemporary. The kind of art produced, the kind of practice that developed there was very much against the grain of the dominant post-minimalist vain, and included the embrace of crafts and of performance that was coming out of consciousness raising groups, and so on— a practice very much focused on the continued production in and of collectivity.

MvO: But still, when you want to discuss what modernism *does* to the art paradigm, you need to admit that the modernist artist puts the art paradigm in question. Modernism created a new methodology. In some ways, it leaves, integrates, transforms, synthesizes the art paradigm. This is a slight provocation, perhaps, but I want to point out that this discussion is near impossible in such generic, if convenient, all-encompassing terms. Much in the same vein of critique, you could see that the incorporation of crafts in and *as* art in your example—a structural feature of modernism—was, to say the least, problematic. These instances must be viewed carefully in each particular case, taking their concrete loci—geopolitical, cultural, gender, class, and other—into consideration, especially if you are interested in finding a translation of vernacular practices, such as crafts or informal living settlements, that is other than mere assimilation into the institution of art or architecture.

TH: I am indeed wary in regard to the available definitions of modernism and modernity; this has always been a modernism countered by the modernist—or avant-garde, rather—artists themselves, in particular with the modernism of urban renewal, of colonial or metropolitan architecture, and so on. Maybe this tension, operating within modernism and repeatedly gesturing at the transgression or destruction of the category as such, its dialectic if you will, continues to be in this kind of critical mode of replacing certain commonly agreed-upon definitions, as the tensions within the modern project—both the "colonial modern past" and the "global modern present," to use your terminology—are being negotiated; a process, to be sure, of struggle and conflict.

MvO: Well, you point out a very important question of how to negotiate and make the present; one that I have tried to tackle but do not have a convincing answer to as of yet. With the *In the Desert of Modernity* project, seeing modernist architecture as a device of knowledge, I looked precisely at these concerns at the time of anticolonial uprisings that formed a new geopolitical paradigm in the post-World War II era. Here, colonial modernity meant an expression of the grand belief in the "planability" of a society, for which the colonial territories functioned as laboratories for experimentations of ostentatious proportions. The critique of (high) modernism from within and the hostility toward the hierarchical impositions of urban development that came about in the era of decolonization led to a shift, providing an impulse for (western) architects to attempt thinking from the territory, from the local context, from the ground, as it were. This resulted in ethnological and anthropological fieldwork with a very colonial outlook at the end; an outcome of a bizarre series of efforts to learn from "non-experts," as they called them—from the competencies of other sorts, in other words—how everyday life was organized, yet barring these very same locals from participating in any related decision-making processes. These appeals to "non-experts" included the *baumeister* organizing a building process without overseeing the overall design in conceptual terms. That is how architecture without architects[9] came about, installing a massive crack in the modernist conception of top-down architectural planning. I think three types of practices—or three paradigms, if you will—have emerged from here. One has continued to uphold the architect as the hegemonic figure who designs, using all this knowledge accumulated on the ground, to "improve" western design—and to design even more; it is a trajectory from within which a great deal of satellite cities have been built. The second says: "Let's look at what people are doing," and then translates the study of local vernacular settlements into a

9   Marion von Osten, "Architecture Without Architects – Another Anarchist Approach," *e-flux journal*, no. 6 (May 2009), online at: http://www.e-flux.com/journal/06/61401/architecture-without-architects-another-anarchist-approach/.

mode of western knowledge that ends up packaged mostly in product design or books as commodity-intellectual work. The third paradigm concerns participation, proposing a form of governance and architectural practice that would "allow" people to have their say in the architectural process. My questions are as follows: Are we still moving between these three options, or have we moved beyond them? Do they still define our vocabulary—from theory to everyday life—in architecture, in artistic practice, and in how we conceive of institutional infrastructure? Or have we moved toward new forms of organizing? Have we moved beyond—and if so, what is this "beyond"?

MH: This thinking about "architecture without architects," or, formulated conversely, if you will, a condition in which everybody is an architect, seems to open up an interstice for reflecting on another political possibility. For here, the notions of both coloniality and modernity get redefined through self-built, spontaneous, makeshift, improvised, commonplace practices of bringing to life the infrastructures for living and being in common—be it by building or squatting or inhabiting or reclaiming or hacking or just simply using whatever there is— that dissent from the expert cultures as we have known them. I recall our previous discussions on the notion of the *open form* as a method—the form to which everybody has a competence to add, intervene, change, adapt—confronting our field with what you have called an "unfolding practice." This brings about another logic altogether, and I wonder to what extent you see parallels among architects in the discussion of the colonial modern and artists?

MvO: This shift in perspective indeed suggests possibilities for reworking a number of political concepts, amongst which that of the artist. And it is indeed critical to keep asking who exactly "the expert" is, what we understand under the notion of

an expert culture when modernity and colonialism get reformu-
lated not just through informal daily practices, but, radically, by
mobilities and migrations in their various expressions, including the present-day war-driven refugee force that puts under
pressure "established" and "settled" societies, transforming
these societies into interlinked transnational political spaces.
It is less about a political possibility, as you put it, than about a
new political demand. That is how I see the making of the present: through the migratory reality that shapes globalization
from below, through the network of micro-economies and the
flows of capital through Western Union that assure that small-
scale infrastructures are built both here and somewhere else,
that survival of family members is assured at distant places,
and so on. We, the so-called cultural practitioners, too, are all
in different places and in different collaborations than we were
in the 1990s, as we are driven by the urgencies we share in
common with others: self-organized in hybrid constellations
not just with those who once were artists, but with people from
very diverse backgrounds and places.

MH: Could these hybrid constellations around common concerns be seen as critical—everyday, hands-on—commentaries
on the imperatives of colonial modernity? That is, through
practice, that which puts under pressure notions such as
authorship, ownership, spectatorship, and, as you said, expertise? And how about, for example, the format of the exhibition;
is it still capable of being a critical platform for accommodating
the urgencies of the present?

MvO: I share these questions and concerns and likewise I am
still interested in exhibition making as a practice for commoning
and diversifying ideas and social relations; the exhibition as an
open form that moves us away from stable bodies of knowledge,
from what we already know, from delivering on the protocols of

cognitive capitalism. And if I speak about ideas and relations, it is about imagining and testing out how we could be together differently, which is not a matter of purely artistic invention, but of movement; movement in and out of the fields we know as art, theory, politics. It is this transversality that interests me, and this is not limited to exhibitions or events or projects, but includes new forms of self-organized infrastructures, micro-organization as I have called them, through which difference is organized. Both within and beyond the field of art and architecture, I see new collective structures of small, translocal micro-organizations that are neither artist collectives nor artist-run initiatives, nor art centers that the colonial modern used to produce, and that are being generated for research, production, learning, gathering, dissemination, and action. They mark a new experimental field that is transversally and transculturally interconnected, both geopolitically and across the fields of art, architecture, design, pop culture, crafts, research, Internet culture, pedagogy, and institutional work, acting in the refusal of a monocultural conception of art and experimenting, through affective practice, with propositional vocabularies as to how to move about the present. Informed largely by feminist perspectives and the practices of de- and off-centering, these micro-organizations escape categorizations settled in and by the field of contemporary art. Any attempt at definition falls short of capturing their dynamics and radical diversity, and, as such, does disservice to the socio-cultural work they deliver. As platforms for convening, they begin from asking: What do we have in common? What do we have in common, not just amongst cultural producers, but with other societal members? That is a pathway into other modes of doing culture—culture in common; one in which those of us who once were artists have a lot to offer and share, albeit without taking charge or ownership of any such process or relationality underway.

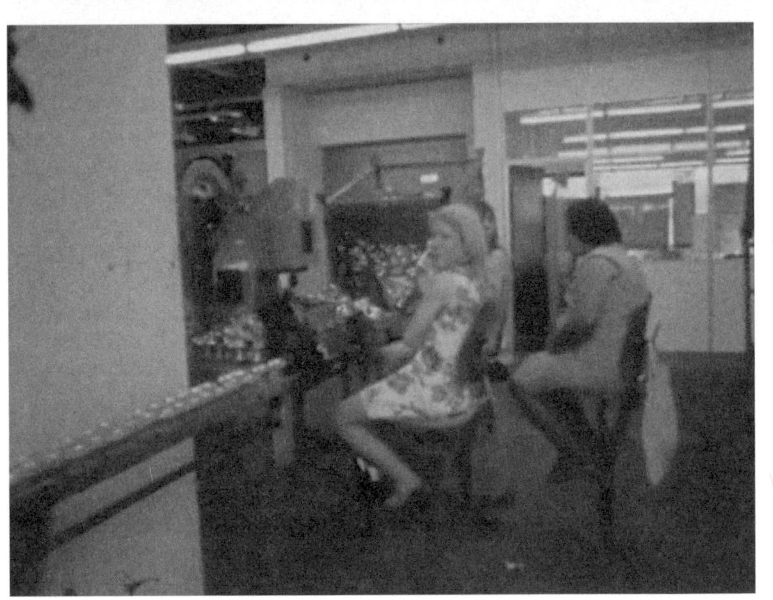

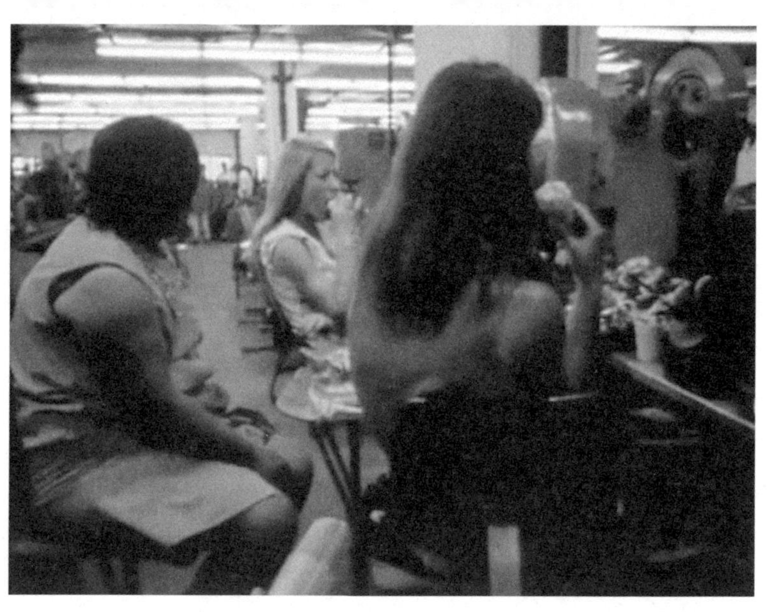

Pierburg: Ihr Kampf ist unser Kampf
(1974/1975), directed by Edith Schmidt and
David Wittenberg, video stills, courtesy Die
Buchmacherei

Tom Avermaete, Serhat Karakayali, and Marion
von Osten, *In the Desert of Modernity:
Colonial Planning and After*, 2009, research
and exhibition project, installation view
Fabrique Culturelle des Anciens Abattoirs
de Casablanca, Casablanca, photo: Marion
von Osten

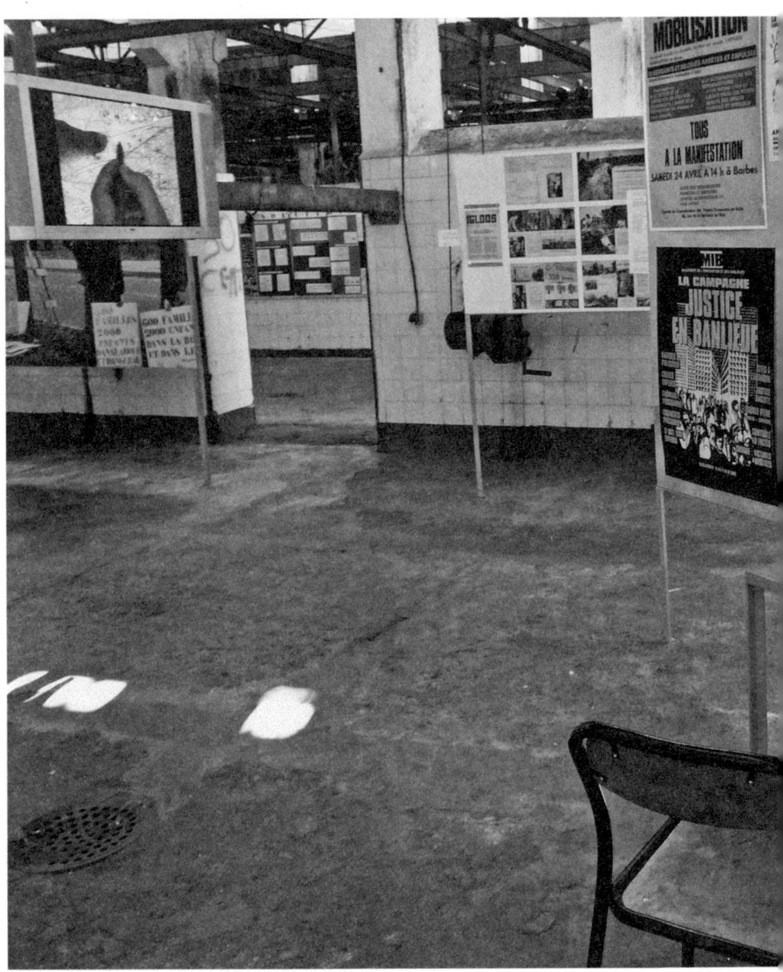

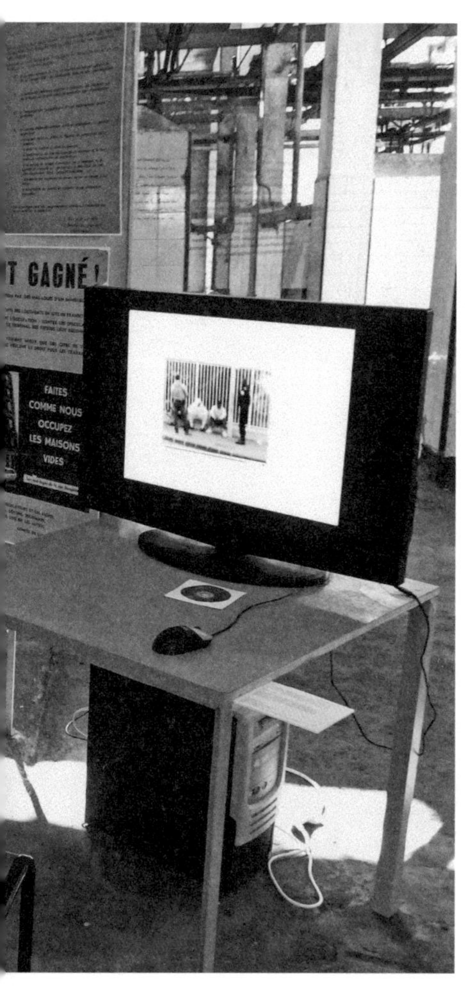
T GAGNÉ !
FAITES
COMME NOUS
OCCUPEZ
LES MAISONS
VIDES

Kader Attia and
Marion von Osten
Interview

<u>Kader Attia</u>: This conversation could begin on an American road between Los Angeles and San Antonio. You know, the endless roads scattered with old cheap motels, like the ghosts of the modern dream designed in 1950s aesthetics and acting as a link to a so-called era of great progress. Back when the west was a symbol of conquest, and capitalism was an ideal. . .

I thought about you when I was in San Antonio. I visited several seventeenth-century Spanish Christian missions, or rather what was left of them. Most of these beautiful architectures can easily be compared to any Mediterranean Christian architecture. If you remember that Spain had been colonized by Muslims for five centuries, you can see and understand better how Spanish colonial style took root in America thanks to characteristic Arabian-Muslim vernacular architecture. This brings up my first question to you, instigator of the amazing project *In the Desert of Modernity: Colonial Planning and After* (2008–2009): Is colonialism responsible for the evolution of architecture through and toward a modern agenda?

<u>Marion von Osten</u>: Historically speaking, the purpose of any colonial plan was to create new settlements and to bring new housing solutions for a distinct non-indigenous population arriving from some other part of the world. When I say "distinct," I mean separated. These constructions were created for colonists—colonial settlers—and separated them from other, already existing habitations and social communities. The colonial settlement is thus a biopolitical entity, a satellite community in a partially unfamiliar area and one that does not want to mingle. But as it has been proved, this will to segregate itself from the local environment always fails. In relation to your comment about Spanish missions, I just visited the historical Franciscan missions in California, where I learned that the church and cloister in Santa Barbara, for example, were built by local Comanche tribes.

This is important, for the Franciscan monks would not have survived without the Comanche, as the latter fed them when they arrived in the eighteenth century. Also, the First Nations handled the construction of the cloister, church, and houses while teaching the monks how to craft textiles and pottery. After the mission was established, the natives were given free food and Christian education as a reward for their labor. Here it becomes interesting because, even though their survival was completely dependent on the Comanche's local knowledge and food, the monks assumed native people to be naive people who needed education and to be taken care of. This is what makes any colonial civilizing mission so paradoxical, as it depends on local people's knowledge, yet it does not acknowledge them as de jure subjects. This is also expressed in architecture. You can find some transcultural translations in these specific places. The church design is based on drawings from Vitruvius's famous architecture book from ancient Rome. However, the monks only followed Virtruvius's model of a Roman temple because they had no other example. Plus, in this strange church-temple you can find small transpositions of Comanche ornaments on the ceiling and Mexican figurative elements beside paintings with belated baroque aesthetics. This eclecticism or conscious or unconscious translation—praised as California's multicultural heritage—conceals that Christian and Roman aesthetic traditions remained hegemonic, while other transcultural elements remained marginal. This hierarchy in the use of aesthetics is mostly expressed in the settlement designed by monks for First Nations converts. The Comanche housing facility next to the cloister showed very modern lines; it was designed like a camp built in a grid-like structure. This small-scale housing grid, specifically created for the natives, echoes philosopher Jacques Rancière's words about distributing the sensible[1] and, therefore, about domination.

1 Jacques Rancière, *The Politics of Aesthetics: The Distribution of the Sensible,* trans. Gabriel Rockhill (London: Continuum International Publishing Group, 2004).

Even when we need to constantly highlight transfers and exchanges created through specific cross-continental encounters like between the Comanche and Franciscans, as they later
became a particular Christian group following early communist
ideals, architecture still reveals this hierarchy and dominance
that denied the Comanche's rights to be represented as gifted
fishers, sailors, and farmers or as spiritual collaborators, political
allies, or even fighters. When the economic and military interests
of Spain, Russia, the Mexican Empire, and, later, the United
States caused never-ending conflicts on this territory, the first
to suffer abuses and die were the Comanche.

And there, again, what is striking is the specific rationality in
the Comanche settlement from the Santa Barbara mission,
for it consequently used this same grid pattern. The grid, as a
planning principle, is to be found in the organization of most
colonial processes. It already existed during the Roman Empire,
so in the end, Spain was not the first one to use it. This grid
structure is an artificial and rational pattern free from any context
and can be expanded any time. It is about expansion, identifying
and conquering new territories in any part of the world. It is
about housing a great number of people, about future population
growth, since the grid can easily spread into any direction. It is
also the same pattern as the famous Philadelphia grid developed
during the eighteenth century, and yet when you come to studying colonial cities, you realize it had already been adopted for
years in each and every one of them. A village or town based
on this structure is the very basis for creating any new artificial
site or, just like in Caracas, for example, a colonial town similar
to many other places you might add to your own research.
New town planning and the grid structure that are nowadays
perceived as high modernist aesthetic items were brought
into building practices and modern discourse through colonial
expansion.

KA: Your answer reminds me of how Spanish Emperor Carlos Quinto ordered Mexico's city planning, following a parallel and perpendicular street pattern. And do you know why? To have control over the population. When Tenochtitlan was taken over by the Spanish they decided to slowly develop their new city on top of the former Aztec capital. These days, some architecture from these colonial settlement projects, such as the *Catedral del Zócalo*, are slowly falling down because of the old Aztec temples underneath. These "conscious and unconscious forms of cultural translations" seem to be another kind of "repairing," because they act as endless cultural translations from one cultural space/time to another. To come back to this colonial settlement planning and to why it reminds me of the first urban plans in Mexico during the early sixteenth century that aimed at controlling people, do you sometimes think that architecture consists of filling a given space, while actually it is the contrary, thus making urban plans more important than the buildings themselves in the end? Do you think that projects led by you and me, among others, like the architect and urban planner Michel Écochard in Casablanca, aim at controlling people through some vertical panopticon or, on the contrary, providing intimate spaces for the inhabitants? And eventually, what drew them to totally close their own balconies?

MvO: Yes, I think you are right, colonial settlement is mainly about organization and urban landscaping, but not so much about establishing an individual house for one particular settler. Biopolitical implications are quite obvious when we think of them as closed entities. What most people ignore, as your question pointed out, is that this vision of colonial planning has considerably influenced modern building concepts like, for instance, city planner Ebenezer Howard's famous garden city. A book entitled *A View of the Art of Colonization: In Letters Between a Statesman and a Colonist* (1849), edited and co-written by

Edward Gibbon Wakefield, which also served as propaganda to convince the British government to build a settlers' colony in New Zealand, mainly influenced Howard's concept. But the latter's goal with the garden city that actually started his career in the US before being published in the United Kingdom went even further than its colonial blueprint. The idea was to sustain, through a satellite city concept, "a healthy, natural, and economic combination of town and country life"[2] thanks to balanced working and relaxing times. This concept aimed at getting away from the contentious relations between industrialization and countryside. Just like in future replicas of the garden city—such as the satellite city or the *cité nouvelle*—life, production, and education were strongly connected. Moreover, spatial organization of confined islands, segregated from the heart of the city and from other social groups, must have been based around new ideas about labor conditions and accumulating wealth as well. In Howard's original vision of a confined settlement, discipline and control were obviously part of the strategy. It is also strongly related to hygienic and epidemic argumentations. Only later was consumption added to the garden-city movement, following new town-planning systems created in the twentieth century. From then on, the new town emerged not as a sign of total enclosure, but as a place that was organized from A to Z. The principle of neighborhood units also appeared there and then developed in the US with urban planner Clarence Stein.

When living in Casablanca under French protectorate, Marshal of France and colonial administrator Louis Hubert Gonzalves Lyautey followed ideas close to Northern American industrial development plans and Howard's garden city concept in his

2   Ebenezer Howard, *Garden Cities of To-morrow*, second ed. (Adelaide: ebooks@ Adelaide, 2012), p. 11, online at: https:// ebooks.adelaide.edu.au/h/howard/ ebenezer/garden_cities_of_to-morrow/ index.html.

vision of the European colonial town, Casablanca. This concept, first introduced in European cities, was later used as a strategy to shut the local community out of the center when building what they called the *Habous* neighborhood or the new medina. Later on in the 1940s, Verlieer, a French town planner and socialist, appropriated the garden-city model again in his new planning of the huge Aïn Chock settlement, a fantasy of a Moroccan village using the grid plan; local workers then lived far away from the heart of Casablanca. A few years later, Écochard established a housing grid for his constructions —applying the "Housing for the Greatest Number" principle— because of the increasing number of colonial factories or even service workers. This housing grid, as the main instrument for new urban neighborhoods, was also meant to replace the numerous slums from the late 1940s to the mid-1950s that were mostly inhabited by rural migrants. In fact, the large-scale housing programs were the French protectorate's attempts to build modern settlements for the colonized just when anti-colonial uprising emerged as Morocco obtained independence in 1956. In those times of resistance, the French urban planning services strategies varied from reordering the slums (*restructuration*) to temporary re-housing (*relogement*) while also creating new housing estates with controlled rents (*habitations à loyer modéré*), all according to Écochard's grid. His master plan applied notions of "culturally specific" housing, making—according to his vision—local construction practices the starting point for developing a variety of housing typologies adapted to each category of inhabitants. These categories were still confined to already existing definitions of cultural and racial differences. However, it was only under colonial rules that categorization reinforced and was turned into a means of exercising governmental power. Écochard's plan divided the city into different residential zones for European, Moroccan, and Jewish residents, as well as industrial and trading areas.

Only "Muslim" housing estates were built far from the "European" colonial city by creating a so-called *zone sanitaire* (sanitary zone), the boundaries of which were actually the newly built motorway. This spatial separation was also inherited from the colonial apartheid regime during which Moroccans were forbidden from entering the protectorate city unless employed as domestic servants in European households, and, likewise, that constituted a strategic measure, facilitating military operations against any possible resistance.

<u>KA</u>: Do you remember, Marion, how we first met many years ago? I think it was for a video work called *Normal City* (2003) (depicting social building facades from my teenage years in Paris's suburbs). Could you find a link between European western or eastern social architecture aesthetics and what has been functionally experimented as a modern housing ideal for the native people and "adapted" in former colonial areas (during pre-independence times)? Again, I am thinking about Écochard in Morocco or architect Fernand Pouillon in Algeria, who apparently tried to adapt their designs to local indoor and outdoor living traditions. I always have the feeling that it is only possible to live in (not to say survive) such a neighborhood, just like in millions of other social housing blocks built for immigrants in the west, because the inhabitants re-created a social structure identical to those of the villages most of them came from. Everyone knows each other and says hello, and if something wrong is about to happen, someone can see it from their window and, for instance, advise you to remove the bag you forgot in your car or park it in another place so that you can keep an eye on it. So, again, here is my question: How do you deal with this dialectic between social housing aesthetics and ethics, this complementarity of minimal functionality and aesthetics? Does it make sense to you? Does this aesthetics fit its own time, which was considered "nice" or stark on the contrary?

And last but not least, could this aesthetics have been part of the control project that happened through standardization of the subjects (the inhabitants) as the objects of the modern social order. . . ?

MvO: I think you are right in both cases, since the modernist project was and is about ambivalences, on the one hand, to grant people with a better life but, on the other, to control and educate them. The Écochard grid was dimensioned according to a typology of houses with courtyards believed to be appropriate for future inhabitants who will live in slums. His so-called culturally specific "Housing Grid for Muslims" measured eight meters by eight and consisted of two rooms and a wide outdoor space related to Arabic patios. Part of the ensuing 64 m² was organized as a so-called neighborhood unit resulting in an intricate, ground-level structure of patio houses, alleys, and public squares. A single house in this grid consisted of two or three rooms and a patio by way of entrance. Using a variety of combinations, it was designed to be flexible enough to eventually adapt to creations seen in other housing types (individual or collective), states the architectural historian Catherine Blain. The patio house in Écochard's vision allowed "growth" through usage. As psychologist Monique Eleb stated during the conference "The Colonial Modern" at Haus der Kulturen der Welt, Berlin—which you attended in 2008—the patio reference was not a copy of a traditional courtyard house but a European (mis)interpretation. On the other hand, the patio house structure developed in French colonies should be understood as a modernist synthesis, a Eurocentric translation that also carried pedagogical intentions to teach people modern industrial production and consumerism.

Though housing programs in French colonies from the 1950s/ 1960s did take certain specific local, regional, or cultural conditions into account when they were conceived, with decolonization these conditions turned out to be much more complex than originally thought. The single-floor, mass-built modernist patio houses, intended to facilitate control over Moroccan workers, are now so altered that one can no longer distinguish their original base structures. The builders simply used the base of the original design and foundations to construct three- or four-floor apartments. The many ways of appropriating space and architecture by people can also lead to assume that neither colonialism nor postcolonial governments ever managed to establish complete control over the populations.

<u>KA</u>: I agree, and it sounds very interesting, as an investigation process, to reveal how and why reappropriation emerges. As far as I am concerned, it took me years of thinking to be able to observe early "signs of reappropriation," from architecture to any items, even human behaviors. Rancière offered an interesting analysis in *The Emancipated Spectator*,[3] which is a reference to another article called "Le Tocsin des travailleurs" (The Tocsin of Workers), published in the nineteenth century in an old French union newspaper. . . To sum it up, the article describes a worker cleaning the wooden floor in a bourgeois house, removing the old surface with a large blade (tough job). After long hours of efforts, he decides to stand up and then looks out the window. He slowly ends up appreciating the view, as well as the perspective leading to the horizon of French "classic" gardens. The pleasure he takes there makes him dream of how he would set up all the furniture in this room, just like he would at home, following his own tastes to decide the kind of furniture he would buy, as well as where and why he would put a given item in a given place, etc.

3   Jacques Rancière, *The Emancipated Spectator*, trans. Gregory Elliot (London: Verso, 2009).

Rancière explains how, from bending on the floor and working hard to standing up in order to stretch a bit and look out the window, the worker switches from one state to another: from "the manual state" to the "visual state." At this very moment, he stops being only hands executing orders so as to "reappropriate" his own self by watching and coming up with his own conclusions. From the hands to the eyes, his individuality reappropriates its freedom by reappropriating the perspective his social position has shut him out of and from which his eyes had been taken off. Founder of mutualist philosophy Pierre-Joseph Proudhon was the first to highlight "reappropriation." Remember his "property is theft"?[4] It also meant social struggle is a reappropriation of what has been dispossessed by the bourgeois and bureaucratic system. . .

Another personality you made me discover in one of your essays, "Architecture Without Architects—Another Anarchist Approach," published in *e-flux journal*, issue no. 6, in 2009, is the British anarchist and architect Mark Crinson (perhaps you did it on purpose). The questions such an interesting political figure and personality raises within the understanding of contemporary social architecture are in the continuity of Proudhon's thought. I would definitely compare him to Paul Robeson, a multitalented personality. This African-American former athlete, who was physically impressive due to his height and voice, was an actor, a singer, and an active communist. In a movie, I saw him sing the Chinese national anthem on a stage right in the middle of the street! The notion of cliché might not exist in human nature; it is probably a product of the modern mind as a consequence of rationalism based on two obsessions: measuring the world with classification (through categories) of things and the fantasy of progress as a pure sign of evolution.

4   Originally published in 1840 in French as "*La propriété, c'est le vol!*"; Pierre-Joseph Proudhon, *What Is Property?: An Inquiry into the Principle of Right and of Government*, trans. Benjamin R. Tucker (New York: Humboldt Publishing Company, 1890).

Philosopher and literary critic Edward Said has beautifully summarized the relationship between anarchism and architecture through the western cliché of Orient with his recognition that the Orient has been Orientalized by Occident. It sounds like a legacy of the western desire to control otherness, first culturally, then politically.

The way windows and balconies were arranged in so many social housing buildings designed by European minds in non-western, colonized contexts from Asia to North Africa (in Casablanca, for instance) raises two questions. If these transformations of balconies into kitchens or closed, inward facing rooms are "reappropriations," then what about freedom? In the *cité verticale*, why have all the large and comfortable balconies, which aimed at opening each apartment to the outside so as to take advantage of both public and private spaces at the same time just like a private courtyard, been covered and closed by the inhabitants? Was it for self-protection, for moral issues (which are linked to Islam and privacy) in response to a design generated by another culture from another time, the culture of colonial domination imposing its utopian vision on another culture?

Could we say that adding confinement to these constructions is a "reappropriation"? When in Arabian Berber Muslim culture, domestic privacy cuts women off from outside eyes so there is no way to see their faces and bodies in their private apartment, could we say that the modern European architecture gender issue failed here? Or as Said investigates in his essay *Orientalism*,[5] is it a purely western fantasy to think it is easy to reach Muslim Arabian women?

5   Edward W. Said, *Orientalism* (New York: Pantheon Books, 1978).

I am sure you have seen examples of these thousands of old colonial postcards representing such "western fantasies," like half-naked women in their apartments. . .

<u>MvO</u>: I vaguely remember an article about veiling in North Africa, stating the first forms of veiling noticed by natives were English ladies covering themselves from the sun and sand. And the author then highlighted the invention of sunglasses with which you can look around even though no one can know what you are looking at, since your eyes cannot be seen. So, I have no answer to your last questions, but perhaps some more comments on your first one that might lead to a whole set of future investigations on what we like to call production and what is called appropriation.

There is a concern about the use of the word appropriation and its concept: in it sleeps the very notion of property, as you pointed out when you quoted Rancière. The concept of appropriation thus suggests that something used to belong to something/somebody and was later developed by somebody or/and used in another geographical context or fashion. This concept suggests no original articulation in itself. Notions such as copy, imitation, and appropriation deny any immediate emergence, yet in the meantime, this emergence is claimed by western modernists, like the architects we were talking about. In the last decades of cultural anthropology and postcolonial thinking, appropriation was used to mark tactics and strategies in a de Certeauian sense, I believe, to show that programs and concepts from above can be altered and subverted from below. But somehow it also suggests that there would be no "first" voicing, but always a belated reaction, only existing because there already was a first voicing by somebody else. The problem I have started to have with this concept is that it is mainly used for describing social class relations or in non-European articulations. When you talk about reappropriation, it aims at making this all a bit more complicated, since it is not clear who a concept and idea originally belonged to. And, as I discuss it in my own research, this is also true about modernism, as it can only be understood as a constant translation or synthesis of vernacular practices into a more rationalizing and universalizing concept that was later called modern. Still, it was a concept that appropriated the Arabian kasbah, the Indian bungalow, the courtyard house, arts and crafting from the colonies, etc. According to this, it escaped the classical and renaissance past, but in the same way the classical era claimed to have higher taste and value, to be more civilized and universal in the end. What I try to highlight is that it is a product of worldly relations and many forms of transculturation mainly triggered by colonialism. But when we think about the uses and adaptations the inhabitants made that can be so easily spotted in Casablanca, it becomes incredible. Actually, the modifications are not mere changes or adaptations; some houses have been completely overworked. Then it brings us back to different issues about biopolitics and government matters specific to each society.

One could say people who lived in Écochard's grid in Casablanca adapted a non-functional house and rebuilt it. Écochard surely thought his system was functional and so people would get used to it. But what actually happened is that they built a new house upon an old structure that did not offer many possibilities because it was too small, as it aimed at creating nuclear family households. Therefore, one could agree on the fact that inhabitants have altered, adapted, and appropriated existing structures to their needs, thus subverting European programs. But when you sort of ignore the original structure, is this still appropriation, is this not production? Nowadays, scholars tend to link appropriation to the concept

of freedom. Yet, it can only be done in such a case as the one
I am talking about—this is what I am criticizing here: European
ground structure is considered the ultimate model from which
all other activities have emerged. If you do not follow this
Eurocentric idea, you need to accept that the inhabitants have
built new structures on top, if that was possible. Until now, this
local "growing house" building practice or culture has been
associated with the already existing construction methods in
the northern African medina. Many studies have ended there
so far. But when you read documents that show more concern
about the history of the medina as a transcultural encounter
site than about French colonial cultural politics aiming at
Orientalizing and museumizing the medina as a site of pre-
modern forms of production, it gets even more complicated to
distinguish whose building practices and cultures we are talking
about. And this is what lies at the heart of the problem: that
architecture was and is still read as the expression of one cultural identity and not of a different way of living, trading, and
articulating that had been exchanging with other cultures long
before the beginning of colonial modern projects and in which
the northern hemisphere was not always the ruling, colonizing
power since other local imperial forces had their own ways
of governing people and handled war, trade, and exchanges
in their own fashions. These transcultural traces are seldom
found in current discourses, as they are mainly based on binaries
of the modern and pre-modern, on political identity, and do not
focus on transfers, translations, and exchanges.

KA: Philosopher Achille Mbembe has spoken of boundaries
referring to the Berlin Conference of 1884–1885.[6] Before that,
the nature of boundaries was different. There were areas

6   See, for instance, Achille Mbembe, "At the Edge of the World: Boundaries, Territoriality, and Sovereignty in Africa," *Public Culture*, vol. 12, no. 1 (Winter 2000), pp. 259–284.

between ethnic groups that were meant to both separate and bind them. In fact, these were places for traditional trade, war, language exchanges, etc... They were exchange areas of a different kind. They would revitalize both cultures...

I would like to come back to the complex reappropriation concept and whether any situation or item that embodies it is born from nothing or, on the contrary, is linked to some already existing thing or not.

Let's take the example of Écochard's *cité verticale* and the balconies that have been "re"-covered by all inhabitants.

Indeed, the use of "re" (for reappropriation or repair) as an intellectual western speculation and deduction occurs through the prism of western modern intellectual values and references. From philosopher Immanuel Kant's critique of philosopher David Hume's analysis we know that the way we read the world is based on the relationship between cause and effect: "causality" ... It is true we are unable to think things from within themselves. If you watch a house or a flower, you can be sure that neither of them will be able to think of what it is... And so there is no human mind able to think this house or this flower by and within themselves. It always has to think them through the "relation" that exists between this thing and the mind. The relation between themselves consists of both the experience of the object and all the references linked to this relation. This relation is called "correlation"...

So when we have a close look at a house and a building that have been "rebuilt" by the inhabitants, then we are just part of this "correlation"... Thus, if social architectures that developed through a modern political agenda in North Africa tried to provide the natives with a western vision of modern housing but have been quickly "re"-adapted by them, then it is just an endless process of human knowledge based on "correlation"... Indeed, you can do a very simple analogy to link such a behavior by native people to modern western "new" architecture: This is how traditional homes and cities (medina) were built... There is not a single house isolated from another in a medina. Each one is built against another so as to provide both a strong, load-bearing wall to the new house and a connection to another area from the terrace... Even when the first one is in construction, the second one is being built at the same time... In vernacular urbanism, the notion of "city" is the accumulation of houses built "one against another," which I have been able to observe in North and South Sahara... What architect Charles-Édouard Jeanneret, also known as Le Corbusier, found fascinating in a city like Ghardaïa (Algeria), for instance, is the fact that every street of this medina puts town facilities (market, madrassa, mosque, grocery store...) within walking distance. When he created his first *cité radieuse* in Marseilles, he claimed it to be a "vertical Ghardaïa," and each corridor in this modern social housing was called a "street," as they linked all flats to social facilities you can find in the building, such as a swimming pool, a kindergarten, a school, a church, etc. In fact, he even used to say this is a vertical *"Beni Isguen"* (Berber name for Ghardaïa). Just as people from North Africa constantly adapted to their natural environment for centuries, they did adapt to their new artificial environment... And to push the "re"-adaptation process further, I would add Le Corbusier's "reenactment" on a so-called personal creation, which sounds just like a repair of his modern building project, yet with traditional functionalism.

When you pointed out that the first veil story we heard about was a British woman protecting herself from sand, you also meant that, in the Sahara, men are veiled, too. Therefore, indeed, what you see is never what reality is. Especially from a western insight. . .

I recently came upon an interesting story about a vernacular, iconic architecture made of clay in the Sahara. . . A story I had already heard but that was never established as true. Did you know that Djenné's mosque in Mali is a fake? Actually, what looks like an authentic twelfth-century mosque is not. . . This beautiful architecture was "re"-built by the French at the beginning of the twentieth century in 1907.

As far as I am concerned, this is extremely interesting, as we always point out that there is "reappropriation because of dispossession." But what if the reconstruction of a mosque that has been destroyed several times by local people and foreigners is ordered by a colonial power—in this case, by William Merlaud-Ponty, the French governor?

People in Mali do not complain, but in all former colonies, especially French ones, relationships to colonial architecture are highly problematic. In Morocco, associations such as Casamémoire are doing a great job protecting architectural legacy, but in Algeria, protecting construction built under the former colonial administration is considered nonsense, except for religious buildings. As a matter of fact, most churches were saved due to the fact they became mosques. This is another process of reappropriation, just like so many Ottoman mosques were turned into churches during colonization. . . It is an endless process, and reappropriation is a loop, too.

<u>MvO</u>: Cultural articulations always have these incredibly rich, multiple trajectories, but traces and transfers are likewise valued differently than the people producing culture: the architect earns cultural and symbolic wealth; the carpenter does not.

On colonial grounds, this perception or creation of value starts with the ideological construction of traditional behaviors and acts against modern behaviors. In this binary pattern, there is competition between two value systems. This pattern is mostly due to European scholars. French Orientalists' analyses and texts about local economies, crafts, and building traditions either state Moroccan local productions were non-original copies of an Arabian style or call Berber crafting authentic indigenous art as long as it had no disturbing contact with Arabian aesthetics. These Eurocentric and anti-Arabian classifications caused great problems for the post-independence generation, and also do not help to understand what a non-capitalist local economy is even nowadays.

Still, crafts production—the way French powers categorized it—was the local Moroccan economy playing a part in trade relations and style exchanges over centuries. In opposition to what French people believed, not only was it more than a mere stable canon reproducing itself and simply influenced by the Ottoman Empire, but like in the medina district, local production was also an expression and meeting point for different aesthetic trajectories and translocal trade relations with Africa and Europe. Moreover, guilds were in charge of controlling the local market, rewards, trades, and production standards in Morocco over centuries, too.

When the French protectorate took over the government, one of the first interventions concerned guilds; that is to say, local economy and local production. New goods were introduced from other markets. Shoes produced in Asia, for instance, partially destroyed local shoe production. That had an impact on European markets because Moroccan leather products were imported to Europe as well; however, trade relations changed with the introduction of Asian products. Therefore, it also modified the classification of local production, trade relations, and local and traditional crafts, since the intervention into Moroccan guilds by French officials caused these manufactured goods to be seen as traditional and belated. On the one hand, the local economy was now considered traditional/pre-modern, and on the other, the French argued that these forms of "cultural production" would need to be protected and supported by French officials in the future when Morocco would be completely modernized. This double-faced destruction—devaluing and finally protecting local economy—made it possible to declare it a mere extra, a boutique element decorating the real thing that would be consumer goods made from industrialization.

For all of these reasons, the medina district was protected by Lyautey as a kind of living museum about ancient living habits, surrounded by the *cité nouvelle* built for French colonists. To help Moroccan local trade, Lyautey had an Oriental-modern Habous neighborhood constructed; by the way, it still exists as a central market area isolated from the former European city center. I am talking about this because it is linked to your last comment—the fact we missed this very point in our first project in Berlin at Haus der Kulturen der Welt in 2008, as we did not focus on who actually were the construction workers involved in building the new modern city of Casablanca. We were focusing on governance ideologies and anti-colonial resistance, but not so much on how working relations dramatically changed after French intervention. So how were these workers recruited? Obviously, most of them were Moroccan, while the planners, architects, and technicians were European. I only understood it after reading about it, but the Moroccan workforce was there because of the same intervention in the local economy and because of the catastrophic decrease in handicraft skills that occurred after protectorate intervention in Morocco. So, first you have to destroy local production and value systems, then you have a highly skilled workforce build the new city for Europeans as well as some houses for the Moroccan workforce.

But these free-floating skills were not just used in the name of colonial powers; they also served a lot of other purposes. As you know, the medina house has always been an adapted and growing house. It was always accommodated according to a family's need, then it could be made bigger when it became too small. This actually was the local building practice, and you can find it in the whole Mediterranean area. Italian villages and smaller cities were built the same way, thanks to adapted construction practices through which buildings can grow. This practice has not been erased by the colonial power; besides many others, this skill survived industrialized means of production and can still be found nowadays. But as a result of colonial rule, local production, being in the margin of industrial chains, has been turned into folklore and transformed into a souvenir culture. But still, this is an economy with its own logic besides other globalized forms of production, and it also makes it possible for people to let houses grow and adapt to the population's needs.

This conversation first appeared in Kader Attia and Léa Gauthier, eds., *RepaiR*. (Paris: BlackJack Éditions, 2014). It is reprinted here with permission of the authors and BlackJack Éditions.

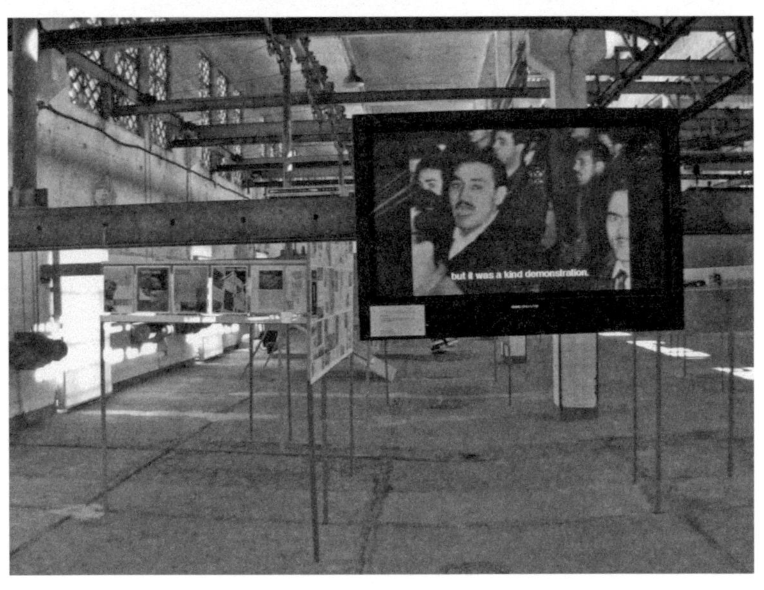

Tom Avermaete, Serhat Karakayali, and
Marion von Osten, *In the Desert of
Modernity: Colonial Planning and After,*
2009, research and exhibition project,
installation view Fabrique Culturelle des
Anciens Abattoirs de Casablanca,
Casablanca, photo: Marion von Osten

Sabeth Buchmann and Judith Hopf
Friends in Context

<u>Sabeth Buchmann</u>: This is not our first email conversation. In 1996 or 1997—when you and I were still living together— we had one about the film *Female Perversions* (1996) by Susan Streitfeld that had just been released. Maybe this also provides an opening for our conversation about Marion von Osten's work: the ways in which we talked about and processed theory (especially gender studies), pop music, literature, and film then. Art was not necessarily more important than other creative and social fields at that time. And maybe it was this way of thinking, prevalent at that time and in our context, that was not interested in categorical distinctions between forms and media of articulation that most clearly distinguished you and Marion from preceding generations of artists coming from the academy that favored media such as painting and sculpture.

<u>Judith Hopf</u>: It was certainly one of the most essential experiences for many artists and cultural producers in the 1990s in Berlin that the boundaries between various art genres increasingly began to blur. Experimental filmmakers and theater practitioners often got involved in what was happening in contemporary art or interpreted text productions and theories from the discursive surroundings of art in their theater pieces and films. Conversely, the stage designs by Bert Neumann at Volksbühne Berlin, for example, substantially inspired my understanding of art. Neumann understood how to create wonderful arrangements with things produced in the gray area between kitsch and pop. I interpret his aesthetics as being related to the language of the art installations by Isa Genzken, for example, or even to early artworks by Mike Kelley. Art was often equated then with "installation" anyway, and this form of presentation frequently had a certain affinity to stage design. The art debates of the 1990s that we are talking about here also called for a new observer role: the contexts in which art was made and its political and social conditions were posed

for debate in many works. Alongside the image experience, there was often also an intellectual question raised that addressed the fields bordering on art, social reality, and politics. Let's say at least there were *attempts* to take these adjacent plateaus into consideration. In general, performance gained new attention in the field of contemporary art. This was a phenomenon that was certainly to be found in many artists' interests in pop culture and pop music, as performative gestures and role models were attentively observed. The interest in performance was also rooted in the recollection and research of conceptual and/or feminist art history of the 1960s and 1970s (and their omissions, which we dug up). It should not be forgotten that contemporary art in the 1990s was not a clearly delineated or predefined social territory: it was not unusual for informal, usually illegal bars where house and techno music was played and developed (and played and shared by artists such as Julian Göthe, Mo Loschelder, Daniel Pflumm, Betty Stürmer, or Wolfgang Tillmans) to defend their terrain against the police by pointing out that an art exhibition was being opened on their premises, so the place was not "only" a bar. The words "exhibition opening" and "art" provided an umbrella that worked relatively well for a brief period as a shield against bureaucratic regulations.

At that time, Marion herself cultivated friendships with theater people who were also active before the fall of the Wall in East Berlin. With them in a working group, for example, she attempted to regain public interest in the Festspielhaus Hellerau in Dresden's Hellerau district: a venue left in quite a desolate state following the withdrawal of the Soviet soldiers stationed there until the fall of the Wall, and where performances and exhibitions were to be planned again. After the fall of the Wall, exhibitions took place in Berlin in locations marked by history. I am thinking about events in the buildings of the former embassy district in the new center of Berlin, which had lost their purpose. Some cultural producers, such as the artist collective Botschaft, moved in there and initiated a very influential bar/cinema/exhibition space. Or exhibitions and screenings organized by the artistic collective around the magazine *Starship,* who invented a cinema, a radio station, and an exhibition space called Pirate Cinema, which was housed in buildings of the former German Democratic Republic (GDR) district, of the post office, etc. The buildings often looked like ruins and were then—usually without much budget but with all the more ambition—newly "occupied" with contents and culture. In the best cases, as I perceived it, it happened in the sense of an expanded concept of art that was aware of its political conditions and could not rely exclusively on the design of modernism or the white cube. In the worst cases, these places triggered the gentrification of Berlin's Mitte neighborhood first, then later other neighborhoods as well. It was in this atmosphere that Marion and I met in the early 1990s—I think at an exhibition opening of the artist Susan Turcot in a project space on Invalidenstraße called Muzek Musenküsse (1993), which was located exactly at the intersection described above, between bar, cinema, and exhibition venue.

Marion and I shared with many "cultural producers," as they were called then, a special awareness of the cultural and political restructuring of Berlin. In the course of this, we radically questioned the old, familiar subject proposals of the individual artist, and we developed an understanding of art that included many different cultural practices. For example, we formed a loose performance group with a number of artists and theorists: Mercedes Bunz, Lukas Duwenhögger, Martin Ebner, Julian Göthe, Ariane Müller, Gunter Reski, Alexander Schröder, and Katharina Wulff. In 1998, we did a performance involving "living" furniture in the so-called WMF-Haus—an empty, formerly occupied studio in Berlin's Mitte district that was to be restored

to its former owners. We substituted the missing furnishings
with our bodies. Together, Wulff and I represented a shelf, for
example; Göthe, a tiger-fur rug; Ebner, a lamp; Reski, a chair;
Duwenhögger, a tea cart; Marion, a sink; Bunz, a wall clock;
Schröder, a refrigerator, etc. In the same group, we moved
to Hamburg to take part in the project *Park Fiction* (1994–
ongoing), initiated by a group of activists and artists such as
Margit Czenki, Hans-Christian Dany, Christoph Schäfer, and
Annette Wehrmann. This project was a matter of preserving
for the residents a small "gap" with an open view of the Elbe
in an urban building development in the St. Pauli district of
Hamburg, and reconfiguring it as a park. Artist-friends were
invited to exhibit art in the surrounding cafes and businesses
to draw attention to the project and to gain support. Our group
decided to approach this task in a less product-oriented way
and to perform in the gap itself. This resulted in a performance
titled *Walk and Talk* (1998). It went something like this:
Duwenhögger (dressed as the French author Sidonie-Gabrielle
Colette) and Schröder (dressed as the artist Daniel Buren),
with his assistant (played by Bunz), pick up the Hanseatic
audience at a meeting point and lead them to the gap, with a
memorable debate taking place among the protagonists all the
while. In the course of this, Colette complains bitterly to Buren
about his redesign of the inner courtyard of the Palais-Royal in
Paris. Between 1985 and 1986, Buren had realized the controversial work *Les Deux Plateaux* exactly there, and Colette,
who lived in an apartment in the Palais from 1926 to 1954,
complains posthumously to Buren that she now has to look
at the work every day, which took the life of several of her cats
and distinctly disturbs the expanse of the place. Buren and his
assistant courageously defend the columns and stripes in the
square, a conceptual design of modernistic character, and point
out the highlighting of the contemporary, urban infrastructure
below it, which reflects sculptures from the underground up to

the surface, so to speak. The group around Colette and Buren reaches the building plot, and there they find, sloping down toward the Elbe, planted in the ground like plants or trees, Ebner, Müller, Reski, Marion, and me. Marion and I take over the performative action. Marion in the role of artist Richard Serra and I in the role of a commissioner negotiate an intervention on Serra's sculpture *Tilted Arc.* Here, we allude to the sculpture that Serra placed in the Foley Federal Plaza in Manhattan in 1981, which had to be removed in 1989 due to public protests and court cases. The protests were especially directed against the size of the sculpture because it purportedly hindered the everyday life and the paths of the people based there. The artist and the commissioner thus discuss a fictive intervention by unknown persons on the sculpture: a pair of tennis shoes tied together by the laces, thrown over the sculpture, dangles at a height of four meters, provoking questions about public acceptance, usability, and the task of sculptures. Following this, Müller and Reski read passages from the psychedelic novel *A Separate Reality: Further Conversations with Don Juan* (1971) by Carlos Castaneda until we are symbolically mown down by a lawnmower. The friends and colleagues who had invited us were not necessarily highly supportive of the performance during the preparation phase because there were concerns that it would be too "challenging" for the Hamburg audience, but the audience accepted the performance with interest. Or at least they didn't just walk off and leave us, and it seemed to me that they followed what was happening with astonishment.

SB: I find it telling that constellations of themes that would become relevant in Marion's later exhibition projects had already appeared in the actions and performances of that time. Although then they were still characterized as being playful and situation-specific, which were, of course, qualities that the "Hamburg artists" claimed for themselves in contradistinction to the more discourse-based art of the "Berlin artists," "Cologne artists," and "Zurich artists." At the same time, these projects had an affinity with the absurd that had more to do with theater than with art. In this context, you also mention the different attitudes or conflicts that became apparent among the actors in regard to addressing the audience. The pivotal point, which is found in practically all of Marion's exhibition projects, was always the possibility of art as a social and collaborative practice. In this, modern and contemporary architecture, in diverse manifestations (residential buildings, cities, landscapes of labor, parks, etc.), becomes a literal and metaphorical stage on which to reflect upon cultural, social, and media-history factors of social subjectification. This was equally evident in the exhibition project *Studio Hellerau* (1994–1995) and the projects that Marion developed in various constellations, often with her partner, artist and designer Peter Spillmann, and with bookstore Pro qm's Katja Reichard, curator Axel John Wieder, as well as architect and artist Jesko Fezer and the group Freies Fach that he co-founded. What also comes to mind here are the interdisciplinary collaborations of Labor k3000 in Zurich (essentially run by Marion and Spillmann). In her intermittent function as a professor at the Institute for Education in the Arts at the Academy of Fine Arts Vienna, Vienna, Marion has enlarged those projects within other institutional contexts. Recently, she has worked together with students and teachers on the research project *Model House—Mapping Transcultural Modernisms* (2012–2013) about the transcultural character of modernist architecture in the context of decolonization movements in Africa, China, and India.

So what you did in your performance *Walk and Talk*, specifically the bodily appropriation and reinterpretation of sociocultural cartographies, is what Marion later developed into more extensive forms of historical-critical knowledge production, in which the tension between the artistic and the educational is especially prominent. For instance, Marion deals with this in the book *Das Erziehungsbild: Zur visuellen Kultur des Pädagogischen* (The Education Image: On Pedagogy's Visual Culture) (2010), which she published together with Tom Holert. Their reader also involves the question of whether and how artistic-theoretical discourses can critically intervene in the pedagogical cultures in which they participate in terms of image skills and art education, for instance.

JH: Yes, it is curious that the themes already crystallized so early. The projects that you mention and that Marion developed with so many colleagues and activists are certainly not to be understood in a strictly linear way as beginning from a "starting point." Instead, they should be read as a "weaving" or a "fabric" developing and forming from many different fields of knowledge and practices. But what is certain is that, at that time, Marion was already involved as a driving force in negotiating these themes.

SB: It seems we could speculate on whether and to what extent the founding of collectives like Labor k3000 in Zurich, the Free Class (founded by former students from the Academy of Arts, Berlin and their friends, including yourself, Judith, as well as artists and theorists Katja Diefenbach, Katja Eydel, Nico Siepen, and Klaus Weber), or even artist and author groups that emerged in the 1980s, like BüroBert, first in Dusseldorf, later in Berlin, and Minimal Club, first in Munich, later in Berlin (I was a member of the latter), created an expanded "context" (*Zusammenhang*, that was our word for it then), which resembles today's networks, because the groups expanded and interlinked or formed new constellations depending on the project and shared a marked interest in communication formats based on the principle of shared knowledge. How do you see the relationship between a friendship-based practice and a collaborative form that was distinguished by engaging with themes and methods in our/your work (and thus also in Marion's work)? I am thinking, for example, of one of Marion's first larger exhibition projects, *Sex & Space: Space. Gender. Economy* (1996–1997), which she initiated in her role then as one of the curators of Shedhalle Zürich.

A certain connection to our discussion about *Female Perversions* might be suspected here too. Although that occasion was "only" a review published in *Texte zur Kunst* in March 1997, we gave ourselves a lot of time for discussing and writing. This was also true to a far greater extent for projects like *Sex & Space.* Today it often sounds (as with sociologists Luc Boltanski and Ève Chiapello, for example[1]) as though project culture was the new, progressive commodity culture. For Marion and many others, including us, the point was—as you suggested earlier— a fundamental confrontation with the patterns of subjectification offered to us. Those procedures were and are completely different endeavors that were accompanied by much debate but not necessarily by efficient working strategies.

JH: Perhaps the film *Female Perversions* is a good example of which kinds of models of subjectification and role models of and for women were negotiated in the 1990s, as well as the related ideas of friendship (also in professional respects). The film deals with conflicts among three women, to put it very briefly, who are perhaps a bit exaggerated in their contrasts, though they are sharply outlined this way, who want to live (out) their different desires, career wishes, and frames of knowledge. This leads them into harsh, comical, and even absurd situations of conflict with one another, which seem to impede their wishes. Their sexual, professional, and love-related needs are constantly

[1]　See Luc Boltanski and Ève Chiapello, *The New Spirit of Capitalism*, trans. Gregory Elliott (London: Verso, 2007).

turned into bad competition and perverted into dysfunctional displacement activities. The end allows for a little hope that friendships may be possible among women who do not impinge on each other's professional self-realization. This shift in the narrative takes place as the protagonists become aware of their differences and no longer allow themselves to be reduced to certain roles; instead, they comprehend and experience their competition and problems in much more complicated manners. From today's perspective, that sounds a bit like a naïve (self-)management cliché about optimizing a "successful" neoliberal life path, but I think for us artists and cultural producers at the time, it was a bit harder to mutually support one another professionally and to form "contexts" that could not easily be broken down into gender clichés and given conservative "role models." Of course this may also be true for male colleagues who no longer wanted to refer to claims of genius and steep, "top-down" hierarchies.

I think the so-called contexts then struggled to question the conventional hierarchies between curator/museum director, gallerist/artist, music producer/musician, director/actor, etc. From my observations, this is the difference between the networks familiar to us now and so-called social media, which can approach possible questions less critically: who supports whom, why and what that means, how we organize ourselves in opposition to and in conflict with the unwanted mechanisms of inclusion and exclusion of the institutions and/or power positions, etc. If I comprehend digital social networks correctly, then the belief in the possibility of a purely virtual, de-personified support for political and cultural concerns—for instance, in the form of online petitions—is a norm. I am a bit skeptical whether the conflicts that we carry out regarding political and cultural issues really have to take place so "facelessly" (and purely in information and communication technology), but I don't

Marion von Osten, *Human Genome Project*,
1994–1995, mixed media installation,
installation view Shedhalle Zürich, Zurich,
photo: Marion von Osten

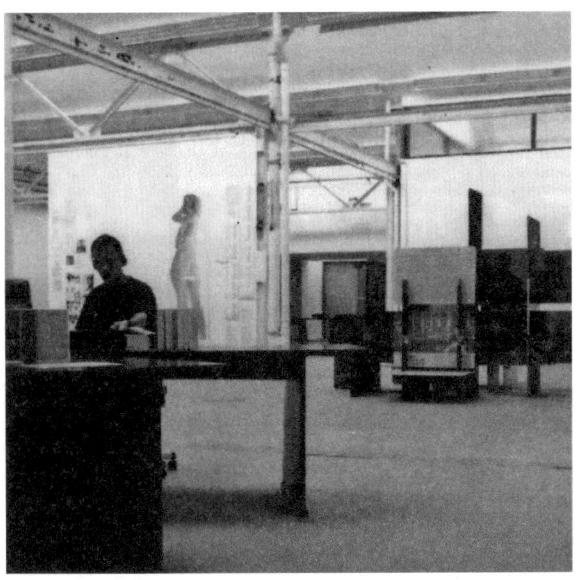

Marion von Osten, *Human Genome Project*,
1994–1995, mixed media installation,
installation view Shedhalle Zürich, Zurich,
photo: Marion von Osten

Invitation flyer for *when tekkno turns to sound of poetry*, 1994, exhibition, Shedhalle Zürich, Zurich, courtesy Shedhalle Zürich

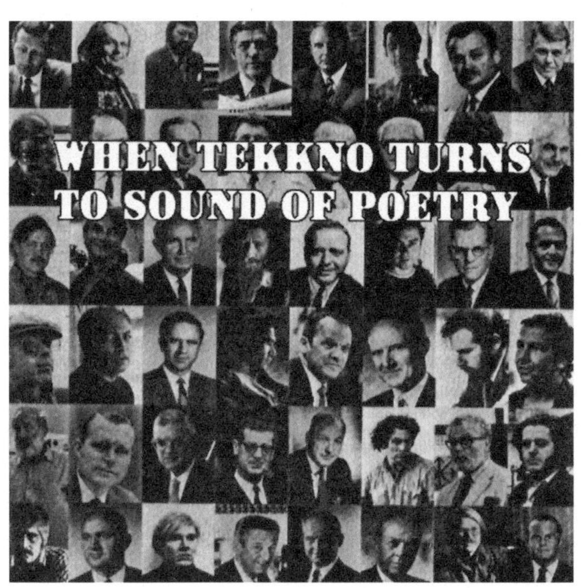

really know enough about social media, because I rarely use them. In any case, the critical "distance" from (presumably?) outmoded artist-subject proposals, the open interest in politics, pop, and art, and the inclination to self-reflexivity typical of the 1990s may be seen from the outside as "context," but we were also heavily caught up in the overly meticulous observation of "mini-differences" between us, which in many cases led to blocks and self-censorship—I'm speaking here from my own experience.

Sex & Space, *Irene ist viele* (Irene Is Many) (1996), and other group exhibitions that Marion and her association of friends developed are, for me today, the foundations of an awareness of cultural, political, and gender-specific conditions and their mutability to which we wanted to relate our artistic activity.

<u>SB</u>: I think the interest in developing new practices within the framework of discourses that were intended to liberate from conventional, modernist notions of art, which we at the same time considered questionable for the aforementioned reasons, never aimed solely for the production of knowledge but rather for a "different," socially and politically informed way of doing art and theory. This interest was certainly also triggered by cultural and gender studies, and, in this respect, Marion was and is a paradigmatic "cultural producer": here was an artist who had already turned away from painting in the early 1990s, when this genre and medium was still dominant in the German-speaking context. When we made the exhibition *when tekkno turns to sound of poetry: Technologie, Feminismus, Konzept-Kunst & Politik* (Technology, Feminism, Concept Art & Politics) with 30, 40 other artists and authors—first in Shedhalle Zürich (1994) and then a year later in Kunst-Werke in Berlin—which revolved around comparisons between the design of (post) conceptualism and biotechnology and genetic engineering,

Marion was already active in a computer art group in Karlsruhe. Yet her work did not correspond to the usual spectrum of media art. It was instead based more—like context art[2] at that time—on themes and methods from cultural studies. I am thinking here of her contribution to our exhibition, *Human Genome Project* (1994–1995), which included references to architect Le Corbusier's housing units, the book *Bauordnungslehre* (1943) by architect Ernst Neufert, and artist Alighiero Boetti's embroidered maps. Everything was already there: tying a theme—the conjunction between techno-scientistic, biotechnological, and reproductive media,[3] which we were investigating at the time—back to heteronormative living and everyday cultures, which she linked at the same time with a view of transcultural production contexts. Marion operated in her artistic works wholly post-conceptually with various media: with installation-based architectural models, with photography and slide projection, with drawing and text. In her work for *Human Genome Project,* she also worked with procedures of mail art, with a fax machine. What was addressed here was exactly the historical connection of art and media practice, which became important to us in terms of the dissemination of information and communication technologies, or digital technologies and their uses, and what they do with our practices as artists and authors,

2   As Rebecca Gordon-Nesbitt explains of "context art": "It is no longer purely about critiquing the art system, but about critiquing reality and analysing and creating social processes. In the '90s, non-art contexts are being increasingly drawn into the art discourse. Artists are becoming autonomous agents of social processes, partisans of the real. The interaction between artists and social situations, between art and non-art contexts has led to a new art form, where both are folded together: Context art. The aim of this social construction of art is to take part in the social construction of reality." See Rebecca Gordon-Nesbitt, "False Economies: Time to Take Stock," in *Curating Critique*, ed. Marianne Eigenheer (Frankfurt: Revolver, 2007), online at: https://shiftyparadigms. wordpress.com/non-fiction/false-economies-time-to-take-stock/.

3   Reproductive media are forms of media that are "reproductions" in theorist Walter Benjamin's sense, e.g., film or photography. See Walter Benjamin, "The Work of Art in the Age of its Technological Reproducibility: Second Version," in *The Work of Art in the Age of Its Technological Reproducibility, and Other Writings on Media*, Michael W. Jennings, Brigid Doherty, and Thomas Y. Levin, eds., Edmund Jephcott, et al., trans., (Cambridge, MA: Harvard University Press, 2008), pp. 19–55.

with our bodies, our relationships, our everyday lives, our languages, our feelings, our sex.

JH: Perhaps here, in the operations of postal services and art, we can tie into the media discourses of the 1990s and their deconstructivist ideas. I don't know whether anyone at all even still uses a fax machine in everyday life today, but a fax machine is unique in comparison with other senders, such as a radio, TV, or the Internet (all of them "senders" and programs that continue sending without interruption, even when you turn them off). The fax machine is always ready to send and receive, but it only turns on or off or receives or sends when an "outside" sends something to its address or, conversely, when someone uses the machine to actively send something. Yet the sender remains "absent" and "invisible" for the recipient. That there can also be something spooky about a fax machine may ultimately be due to the fact that this is a machine attached to a telephonic medium, thus enabling the transfer of writing and image. So receiving a fax works just like a call via the analog telephone, more or less unpredictably. You get a call whether it is convenient right now or not: there is philosopher Avital Ronell ringing me yet again. Secondly, the receiving/sending of a fax, just like the phone call, goes through the same cable that separates the transfer again at the same time. As Ronell says, by receiving and connecting, the telephone cable conjoins what it divides.[4] I like the idea of this paradox, and maybe it also fits with the understanding of artistic practice as Marion pursues it. Her complex exhibition projects and discourses always also involve a search for techniques that enable connecting discourses and aesthetics that are separated from one another in conservative understandings of art: disconnecting art from the bourgeois traditions and the ideas of a work

[4]   See Avital Ronell, *The Telephone Book: Technology, Schizophrenia, Electric Speech* (Lincoln, NE: University of Nebraska Press, 1989).

associated with them. And conversely, detaching aesthetics from an understanding of economics that considers capitalism to be without alternatives, thus making it a condition constitutive for art, etc. Writing on "white papers," illuminating and visualizing texts (in a metaphorical sense, making areas visible that are not—yet—canonically established in academic discourses). All of this has always been part of receiving and sending a fax, which then inserts itself, whether it is wanted or not, as a "document" in the social space, thus also becoming manifest in art.

SB: The works Marion made starting in the early/mid-1990s exhibit features characteristic of context-sensitive spatial installations. An explicit interest in keeping production open as a process of communication is also evident; as though these were situation-specific "workstations" that resist the notion of fixed objects linked to fixed values. Yet this was not due to a rigorous rejection of art production; rather, it was the unexposed moment of a cultural framework "in the making" that Marion did not abrogate at any point: the idea that a theme could be dealt with exhaustively and provided with references to secure significance and with presentation aesthetics was, and is, if I see it correctly, relatively alien to her. So one project has always anticipated the next and referred to past projects, branching off into many thematic fields and thus producing contents that do not occur in academic cultural studies, social sciences, or political sciences, for instance. In my view, Marion's work can therefore not be subsumed under terms like "context art" or "institutional critique," even though she pursues comparable motifs with her interests in architectural, social, and media history. The forms of her work are essentially oriented more toward knowledge practices that cannot be so easily divided into categories but are instead situated in transversal linkages of practice, theory, and activism often pursued for years, if not all the way up to the present. I am thinking here of the publications that she edited with others: *Das Phantom sucht seinen Mörder: Ein Reader zur Kulturalisierung der Ökonomie* (The Phantom Seeks Its Murderer: A Reader on the Culturalization of the Economy) published with Justin Hoffmann, co-curator of Shedhalle Zürich at the time, in 1999, or *Be Creative! The Creative Imperative*, published in 2003 with Spillmann in conjunction with the exhibition project of the same title produced by Labor k3000. Another volume documents Marion's role of providing keywords for changing social and cultural paradigms, which she has assumed again and again together with her respective collaborators: *Norm der Abweichung* (Norm of Deviation) (2003), as well as *Das Erziehungsbild, Colonial Modern: Aesthetics of the Past, Rebellions for the Future* (with Tom Avermaete and Serhat Karakayali, 2010), and *Transcultural Modernisms* (with the Model House Research Group, 2013). These books are manifestations of knowledge production from and with artistic practice and research. They provide content and methodologies often ignored by the dominant academic world. At the same time, they are expressions of the transdisciplinary networking of art-as-project-production, academic educational systems, and an exhibition business no longer devoted solely to art. When I today think of the biennials, for instance, or Haus der Kulturen der Welt in Berlin, that seems to be taken for granted and stands for a political understanding of art that meets with broad consensus. At that time, in the mid to late 1990s, when first artist Renate Lorenz and art historian Sylvia Kafehsy and, later, artist Ursula Biemann, Hoffmann, and Marion worked as curators at Shedhalle Zürich, the art world reacted largely with disinterest, if not with resentment. It was also from this condition that the role of an exemplary representative of a "self-organized field" was later ascribed by the politicized art community to Marion, along with everything that goes with it:

initiating, organizing, communicating, mediating—perhaps also something that narrowed the public perception of her artistic "signature," her pleasurable designs of space and exhibitions. Yet there is an entire series of works showing the extent to which she generated her projects again and again from her artistic self-understanding. In *Sex & Space,* these are Broodthaers-like settings, for instance. Her wall and space arrangements can be compared in many respects to the exhibitions by the artist collective Group Material, artist Renée Green, and others. A predilection for linking pop and youth culture designs and materials with self-made objects and displays is always recognizable as well. However, it seems that these dimensions of her work have been somewhat suppressed under the weight of the major themes that have also always been present or considered from solely functionalist perspectives. Was it important, for example, to you, Judith, to consistently take into consideration, with other means, exactly this problem—namely, the imperative of legibility—in your works? Knowing that you and Marion have consistently maintained a close exchange about the complicated conditions of a politically envisioned art practice, I would be interested in hearing how you see this relationship of tension from today's perspective.

JH: Since the 1990s, I think we have been developing a very interesting relationship of art in the field of tension between control and experiment. It may sound like a contradiction, but there were always very strict ideas—particularly in the so-called "self-organized" field of art and in our "contexts"—about what a "wrong" approach could look like (as "wrong," I imagine artistic and political stances being crushed in a mill driven by mercantile interests and calculation) and an almost manipulative perspective of what "other" people might think of our art endeavors (typical fragments of conversations like this could be: if I depict something this way or that way, I don't want the viewer to

perceive it that way or this way or even think that way or this
way about it), completely ignoring that you can simply never
know what another person thinks or is even capable of per-
ceiving. . . Perhaps this is the crux of an art that wants to be
confirmed in its own stance but is understandably not able to
simply aesthetically implement what it has "clarified" in terms
of content or can perhaps signify and debate in the same "experimental" and "complex" way at the same time. The reason
aesthetic implementation is not possible is simply that one
does not know the techniques or have them available, because
the tendency of experimental aesthetic processes is specifically
that they are not controllable or may not even succeed. Yet all
these aspects speak against an art project that seeks mostly
and primarily to promote its political and social "messages"
and "contents," resulting in unintentionally or intentionally normative ideas about how something can be propelled in the right
direction. So the uncertain, undecided aesthetic positions are
likely to be abandoned because they are considered too little
expedient. I always hope that a flash of exactly this indecision
in political art can still be found in all the "theme shows" and
political insights, because I assume that we actually don't
know "it" (what others think, what is to be avoided, what is
embarrassing, what is beautiful); rather, we can only socially,
politically, and aesthetically negotiate and experience it as
fields of conflict among one another. Because of this potential
for conflict, I also love entertainment or pop and even "beauty,"
especially in their most puzzling manifestations. Marion and
I share, I think, this expectant, perhaps even somewhat hope-
fully-overcharged, view of art. This is why Marion has always
advocated "experiment" and the artistic process in conjunction
with art and politics, as you have described it so well. With this
in mind, when Marion decided to take a position as an artist, as
a curator at Shedhalle Zürich, she did so—along with her great
passion for artistic teamwork, thematic exhibitions, and cultural

education—for the sake of solidifying her own economic independence. At that time and for the same reasons, I worked in the field of graphic art and later at universities, first as a guest lecturer, then as a guest professor. So, ultimately, it was also our economic possibilities and/or compulsions that co-determined or separated our artistic paths, because they led our explorations further again into new and different contexts. . .

SB: . . . which then actually meant and still mean different forms of practice and distribution. As said before, Marion worked on the same themes ahead of time. It also was a qualitatively different sort of engagement than that which we see at the biennials today. A very important engagement was *Projekt Migration* in Cologne in 2002–2006, along with the resultant engagements with the diverse manifestations of globalization and transculturalism. The theme of the border, which is charged with identity politics and which for many years now has had eminent importance, is one that Marion has treated time and again from always new, European-Union-critical perspectives. Perhaps it is the politics of demarcation that so deeply permeates everything that has impelled her work from the beginning in one way or another—perpetually working against insidious discriminatory separations, inclusions, and exclusions that especially apply to the highly professionalized art and discourse field in which we participate. Here, I sometimes wonder whether we do not place too much faith in the transgressive capability of the symbolic, which ultimately benefits the cultural and intellectual milieus more than the worlds we seek to relate to. We thus find ourselves at the beginning of the questions that we raised in the early 1990s, which have something to do, not least of all, with the contradictory and incapable or even openly racist migration policies that are increasingly evident again today. I also always see them from the perspectives of the projects that Marion initiated or was involved in, and there it has always been a search for modes of articulation, agency, and resistance that can take root along the borders that cannot be denied as being between artistic and social perspectives and realities. But maybe we have partly placed too much faith in these kinds of strategies of empowerment and articulation, taken the economic, intrinsic dynamics of symbol and cultural politics too little into account. These have nothing against critical thinking, but know how to neutralize it again and again.

<u>JH</u>: I agree wholeheartedly. I am always completely astonished to encounter a stance in 2015 at the "phase front," the point where transformation starts to take effect, where I currently see myself and which includes participation in contemporary gallery- and fair-related art events, which experiences itself as "lacking alternatives" and—in conjunction with the postcapitalist economy—as constitutive for art and aesthetics. The obfuscation of the boundaries between culture and economy that Marion discusses in the reader *Das Phantom sucht seinen Mörder* has only become denser since its publication.

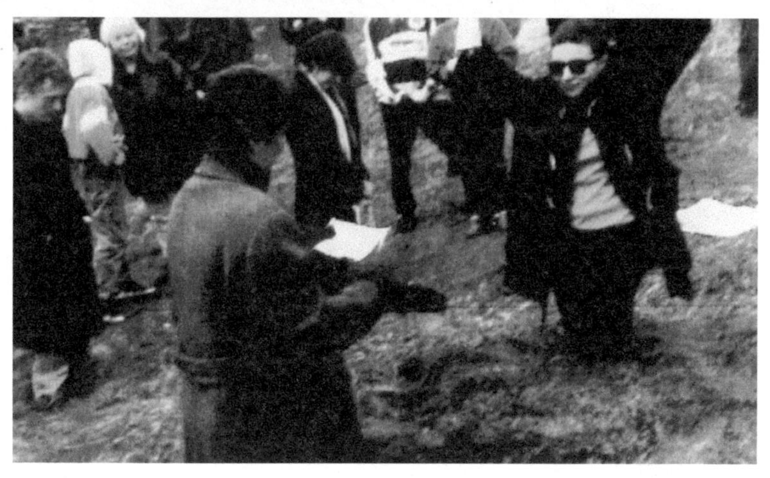

Marion von Osten and Judith Hopf in the
roles of Richard Serra and his commissioner.
Mercedes Bunz, Lukas Duwenhögger, Martin
Ebner, Julian Göthe, Judith Hopf, Ariane
Müller, Marion von Osten, Gunter Reski,
Alexander Schröder, and Katharina Wulff,
Walk and Talk, 1998, performance during
Park Fiction, Hamburg, photo: Lukas
Duwenhögger

International FAXline
of Genetechnology Innovations and Bioethics
in the Shedhalle Zurich, Switzerland
from June 25 to August 13, 1994

The exhibition "When Tekkno Turns to Sound of Poetry' deals with
problems of "dematerialisation and devaluation of the human body and its
surrounding space through bioscience and media theory. The body became
a material supplier for something like "pure" software. What does it mean
when the human body serves as a container for genetic material, reckoned
as information ?" (quoted from the exhibition proposal)

On this background I am planning an international FAXline where scientists,
ethicists and artists join in an information pool to build a base for an intense
debate about the change of our notion of human kind.
The major problem in an objective debate is that the public has no idea what
is really going on in the bio-engineering laboratories. The questions to be
addressed are : Of what kind are the new innovations in biotechnology and
how will they alter the perception of individuality, identity and persona ?

A second string of thoughts entails us to discuss public strategies, as they
are carried out by parts of the scientific community or by the media.
The example of scientists Robert Stillman and Jerry Hall researching at the
George Washington University clarifies this issue: These scientists
reproduced human embryos for the first time. The important fact of this
event is that, to a large degree, the traditional concept of scientific research
has been suspended. Since "Splitting", in biogenetic science, is no longer an
invention, the scientific value of this experiment has been nil. Stillman and
Hall, by breaking the taboo of cloning a human embryo and thus
approaching "the last frontier", has left the realm of fiction and created a
tangible fact. The whole strategy was to evoke a scandal to popularize in a
mass media "happening" the new scientific (or better: economic) possibilities
in bio-engineering.
What influence will such strategies have on further scientific research?

...2

I would appreciate if you or your institution could send an article. statement
or essay addressing these topics.
During the exhibition the arriving faxes of the participants will be presented
like a wall newspaper. In the middle of the project when most of the faxes
have arrived, the whole material will be sent to every participant, so that the
first interaction on the articles could start. The objective of the project is to
document the debate on CDROM . The rights of every author/artist will be
guarantied and the contributions will only be published with the consent of
the author.

To give you an example of participation I would like to mention that Mrs.
Dr. Elisabeth Goedde, a German genebiologist and medical therapist will be
sending a report of a seminar which she is conducting with her students:
The seminar is focused on the evaluation of genetherapeutic applications to
specific prenatal care case studies.

I passionately hope that you agree to democratize and internationalize the
debate of Bioethics. And I am looking forward to your kind participation
in the Information Pool in the Shedhalle Zurich in Switzerland.

A particular FAXline will be installed soon in the museum space. You will
get the number as soon as possible. In the meanwhile the fax number of the
Shedhalle office is available. Catharina Cosin in New York is available for
assistance throughout the duration of the exhibition.
FAX: 011- 41-1-~~182 9210~~ (Shedhalle office, Zurich)
4815030

Marion von Osten 1994

Diedrich Diederichsen
The Best of Three Worlds

In response to questions about her motives, beginnings, or the origins of her work and the work of her generational peers, Marion von Osten often sketches a triangular constellation as intensely taut as it is unbalanced. The first two worlds she draws are the subculture of punk rock and a Marxist-inspired perception of inequality and privilege. The third is a feminism both independent of and averse to the boundaries and questionable aspects of the other worlds' thinking and experiences. This triangle informs the conditions of the late 1970s and early 1980s that von Osten also explicitly references in her few existing autobiographical reconstructions, for example in an interview with researcher, curator, and art educator Barbara Mahlknecht that I refer to later, or in her unpublished manuscript *Wir leben im Computerstaat* (We Live in the Computer State).

I came of age around the same time in West Germany. This is relevant because, despite similarities in the looks and gestures of punks, feminists, and new leftists of the second and third generations in this international context, numerous local discourses and debates made themselves felt in particular ways. This would be hard to discern if only considering the often superficial commonalities. Punk could be a progressive or a reactionary movement in different cities—even in different neighborhoods—in 1979. Feminism could be an ally to or an enemy of it, depending on previous developments, often very specific ones.

In her text "Irene ist Viele! Or What We Call 'Productive' Forces" (Irene Is Many) (2009),[1] von Osten recalls the 1978 film *Die allseitig reduzierte Persönlichkeit–Redupers* (The All-Around Reduced Personality–Redupers) by Helke Sander.

[1] Marion von Osten, "Irene ist Viele! Or What We Call 'Productive' Forces," *e-flux journal*, no. 8 (2009), online at: http:// www.e-flux.com/journal/08/61381/ irene-ist-viele-or-what-we-call-productive-forces/.

Here, von Osten analyzes how a filmmaker in the late 1970s had already characterized modes of behavior that later analyses of cultural production describe as coming from between activist, identity-based, and career-related motives, just like those of von Osten herself. The film is, at the same time, a very clear sketch of the director's own entry into the field of artistic production: going back and forth between journalistic jobs as a photographer, individual artistic claims, and the artistic-documentary collaboration of a group of feminist artists. In other words, von Osten is situated here exactly in a biographical tension between a self that is orienting itself—tethered, setting out—and a self that is later able to recognize, in the origin of its own departure, the early versions of the antagonisms and aporias that would later make up a not insubstantial portion of her own academic-artistic work.

Edda, the key protagonist in Sander's film, is defined in multiple ways, and the film shows how she seeks to escape these determinisms—or at least to tactically deal with them in part. She is a photographer, and this already puts her in a difficult position. On the one hand, she understands photography as a form of political activity—marking something, shifting it into public awareness, where this type of knowledge has either been repressed or not available. This visual knowledge consists primarily of images of the city where all the participants live: isolated West Berlin. The political intentions that motivate her and her fellow photographers also include documenting East Berlin. On the other hand, she works as a press photographer and has to provide professional pictures for news production. In this role, she is commissioned to document occurrences that will be reported on in newspapers the next day—from the last appearance of a type of a Russian diesel locomotive going from Moscow to Paris and passing through Berlin, to a business event hosted by the city. She is able to earn money as a photographer, but she lacks the freedom to interpret her commissions. Instead of interrupting or enriching public knowledge, she is helping to affirm what everyone already knows. And on yet another hand, she has the possibility of defining her photography as art in an exhibition that she tries to organize with her collective, a group of four women.

These three positions—activist, journalist, artist—are then complicated in the film by its central narrative: the organization of the everyday life of a single mother and producer operating alone. The protagonist argues—in meetings with friends but also in inner monologues, although sometimes touched by a certain skepticism—that this situation can be overcome through collective action. The group of four women enables agency—both in respect to the power hierarchies in which Edda carries out her profession (which, as we already know, actually consists of three professions), as well as in response to the general patriarchal social conditions of the time, which required determined action from women from the most diverse lives or worlds to assert feminist demands: outside of the intellectual world, a more general feminist consciousness had just started to spread after very popular protests against abortion paragraph §218 of German law. The type of demonstrations following this have far more popular feminist concerns than the specific debates among the group of artists. Another parameter to consider when thinking with this film is the Marxist matrix—the pre-history of West Berlin feminism: it has not only influenced these ideas of collectivity but also, in a complex way, the entire project of persons taking action, such as those in the film. The idea of only producing art collectively was semi-normative in certain post-SDS circles (the neo-Marxist Socialist German Student League or *Sozialistischer Deutscher Studentenbund*) because of their nostalgia for 1920s-communist-collective practice before it became part of a feminist agenda.

The feminism of West Berlin at this time arose from the highly publicized and much discussed dissatisfaction of women within the "revolutionary" SDS of the 1968 student revolts. This feminism reacted, first of all, to the exclusion of women from the revolutionary project, which was supposed to be secured by the Marxist discourse of the secondary contradiction, as interpreted by the SDS.[2] Especially after a more general and popular feminism became visible with the anti-218 protests after 1973, it became more relevant for feminists to engage in the improvement of women's living conditions. This is a much broader social struggle that basically calls for a concept of solidarity and alliance that the Marxist-universalist tradition might prescribe, but is incapable of providing in its practice and actually tends to undermine by implicitly (and explicitly) accusing women of dividing the working class.

Those in the SDS may have been similar to the women portrayed in the film in terms of class and culture, but the feminist politics of the late 1970s seem politically more successful and popular than the politically isolated nostalgia for the working class of the male post-SDS Communists and Maoists. The non-isolated feminist position of the film's protagonist is later supplemented by another, also Marxist-influenced stance, namely that of the German Democratic Republic and the almost inaccessible other part of the city, East Berlin. The film takes its title from a radio program from East Berlin that Edda listens to, in which someone speaks of the "all-around developed personality in Socialism," leading the protagonist to experimentally conclude that she lives in capitalism as an *all-around reduced personality*.

2   I refer here to *nebenwiderspruch* or the notion that there are secondary contradictions, such as gender or race, as opposed to the primary contradiction of capital or labor.

This *all-around reduced personality* proves to be tied to multitude forms of living, modes of existence, and their associated battlefronts, each with a specific form of isolation. This is the (not entirely undialectical) foundation for a different orientation from which von Osten's work, according to her own statements, takes its starting point. Born later than the fictional Edda, von Osten was a child and/or did not have to work between 1968 and 1978. For her, engaging with forms of rebellion and resistance began with the culture of punk rock, which she became increasingly interested in around 1980. In many respects, punk rock as a counterculture was something like a summary answer to the cultural aporias of late 1968, sometimes also to the feminist, artistic-political labyrinth of "redupers" (reduced personalities). This generation needed to continue a culture of protest, but also separation and secession. It was also a generation that needed to distance itself from the seemingly stalemated forms of a given protest culture.

Punk rock paid a high degree of attention to fighting for and spreading possibilities for articulation. The frequently invoked do-it-yourself ethos is considered today to be a fad, a purely aesthetic preference for noise, or an ethics of the self-made, and it is thematized as such in historiography. The point at that time at every level (indie labels, self-production, concerts, and performances below the standards of professionalist conformism of the 1968 generation) was to make audible people and voices that had not been heard because they were either structurally excluded or because they simply did not yet exist as articulated types. At the same time, with punk rock there was a break from 1968 in terms of content, primarily carried out at a habitual level: harsh, unfriendly behavior, sarcastic humor, provocative gestures. Slogans like "kill all hippies" were to be taken less literally than the move from soft, flowing, rocking movements to the hard, erratic staging of bodies.

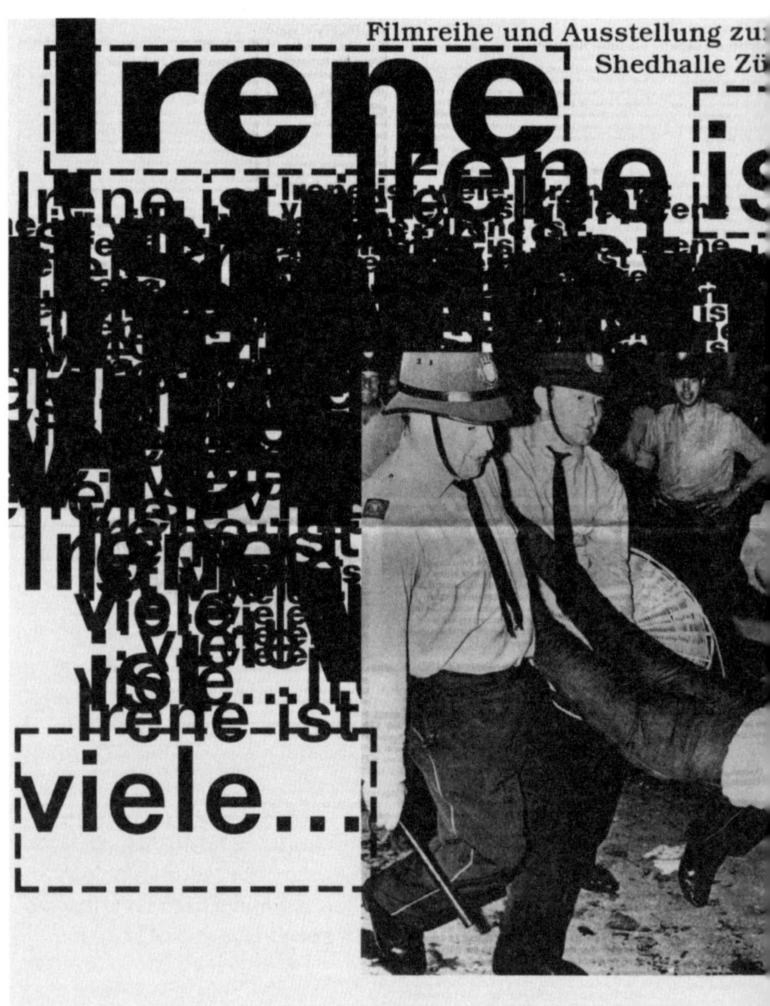

Flyer for *Irene ist Viele*, 1996, screening program and exhibition, Shedhalle Zürich, Zurich, design: Ilia Vasella

Filmprogramm:

Samstag, 16. März 17.00

Eine Prämie für Irene Helke Sander, BRD 1971, 50 Minuten

...Es kommt darauf an sie zu verändern Claudia von Alemann, BRD 1972/73, 54 Minuten

Mit allgemeiner und filmbezogener Einführung von "Übung am Phantom" und Diskussion mit den Regisseurinnen Claudia von Alemann und Helke Sander

Sonntag, 17. März 17.00

Für Frauen, 1. Kapitel Cristina Perincioli, BRD 1972, 36 Minuten

Janie's Janie Newsreel (Geri Ashur), USA 1971, 32 Minuten

The Woman's Film Newsreel, USA 1970, 45 Minuten

Mit Einführung und Diskussionen

Freitag, 22. März 19.00

Susan Jacqueline Veuve, CH 1974, 15 Minuten

Lady Shiva oder: "Die bezahlen nur meine Zeit " Tula Roy, CH 1974, 40 Minuten

Julie from Ohio Isa Hesse, CH 1978, 30 Minuten

Gespräch zum filmischen Umgang mit sexistischen/ geschlechtsspezifischen Rollenzuschreibungen und die Darstellung/Erarbeitung von 'Gegenentwürfen' mit der Regisseurin Tula Roy und der Produzentin Therese Schärer

Samstag, 23. März 17.00

La lotta non e finita Colletivo Feminista di Cinema, Italien 1973, 30 Minuten

L'aggetivo donna Rony Daopoulos und Colletivo Feminista di Cinema, Italien 1972, 60 Minuten

Sonntag, 24. März 17.00

Der subjektive Faktor Helke Sander, BRD 1980, 138 Minuten

Freitag, 29. März 19.00

Lieber Herr Doktor Filmgruppe Schwangerschaftsabbruch, CH 1977, 64 Minuten

Lieber ledig als unverheiratet Tula Roy, CH 1978, 50 Minuten

Diskussion zu Schwangerschaftsabbruch und der politischen Praxis im Umgang mit der Selbstbestimmung und dem Widerstand von Frauen mit Vertreterinnen der aktivistischen siebziger Jahre.

Samstag, 30. März 17.00

Ta' det som en Mand, Frue! (Nehmen Sie es wie ein Mann, Madame!) Mette Knudsen und Kollektiv Rote Schwestern, Dänemark 1974, OmU, 96 Minuten

Swiss Graffiti Jacqueline Veuve, CH 1974, 4 Minuten

Subjektitüde Helke Sander, BRD 1966, 4 Minuten

Sonntag, 31. März 17.00

Abort Vibeke Lökkeberg, Norwegen 1972, 43 Minuten

Macht die Pille frei? Helke Sander, BRD 1973, 45 Minuten

Zu jeder Filmvorführung wird eine kurze Einführung gegeben. Nach den Filmen besteht jeweils die Möglichkeit zu diskutieren. Eintritt: 7.–

Programmänderungen sind vorbehalten.

Begleitende Ausstellung zum aktionistischen Frauenfilm und der feministischen Bewegung der 70er Jahre Shedhalle Öffnungzeiten: Mi - Fr 14.00 - 18.00, Sa/So 14.00 - 20.00

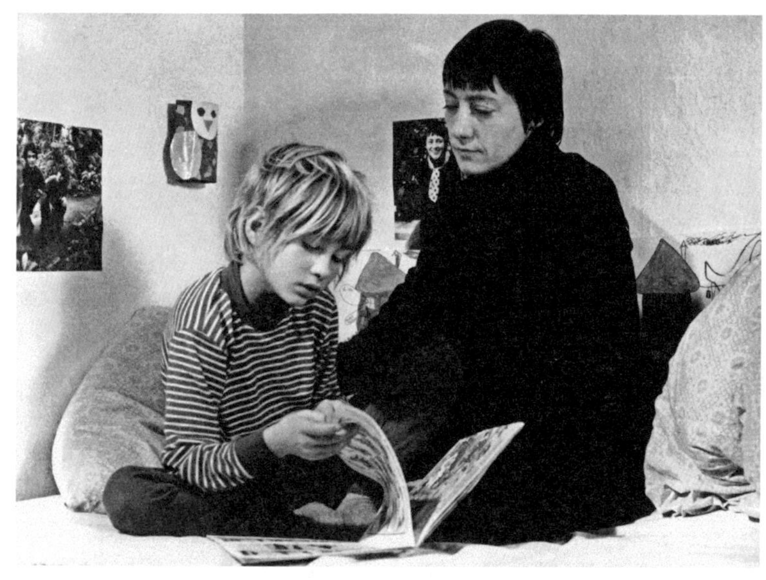

Helke Sander in the role of Edda Chiemnyjewski in *Die allseitig reduzierte Persönlichkeit–Redupers* (1978), directed by Helke Sander, photo: Deutsche Kinemathek

One could say the hippies and generation of 1968 moved as though they were living underwater, while punks jumped around as if in Mack Sennett's slapstick films.

As I remember it, punk—at least in the German-speaking region—was a paradoxical development for subcultural feminism. On one hand, there were far more women taking part in the movement and equally present in its products, but on the other, the feminist values that slowly began to take hold in the late 1970s were scorned along with other ideas from 1968: the whole old-leftist and hippie consensus on a nexus between morals and politics had been rejected by punk. Indeed, women were more and more often artists acting independently of the classical quasi-familial structures still virulent in hippie culture. But punk's self-obligation to unsentimental hardness often allowed emotions only as aggression or exuberance and supplanted forms of empathy and solidarity, which may have dwindled into clichéd gestures but still determined everyday life before punk and were structurally relevant for feminism up until then. The connection with their own feminist history was severed—often more for reasons of taste than content.

Neither self-empowerment, the collapse of content, nor regression are decisive in von Osten's recollections. Instead, she more frequently mentions a positive relationship to the artificial nature of social relations as the crucial kick or lesson[3] that she took from punk, as opposed to an ideology of self-realization with its belief in a "true self." That means—and this is an important point for all her projects—that the normative

3   In conversation with Barbara Mahlknecht, in Barbara Mahlknecht, "Dann bist Du trotzdem nicht gemeint," in *Mahlknecht, Projecting out into the Community*, ongoing web project, online at: www.projectingout-intothecommunity.org, for instance, there is mention of "embracing artificiality." In "Wir leben im Computerstaat," an unpublished manuscript, von Osten speaks of a movement obligated to "negation, dilettantism, and the artificial."

self-invention often (rightly) scorned since the regimes of post-modernism and post-Fordism became targets of criticism (most prominently argued by von Osten herself in the title of her 2003 book *Norm der Abweichung* [Norm of Deviation][4]) had a progressive and positive beginning that could still be recuperated in the core of contemporary "self-inventions."[5] The adjustment relates to something that comes from the later critical impulse to reject normative self-invention after the full panorama of post-Fordist ideology became visible. At the time of punk, this impulse to celebrate artificiality arose from the need to escape the aporias of a 1968 culture paralyzed in a compulsive binarism between adapting to the real politics of the Federal Republic of Germany and unconditional revolutionary eschatology. Indeed, the "affirmation of artificiality"—a formula used by many writers in the early 1980s—stood for various moments of uprising in the 1980s. First of all, it applied to the latent mechanisms of exclusion embedded in the assertion of authenticity, widespread in informal and subcultural movements: Are you really one of us? And of course this question was addressed quite frequently and suspiciously to women. But it also raised the question: Is this really a genuine free space and not just a free space temporarily tolerated by the system that it will actually serve to stabilize in the long run?

This strategy of a conservative self-doubt secured a certain continuity of the movement as outside and oppositional, but also as ineffectual. This strategy still aimed against any successful political pressure and was therefore rejected by a pragmatism of self-empowerment that experienced how taking over cultural spaces enabled political gains—without winning any crucial battles. This discrepancy between quietism

4   Marion von Osten, ed., *Norm der Abweichung* (Vienna and Zurich: Springer and Edition Voldemeer, 2003).

5   See also Marion von Osten, "Einleitung," in *Norm der Abweichung*, pp. 7–19.

purporting to be radical and the concomitant practice of an ultimately depoliticizing critique became a central problem, particularly through its revival in the critique of post-Fordism and postmodernism. Von Osten has succinctly addressed this in the already mentioned *Norm der Abweichung* without putting on the mantle of cultural pessimism the assertion that deviation is finished once and for all as soon as a normative version of it appears. This kind of knowledge, however, can only be gained through a long process and project experience. In the early 1980s, compounded by her studies at the art academy, where she experienced the majority of the teachers as misogynist and homophobic, von Osten realized that certain gains articulated during the punk period came at the cost of political progress that had already been achieved. She had to counter this recognized continuity between a punk culture more or less hijacked by an aggressive masculinity and new painting with something other than the conventional emotions of disappointment over a failed movement. As she mentions in the conversation with Mahlknecht cited earlier, feminist critique of these developments specifically does not follow the all-too-familiar appropriation phantasms, with which so many countercultures process their failures: once we were innocent, but then we were sold out and "appropriated." Instead, von Osten has salvaged a real point of artificiality in punk, dialectically to a certain extent, as a harbinger of the arguments of philosopher and gender theorist Judith Butler, whose texts and influence she later encountered during a longer stay in New York. The artificiality in question is, in fact, not some postmodern self-invention that can later be turned into a productive force and built into the formation of creative industries. It is a very particular artificiality (as it seminally already was in punk) that developed due to a very particular ideological condition that was not able to name the target of its critique from the beginning: the asserted naturalness of the predominant gender order as it continued happily in all forms of rock-masculinity before punk—and in most of them afterwards as well. And thus the "new artificiality" was also only very slowly able to ally itself with some of its logical friends: queer culture, for instance.

This movement, which was carried out in more than texts, projects, or artistic works, led to a form of conviction for von Osten different from opinions in the art business that usually overflow with exchange value. It is also different from the hallowed articles of faith in biographies with which people normally separate what they have comprehended from what they have not comprehended. Critique and objection are still justified in themselves, even if the respectively formulated counter-argument is nothing more than ill-considered material at a certain level of articulation that may even end up also being suitable for the purposes of an opposing side. For even this kind of negation that is often not concrete also always holds an element of concrete negation, even if it crystallizes over the course of time. This can be further developed philosophically, but this insight only becomes experiential knowledge through the long-term, project-oriented action in which it becomes manifest.

As I see it, what von Osten primarily distilled from the discourses of (especially British) cultural studies, postcolonial and migration-related research, and post-operaist theories about labor and the working class, is an emphasis on the relative autonomy and the adequacy and righteousness of an objection beyond its verbal articulation. With the concept of *colonial modernism*, she recognizes not only the familiar aporetic characteristics of modernism and the dominancy of colonialism but also, particularly, the odd effects that emerge when the two projects, which are actually irreconcilable on paper, are conjoined: modernism, ultimately a legacy of a movement that wanted to liberate all people, logically cannot be taken into the service of colonialism, which seeks the exact opposite. Yet precisely this is not only proof of the limited validity of an old western-universalist idea of emancipation, it is also an opportunity to observe local emancipation effects that occur inadvertently or at least unintentionally where the no-longer-bound self-understandings of the aforementioned discursive traditions collide. Then one discourse is no longer discourse to the other, but rather part of a recalcitrant reality.

Von Osten thus writes, together with sociologist Serhat Karakayali and architectural historian Tom Avermaete, in the preface to *Colonial Modern: Aesthetics of the Past, Rebellions for the Future*: "Conceiving colonial territories as a laboratory of modernism therefore means reflecting upon this ambivalence within modernism. Modern projects are not always and not exclusively concerned with domination and oppression. Relationships are not to be seen as asymmetrical power relations between two unchanging parties. The inherent emancipatory potential has also enabled anti-colonial liberation movement. . ."[6] The crucial point of this specific ambivalence of colonial modernism returns in other projects, and in summary this could be noted as a central point in common: discourses are not material realities to begin with, yet there is nothing else to articulate objection. The objection can never be had solip-sistically and asocially. Nor does it survive as a category of discourse in a community of accord that has long since been convinced and agreed not to have disagreements. The purely discursive, cultural objection does have a material core though: a foundation for dissatisfaction that cannot yet show itself in its purely cultural-discursive manifestation. Speaking unveils

6   Marion von Osten, Serhat Karakayali, and Tom Avermaete, "Colonial Modern," in *Colonial Modern: Aesthetics of the Past, Rebellions for the Future*, Tom Avermaete, Serhat Karakayali, and Marion von Osten, eds. (London: Black Dog Architecture, 2010), p. 12.

and veils its material causes. In the engagement with other discourses (beyond pure antagonism) and in the manifestation of irreconcilabilities, this core, this spark also first becomes explicit. From the celebration of artificial identities, eventually an anti-patriarchal political feminism emerges, whereas, from architectonic applications of ideas of usability, the face of instrumental reason arises (as does its rejection). What is necessary for these kinds of processes, however, is that more than two—in other words, at least three—perspectives are involved. Only when there is a third actor, discursive format, type of articulation involved, is there a chance that the political cause and the articulatory attack do not remain in the lame relation between idea and expression, between artificial and authentic. The quality of negation depends on the third party: the female punk rocker learns the meaning of her objection against the ideology of the natural in (earlier, pre-punk) rock only when she meets a patriarchal painter.

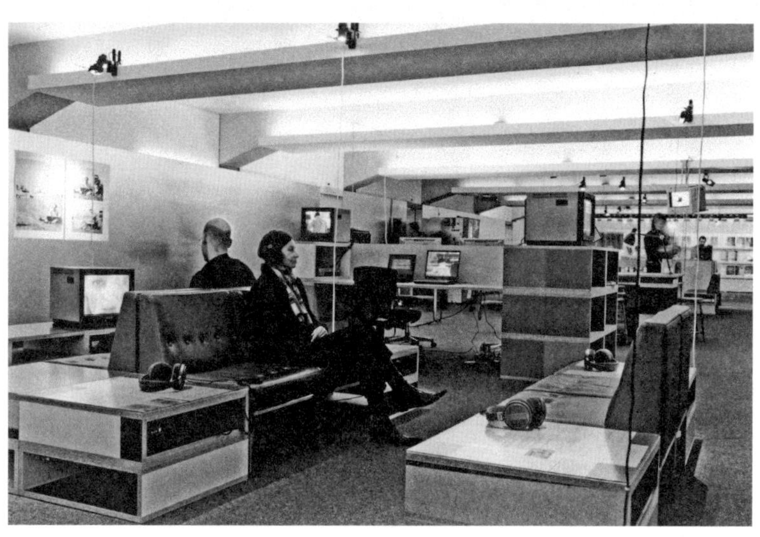

Labor k3000, *Be Creative! The Creative Imperative*, 2002–2003, research and exhibition project, installation view Museum für Gestaltung, Zurich, photo: Betty Fleck, source: Archive Zurich University of the Arts

Tom Holert

In the Company of Others: Marion von Osten's Building Practice

<u>Politics of Friendship</u>
As it regularly happens when writing on the work of friends, the apparently impersonal use of names, written in full or just using the surname, feels awkward for the writing subject. It is particularly hard to write in such an objectifying (or literary) mode when the person in question is not only a close friend but also one whose practice very much relies on breaking down the barriers between friendship and collaboration, between intimacy and professionalism. When I met Marion von Osten for the first time in a café in Cologne (in the summer of 2001, if I remember correctly), I could not by any means anticipate how quickly and to what extent I would be integrated into her world of thinking and acting during the months and years to follow. I had known her name and her work as a cultural producer and as a member of the Berlin and Zurich art worlds for quite some time already, and we might have met before, if only casually, on several occasions. But after having actually made her acquaintance, I simply fell for her engaging, inviting energy and breadth of interests, urgencies, and experiences. I thus became a collaborator in the *Be Creative!* project, including a lecture at the December 2002 opening conference of the exhibition *Be Creative! The Creative Imperative* (2002–2003) at the Museum für Gestaltung in Zurich; in the latter, I participated with two video pieces (one in collaboration with visual artist/illustrator/ thinker Felix Reidenbach) based on my research on the visual discourse around notions of testing, intelligence, and the brain. In the summer of 2002, I was invited to spend three months as a fellow at the ith (Institute of Theory, affiliated with HGKZ, today's ZHdK or Zurich University of the Arts), where Marion worked at the time and where I was employed as an adjunct researcher for two more years, being mostly occupied with work around the conceptual and material history of "the glamorous." From 2004 to 2006, Mark Terkessidis and I benefited from a travel and research grant offered by the *Projekt Migration*

curatorial team, among them Marion, on the basis of which Mark and I were able to write the book *Fliehkraft: Gesellschaft in Bewegung. Von Migranten und Touristen* (Centrifugal Force: Society in Motion. Of Migrants and Tourists) (2006). In 2006, then, Marion and I happened to become colleagues as professors at the Academy of Fine Arts Vienna, Vienna for the following five years. Again, we collaborated on several occasions, most importantly in a lecture series on the intersections of visuality and pedagogy, and the subsequent co-edited publication *Das Erziehungsbild: Zur visuellen Kultur des Pädagogischen* (The Education Image: On Pedagogy's Visual Culture) (2010). Our friendship has grown since then, and therefore the attempt, in this essay, to provide a survey of Marion's work, methodologies, and styles of making-thinking is necessarily informed (and, some would argue, distorted) by immense sympathy, or, more precisely, love. The seemingly distant way of writing about the cultural and aesthetic practices of someone who is, in fact, close to one's own heart will occasionally bear traces of inconsequentiality and oversight. However, this disclosure is meant less apologetically than it may seem, as friendship not only proves to be a crucial productive force in the highly "relational" field of contemporary art (when considered as empowering and resistant and only partially obeying the economic logic of post-Fordism) but also a hermeneutic device that competes with (and sometimes contradicts) the mandatory expectations associated with scholarly detachment.[1]

Group Architectures in Formation
In an inconspicuous brown DIN A0 cardboard box that Marion once offered me as a gift, she had collected selected items

[1] For an insightful essay on the notion of friendship in anthropology, see Henk Driessen, "The Notion of Friendship in Ethnographic Fieldwork," *Anthropological Journal on European Cultures*, vol. 7, no. 1 (1998), pp. 43–62 (of which I have a photocopy that Marion once gave me).

of modernist ideology: design drawings by Le Corbusier, renderings of the architect's legendary small office (*petit atelier*) accompanied by hand-written quotes from his writings; portraits of architect Walter Gropius and artists Theo van Doesburg and Piet Mondrian, pencil-drawn after well-known photographs, surrounded by handwritten text, and subsequently photocopied; another drawing of Mondrian's famous Paris studio; a Xerox of two pages of a book about DIY handiwork, on the preparation of wall paint (including, alongside many close-ups of presumably male hands demonstrating the use of different tools, one photo of a young woman using a kitchen blender, facing the camera with a slightly ironic expression); a Xerox of an aerial view drawing, courtesy of Gropius and architect Rudolf Hillebrecht, of their submission to an architecture competition from 1934, showing a *Haus der Arbeit* (House of Work) designed in vintage Bauhaus style yet prominently featuring swastika banners.

And there is more material to be found in the box: loose, unbound pieces of paper of different sizes and materiality, some of them still bearing the traces of Scotch tape, reminding one of the fact that these materials have been used in Marion's installation *Bauordnungslehre* (The Principle of Building Codes), one of her contributions to the 1995 exhibition of *when tekkno turns to sound of poetry* (subtitled *Technologie, Feminismus, Konzept-Kunst & Politik* [Technology, Feminism, Conceptual Art & Politics]). After taking place originally in 1994 at Shedhalle Zürich, *when tekkno*, organized by art historian Sabeth Buchmann and philosopher Juliane Rebentisch, traveled to Kunst-Werke, Berlin, albeit in a version developed on site that differed significantly from the former one. The two exhibitions featured talks, discussions, and screenings while focusing on a feminist and techno-skeptical critique of conceptual art and its aftermath, dealing with the fascination that the aesthetics and powers of (bio)technology exert, and arguing for (post)feminist self-organization. In an explicit move away from a theory/practice division that the organizers observed in the feminist discussion groups they attended as well as in the emerging post-conceptual genre of "issue" exhibitions in the early 1990s, *when tekkno* was meant to offer a different model for the productive entanglement of texts, collectivities, and materialities.

Although it met with strong defiance[2] or—with the exception of occasional attempts at reading the underlying group dynamics in the context of recent developments in the art world[3]—utter neglect by the public, *when tekkno* figured as a rallying point for otherwise largely heterogeneous practices and practitioners, making manifest the workings of factions of the notorious *Zusammenhang* (context) of mainly Berlin-based artists, writers, and activists gathered around journals such as *A.N.Y.P.* and what would later become the Berlin bookshops b_books (also a publisher) and Pro qm.[4] The experience of a critical, precarious commonality organized along topics that were routinely ignored or repressed in the German art context remained decisive for many participants who went on to curate and organize exhibitions as discursive events. In 1994–1995, Marion participated not only in *when tekkno* but also in the notorious *Studio Hellerau.* Involving approximately the same bunch of Berlin practitioners involved in *when tekkno,* this was a rather

2   See, for example, Marius Babias, "When Tekkno Turns to Sound of Poetry," *Frieze*, no. 22 (May 1995), online at: https://frieze.com/article/when-tekkno-turns-sound-poetry.
3   See, for example, Isabelle Graw, "Gruppenzwänge," *Texte zur Kunst,* no. 18 (May 1995), pp. 51–59.
4   At the same time, *when tekkno* (particularly its Berlin installment) happened to be the arena for crises and fights within this very group, leading to tension and a series of subsequent personal breakups. Soon after, under the career-savvy guidance of future MoMA curator Klaus Biesenbach, Kunst-Werke transformed from a rather obscure, informal, and potentially radical post-1989 project space in Mitte to today's well known KW Institute for Contemporary Art, home of the Berlin Biennale and other art world spectacles.

disastrous attempt to mimic an early twentieth-century artists' colony in Germany's first garden city of Hellerau in Dresden (built from 1909 onwards by architects such as Kurt Frick, Hermann Muthesius, Richard Riemerschmid, and Heinrich Tessenow) and to produce a film on the realities of a post-1989 squatting situation and the utopian models that had led to the original architecture. Nonetheless, it had formative effects as it nurtured Marion's interest in the historical ambiguities of any concerted attempt at reforming society through educational programs and architecture.

It is to be said, though, that in the mid-1990s Marion had already been instructed and prepared by her time as an art student and by encounters with various artistic dead ends as well as progressive practices, which meant she had already passed through several stages of intellectual, political, and artistic development. Prior to her short-lived immersion in the Berlin *Zusammenhang,* she studied painting at the State Academy of Fine Arts Karlsruhe, Karlsruhe, became involved in new media exhibitions such as the 1988 *Unternehmen Dunkelkammer* (Darkroom Enterprises) and the collective MetaAusStelLung (MetaExhibition), and, in 1989–1990, spent decisive months in New York. There, she visited—to lasting effect—artist and activist Martha Rosler's 1989 *If You Lived Here. . .,* a canonical exhibition on homelessness and gentrification at the Dia Art Foundation, and attended the premiere of choreographer and filmmaker Yvonne Rainer's *Privilege* (1990), where Marion experienced, much to her delight, a cinema full of people interested in feminism and film, something that had become rare in 1980s Germany. Back from New York, she moved to Berlin and befriended practitioners of the former East Berlin dissident *bohème* before starting new collaborations within circles from which *when tekkno* and other projects were later to emerge.

The box that Marion made on the occasion of *when tekkno* belongs to a small artist's edition produced in the aftermath of the exhibition, referring particularly to the *Bauordnungslehre* installation. It carries several traces of her experiences in a rapidly changing historical environment, and the particular interests that were triggered by her stay in New York and the subsequent move to Berlin—the issues of housing, of gendered work, of modernism's legacy. On the box's lid, next to a drawing showing Gropius and along with some key terms from historian and architectural critic Sigfried Giedion's 1929 *Befreites Wohnen* (Liberated Living) pamphlet, she had glued a small explanatory text:

The installation *Bauordnungslehre* thematized the production of space and living conditions from a variety of perspectives. For one, a separate, windowless room whose size conformed to the size of Le Corbusier's *petit atelier* was built into Kunst-Werke.[5] This tiny, white space was both a kind of working room (studio/office) and a space of exhibition (white cube). On the work desk, there were drawings that presented some masterminds of modernism and, in abbreviated form, their ascetic concepts of space. On the walls behind the work desk, designs by Le Corbusier for the *petit atelier* and the Couvent Sainte-Marie de La Tourette were mounted next to designs from Ernst Neufert's [1943] *Bauordnungslehre*.[6] On the two remaining walls, there was photographic

[5]   Three years before, in his 1992 exhibition *Vergessene Zukunft* (Forgotten Future) Kunstverein München, Munich, Christian Philipp Müller had likewise reconstructed Le Corbusier's 1947 studio in simplified form; for more on Le Corbusier's working cell, see Karen Michels, *Der Sinn der Unordnung: Arbeitsformen im Atelier Le Corbusier* (Braunschweig: Vieweg 1989), p. 29ff.
[6]   Before Neufert published *Bauordnungslehre* in 1943, edited and introduced by Reich Minister Albert Speer, he had already published *Bauentwurfslehre* in 1936, an influential architectural handbook on building norms and rapid design (later revised and translated into English as *Architects' Data* in countless reprints). On this, see, most recently, Nader Vossoughian, "Standardization Reconsidered: *Normierung* in and after Ernst Neufert's *Bauentwurfslehre* (1936)," *Grey Room*, no. 54 (Winter 2014), pp. 34–55.

documentation of a photo album by a woman who tried to describe her small, single apartment to her relatives in the then GDR, using pictures and texts.[7]

For those readers equipped with rudimentary knowledge of Marion's work as a visual artist, researcher, curator, organizer, teacher, activist, or, differently put, as a producer of culture (*Kulturproduzentin*) and instigator of collaborative processes over a period spanning more than three decades, a brief rendition of her *Bauordnungslehre* will be reminiscent of familiar features and subjects of her practice: references to modernist art and architecture, the insertion of an architectural structure in a given space, and the interest in the efficiency-driven rationalization of lives in capitalism as well as in the historical and basically vernacular tactics of coping with (and challenging) the modernist grid (in this case, through showing the found, photographic self-documentation of a West German woman made with the purpose of communicating the features of her tiny apartment to those living beyond the Iron Curtain).

From Theme to Project
Typically, if slightly misleadingly, the first sentence originally uses "*thematisieren*," a virtually untranslatable German word that was introduced into academic discourse around the 1970s before going increasingly mainstream during the 1980s and 1990s. However, contrary to what may be expected, the use of this term here is not to be associated with the concepts of the thematic artwork or theme exhibitions that tend to rely on a logic of representation. Instead, the institutional and physical space of the art exhibition was conceived by Marion and her fellow participants of *when tekkno* as the template (a defining and disciplining environment, but also a set of methodologies

[7] Translation by author.

and political attitudes) and the platform (an open, malleable institutional infrastructure) for a different mode of address. In the framework of essentially collaborative endeavors (such as *when tekkno*), an approach was developed that critically distinguished between traditionally curated group shows, exhibitions organized around a "theme," and what came to be called "project exhibitions."[8] Theories were not to become themes, but methodological tools of exhibition making.[9]

Some years later, Marion would speak of the project exhibition as a "new artistic practice" that opposes the art world and "unambiguously takes a stand in not illustrating a theme but instead developing its own theses, methods, and formats, establishing a discourse, a practice that radically questions the space of art and the regime of representation linked to it."[10]

[8] The origin of this term is somewhat hard to determine. In German, the terms *"Ausstellungsprojekt"* and *"Projektausstellung,"* though not identical (the former being less programmatic in regard to the contestation of traditional hierarchies and divisions of labor in the art institution than the latter), gained traction in curatorial discourse during the 1990s and have become widely used since then. See, for example, Beatrice von Bismarck, "Haltloses Ausstellen: Politiken des künstlerischen Kuratierens," in *The Artist as...*, ed. Matthias Michalka (Vienna: MUMOK, 2007), pp. 33–47.

[9] In a programmatic statement on the exhibition, Monika Rinck, a member of the participating group Übung am Phantom, formulates: "As a 'theme project' *when tekkno turns to sound of poetry* attempts to work methodically with feminist approaches without turning the theories as such into a theme." See Monika Rinck, "when tekkno turns to sound of poetry," in *Programm 1994* (Zurich: Verlag Shedhalle Zürich, 1995), p. 26.

[10] Marion von Osten, "Changing Methods, Shifting Discourses, Producing Publics: Project Exhibitions as a Feminist Artistic Practice," abstract of a lecture at Kunstraum, Leuphana University of Lüneburg, online at: http://kunstraum.leuphana.de/projekte/ republicart-publicum/abstract-vonosten.html. On project exhibitions, see also Marion von Osten, "If white is just a colour, the gallery is just a sight?," in *n.paradoxa*, no. 16 (July 2002), pp. 46–50. Different versions of the article have been published under various titles in: *Olympe*, no. 19 (December 2003), pp. 59–72; *Multitudes*, no. 15 (Winter 2004), pp. 239–249, online at: http://www.multitudes. net/A-double-tranchant/; Peter Blundell Jones, Doina Petrescu, and Jeremy Till, eds., *Architecture and Participation* (Oxon: Spon Press, 2005), pp. 207–210; Simon Sheikh, ed., *In the Place of the Public Sphere?: Critical Readers in Visual Cultures* (Copenhagen and Berlin: Øjeblikket and b_ books, 2005), pp. 142–169; Gerald Raunig and Ulf Wuggenig, eds., *Publicum: Theorien der Öffentlichkeit* (Vienna: Turia + Kant, 2005), pp. 124–139; Marianne Eigenheer, ed., *Curating Critique* (Frankfurt: Institute for Curatorship and Education/Revolver, 2007), pp. 59–67; and *Afterall*, no. 25 (Autumn 2010), pp. 56–69.

This argument for an intense reconfiguration of artistic practice by way of a process-based, collaborative, transdisciplinary, nonhierarchical, gender-conscious, and generative mode of exhibition making, which is more about enabling a becoming and creating a (counter)public than about displaying knowledge in a representational mode, has been adopted by many cultural practitioners who came of age in the 1990s. However, Marion is arguably the one who most explicitly and energetically made a case—a sustainable, discursive object—out of it. In very clear terms, as well as in a practice that does not shy away from conflict and confrontation *within* the temporary and long-term collaboratives and the often complex institutional affiliations that form their infrastructures, the project exhibition emerges "from concrete demands and social struggles," strives for a "post-identitarian perspective," and benefits from the "artificiality and publicness" of the art institution that is converted, in the process, into "a space for the desire for new subjectivities as a 'ground for possibilities.'"[11]

In retrospect, one could recognize in Marion's work what political thinker and philosopher Hannah Arendt and philosopher and sociologist Jürgen Habermas have theorized from different angles as modalities of publicness, later elaborated upon by queer theorist and literary historian Michael Warner in terms of counterpublics, or, more precisely, "the fantasy of stateless public association" that runs counter to "the normalizing ideal of the social."[12] Equally, the postcapitalist theory-practice developed by feminist economic geographers Katherine Gibson and Julie Graham resonates here. J. K. Gibson-Graham's

---

11 Marion von Osten, "Another Criterion… or, What Is the Attitude of a Work in the Relations of Production of Its Time?," *Afterall*, no. 25 (Autumn 2010), pp. 68–69.

12 Michael Warner, *Publics and Counterpublics* (New York: Zone Books, 2002), pp. 275, 221.

ventured modes of thinking and their fieldwork on different economies and a political imaginary that reaches beyond the paradigm of neoliberal capitalism are not unlike the epistemic-curatorial paradigm whose development constitutes a central strand of Marion's cultural production.

By way of transforming a hitherto innocent, silent, or invisible state of affairs into one of pressing urgency, e.g., into a "theme," political meaning is bestowed on the otherwise neutral "thematization." The discursive work of engendering an issue by juxtaposing seemingly unrelated concepts is a crucial component of a practice that pertains to creating problems, sometimes causing trouble. Addressing the "production of space and living conditions" (mentioned in the brief quote on *Bauordnungslehre*) through an architectural, installation-based intervention in Kunst-Werke and the *when tekkno* exhibition, clearly evinced a Marxist-Lefebvrian sense of material processes, "production" took place and was critically investigated at the same time. A hybrid space—white cube and work place—"was built" by Marion herself with the input and help of others to gain insight into the ideological and aesthetic operations of inclusion and exclusion, of claiming and denying authorship in spatio-political matters against the backdrop of modernist planning, architecture, and the visual arts.

Creating Space

Emphasizing the actual process of making-building in Marion's contribution to *when tekkno* is appropriate because the material practice of putting up installations and exhibitions should play a major part in the understanding of it. In other words, the obvious conceptualist approach of an installation such as *Bauordnungslehre*, with its multiplicity of associative and investigative layers, should not block an appreciation of the very made-ness of the created space, its low budget textures, and

Marion von Osten, *Bauordnungslehre*, 1995,
mixed media installation, installation view
Kunst-Werke, Berlin, photo: Marion von Osten

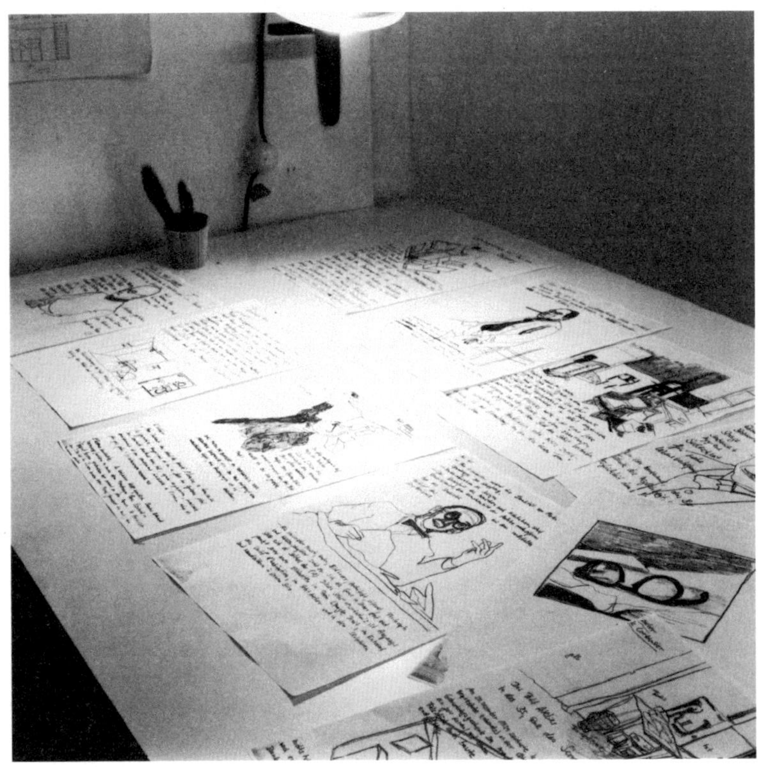

DIY aesthetics. Although Marion, in her feminist commitment to issues of service and care work, would question the equation of production (*Produktion*) and fabrication (*Herstellung*) as maintaining a stubborn legacy of masculinist labor politics,[13] she is herself an ardent builder and maker of physical things.

Producing culture here is considered to be material in more than one sense. For one, it is seen as an essentially reproductive type of labor informed by various economies and ecologies: libidinal, financial, social, and epistemic. If modernist architecture and other kinds of built and made environments are being considered, this is done from the point of view of those inhabiting them for largely reproductive reasons. Moreover, creativity, the romanticist and pedagogical notion that has taken center stage in contemporary societies that are organized around notions of the performative self, is read in terms of reproduction rather than of original creation. Marion's critique of the neoliberal mythology of creativity resulted in the Zurich 2002–2003 *Be Creative!* project, which emphasized the concealment of the sphere of reproduction by a late-capitalist governmentality that had successfully co-opted artist Joseph Beuys's "every man is an artist" slogan to produce creative subjects as the ultimate free agents for the cultural capitalist market.

In 1995, the "theme" of the physical environments where acts of making modernist architecture and painting happen was displayed via the annotated drawings of Le Corbusier's and Mondrian's studios and the built, three-dimensional space of *Bauordnungslehre*. This constellation not only invites a

13 See, for example, Marion von Osten and Elisabeth Stiefel, "Arbeit Arbeit Arbeit—und was kommt danach?," in *Das Phantom sucht seinen Mörder: Ein Reader zur Kulturalisierung der Ökonomie*, Justin Hoffmann and Marion von Osten, eds. (Berlin: b_books, 1999), p. 160.

critical reading of modernist mythology and the heroics of male-creativity-in-splendid-isolation, but also points to the libidinal economy of making, the affectivity of handiwork, the engagement with different materialities, the practical problem-solving on the spot, the (sometimes tedious, often delightful) dependency on others who assist and advise. Practice, in these instances, is the very manner in which the body is put into action—behind, rather than on, the stage—but in full acknowledgment of its vital importance as the constitutive factor in the occupation of time and space in the company of others and, therefore, the ground of historically (in)formed subjectivity.

Exhibitions, in all of Marion's endeavors, are treated in deliberate analogy to architects' or artists' studios, or even more, to craftswomen's workshops. In *Atelier Europa* (2003–2004), the very notion of the studio even figured in the title of the project that also featured a decidedly sculptural (and doubtlessly funny) mock-monumental installation of decommissioned furniture from the offices of one of the largest German insurance corporations. Marion, for once enacting her gallery "artist" self/role while inviting visitors of the show to take home a table or a chair, devised the installation. The context of this sweeping, generous, and even somewhat careless gesture, however, was a manifold, translocal undertaking. Aptly subtitled *a research and event project for the Munich Kunstverein, Atelier Europa* was hosted by Kunstverein München curator Søren Grammel and co-organized by Marion and feminist cultural studies scholar Angela McRobbie. Here, to increase the complexity of the social and productive arrangement, Marion collaborated with artists Pauline Boudry, Brigitta Kuster, Katja Reichard, and political theorist Isabell Lorey, the latter three of which, alongside Marion, constituted the group kleines postfordistisches Drama (kpD) between 2003 and 2006. Via interviews and the scripted 2004 video *Kamera läuft!* (Rolling!), kpD investigated

the "lines of potential collectivization"[14] amidst pandemic individualization in the field of cultural and knowledge production.

Atelier Europa involved experts from various disciplines and
backgrounds who gathered to discuss the changing percep-
tions and practices of cultural producers in the post-Fordist
work sphere. I recall the meetings as intense and sometimes
controversial encounters of quite different language games
(activist, scholarly, "artistic"). These were nonetheless marked
and arranged by the built (and staged) surroundings of the
Kunstverein and the work that had gone into the production of
an environment designed to elicit the kind of exchange that in
the early 2000s increasingly—not least of all thanks to Marion's
insistence on imagining discourse in terms of materiality and
aesthetics—had become a desired outcome of project exhibitions such as *Atelier Europa*. The collectivity in the making and
the generativity of building physical structures and organizing
objects and bodies in space are characteristically highlighted
in projects ranging from *Sex & Space: Space. Gender. Economy*
(1996–1997) to *In the Desert of Modernity: Colonial Planning
and After* (2008–2009).

Informal Modernism
Quite likely starting with *Bauordnungslehre* and her second
contribution to *when tekkno*, the work *Human Genome Project*
(1994–1995) was an investigation of Le Corbusier's *unité
d'habitation*, relating it to the technology of genetics. A main
strand of Marion's transdisciplinary practice became an exploration of the distinctions between the planned and the built,
the conceived and the realized. The vernacular modernisms

14 kpD, "Wenn die Arbeit so ins Leben
sickert," *Arranca!*, no. 31 (January 2005),
online at: http://arranca.org/ausgabe/31/
wenn-die-arbeit-so-ins-leben-sickert. The
German phrase in the original reads: "*nach
kollektivierbaren Linien zu suchen, die aus
der individuellen Erfahrung hinausführen.*"
Translation and emphasis by author.

that have sprung from the non-regulated activity of the subaltern, colonized, and decolonized populations not only evidence how the realities entailed by modernist planning can be subverted and rerouted, but also how this is taking place on the level of material interventions in buildings and infrastructures. Referring to her interest in the histories of colonial and postcolonial planning in Morocco and elsewhere, Marion writes that "the most radical form of design emerges when the people begin to represent themselves without mediators and masters."[15]

The vernacular, as conceived by Ivan Illich and other theorists of informal economies, is one of the categories that most informed Marion's political project of excavating ever more "lines of potential collectivization"—as mentioned above in relation to kpD—in the counter-archives (and on the battlefields) of anti- and postcapitalism and decolonizing movements. Repeatedly transformed from a site of resistance (or resilience) into one of economic productivity in the modernist sense through innumerable enterprises of the learning-from variety, the vernacular has proved to be a particular dialectic, a shifting figure of domination through integration, as well as empowerment through acts of *détournement* by people-experts who use the architectures and infrastructures that were foisted upon them in unexpected, desublimating, and critical ways. A central and ultimately optimistic hypothesis underpinning Marion's pursuit of deindividualizing, transnational, and transhistorical modes of solidarity and collectivity seeks the benefits of such dialectics: as much as it is susceptible to being co-opted and commodified, the vernacular or "common culture" as addressed by Paul Willis[16]

15 Marion von Osten, "Architecture Without Architects—Another Anarchist Approach," *e-flux journal*, no. 6 (May 2009), online at: http://www.e-flux.com/journal/06/61401/architecture-without-architects-another-anarchist-approach/.

16 Paul Willis, *Common Culture: Symbolic Work at Play in the Everyday Cultures of the Young* (Boulder, CO: Westview Press, 1990).

may subsist as the very dimension of action, organizing, and thinking-making that provides models of refusal in the contemporary condition of a capitalism based on the exploitation of individual and cultural difference. The historical moment of resistance through rituals and similar formulae for renewed class struggle might be gone forever. However, the new spirit of capitalism has proved to be less monolithic and all-absorbing than often assumed. The inventiveness of those suffering from the real social and environmental catastrophes inflicted upon them by the same ideology that has successfully devalued politics in the name of the market continues to hold strong.

This utopian remainder of such latter-day feminist Marxism, however, needs to be constantly wrested from the rather bleak results of the analyses of neoliberal governmentality and expanded value extraction. As Marion puts it in a complex essay on issues of gendered consumption/production, the informal economy of cross-border fashion trades at the outer limits of the European Union and the development of the creative industry in Zurich. Writing in the context of the *MoneyNations* project (1997–2001), Marion states, "subcultural deviation has . . . not only become lifestyle and fashion today in the sense of commodification, rather, individual paths of life have become 'productive' today for surplus value generation."[17]

However, the search for the cracks and fissures in the capitalist building does not stop here. The kind of collaborative, cross-border cultural production that was realized in projects such as *MoneyNations* would hardly have worked if it had taken place solely on the basis of a negativist approach. The thorough

17 Marion von Osten, "Fashion Is Work: Some Thoughts on the Gendered Relationship between Production and Consumption before the Backdrop of the International Division of Labour," in *MoneyNations: Constructing the Border – Constructing East-West*, Marion von Osten and Peter Spillmann, eds. (Vienna: edition selene, 2003), p. 76.

critique of the EU border regime may have served as a common ground for international participants, but at the same time, *MoneyNations*—like any other project addressing an unacknowledged, ideologically distorted, problematic issue—drew most of its energy from the shared sense of a necessity to work from a new, presumably more productive angle that broke with inherited conceptualizations and categorizations. Here, in the first project that was conceived, developed, and realized in tandem with artist and educator Peter Spillmann, the basic ideas involved critically overcoming any west/east binarism, making available transdisciplinary knowledge of the political economies of the "former east" as well as the "former west," enabling the "formation of networks across the Schengen border,"[18] and developing the project in such a way that the "theme" being researched does not overwhelm the reflection on the positions from which each participant speaks. The particular drive and energy characteristic of such projects not only stemmed from the confidence in addressing big issues such as "Eurocentrism" from a fringe perspective, but also from the discovery of other possibilities (of acting in informal economies, of working in collaboration and correspondence, of using the Internet to new effects, etc.), of moments of experiencing the surplus of producing around a shared urgency and in an unexpected, experimental commonality.

Being in a Room, Together

There is a reason that the publications edited by Marion and her collaborators time and again feature photographs of such situations of commonality, of exchange, of working together. Despite having become conversation pieces portraying an often self-indulgent, depoliticized culture of exchange and "relational aesthetics" in a biennialized art world ever since the 1990s and

18 Marion von Osten, "Introduction," in *MoneyNations*, p. 9.

early 2000s, for a limited period of time such images worked as a means of communicating a different understanding of art practice *as* cultural production. The sensation of being in a room (and in a constellation of common interests) with cultural producers from other countries, milieus, or fields of expertise, and whose experiences and knowledge supplement one's own in unforeseen ways, ranged among the key factors that propelled this practice forward. At the same time, Marion never believed in the "good" commonality as such, but has always been critical of any illusions pertaining to claims of a political, ethical, or aesthetical superiority stemming from just being together for no particular reason. Her approach cannot be separated from the urgent quest for knowledge that seldom comes without concerted effort but does not declare commonality a prerequisite as such. The collectivities entailed in her projects are strange hybrids of research teams, friendship circles, elective affinities, and construction crews, but they never aim at any self-sufficiency or a misconceived notion of autonomy.

Amidst all the characteristic earnestness of critique and questioning, however, there is a pleasure in the glamorous and the beautiful that shines out through the fiercest struggles for recognition and change. Most of the projects that Marion has been and is involved in bear marks of such moments of pleasure otherwise absent from sociopolitical discourse (and that contribute to an insistent resilience despite any subsumption by art world or institutional logic). Just consider the fold-out cover of the voluminous, 888-page catalog published for the final show of *Projekt Migration*, the 2002–2006 Cologne-based exhibition and research endeavor for which Marion was hired as a co-curator alongside archivist-activists Aytaç Eryılmaz and Martin Rapp, curator Kathrin Rhomberg, and anthropologist Regina Römhild. It featured a blown-up photographic still used in a documentary (*Pierburg: Ihr Kampf ist unser Kampf*

[Pierburg: Their Stuggle Is Our Struggle] by Edith Schmidt and David Wittenberg, 1974/1975) about the 1973 wild strikes at a car parts supplier in the city of Neuss. The still shows two women—presumably migrant workers—one of them caressing her hair as if the camera were a mirror, the other smiling and smoking a cigarette, beaming confidence and determination.[19] Florian Lambl, who designed the catalog, opted for silver, embossed lettering, combining the rather surprising image of the women with the bold and glitzy words "Projekt" and "Migration," thereby generating an awkward, individualized, yet collective political spectacularity where one might have expected straightforward images of misery or protest.

Speaking differently about (or, better, *from/alongside*) migration, feminism, capitalism, and labor, using visual means (in book and exhibition design) and discursive strategies (in research, writing, communication) that reach beyond the usual tonalities of science and politics were declared goals of *Projekt Migration*. The introduction of concepts such as "visual regime" (*Blickregime*) into the discourse was part of a concerted, transdisciplinary effort to change the perspective, invert the national gaze on the issue and inhabit the point of view of migrants.[20] Acknowledging by "making visible," the fact that migration had become a "central force of societal change" was made tangible by combining the "imaginative potentials of artistic production, the accuracy of historical research, and the theoretical challenges of research in social and cultural studies."[21]

19 Marion once told me that the images of the women on strike at Pierburg reminded her of the women cultural producers installing the *when tekkno* exhibitions in Zurich and Berlin in 1994–1995.
20 For a methodological reflection on the concepts used in *Projekt Migration*, see Marion von Osten, "Eine Bewegung der Zukunft: Die Bedeutung des Blickregimes der Migration für die Produktion der Ausstellung Projekt Migration," in *Turbulente Ränder: Neue Perspektiven auf Migration an den Grenzen Europas*, ed. Transit Migration Forschungsgruppe (Bielefeld: transcript, 2007), pp. 169–185.
21 Aytaç Eryılmaz et al., "Vorwort," in *Projekt Migration*, Kölnischer Kunstverein et al., eds. (Cologne: DuMont, 2005), pp. 16–17. Translation by author.

Aytaç Eryılmaz, Marion von Osten, Martin
Rapp, Kathrin Rhomberg, and Regina
Römhild, *Projekt Migration*, 2005–2006,
research and exhibition project, installation
views Kölnischer Kunstverein, Cologne,
photos: Kölnischer Kunstverein

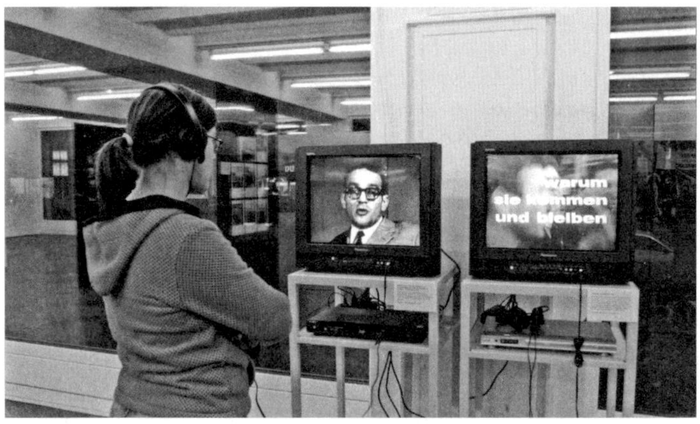

warum
sie kommen
und bleiben

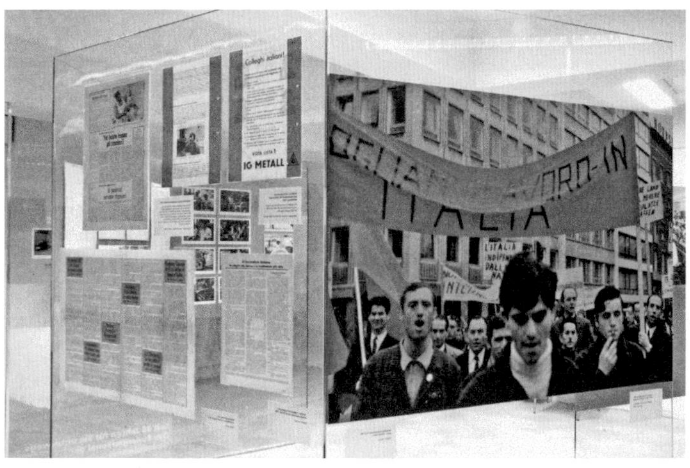

Colleghi italiani!
IG METALL
ITALIA
LAVORO-IN
L'ITALIA
INDIPEN
DALL

Projekt Migration at the time, but even more in retrospect, was a daring, colossal undertaking. It managed to upset and confuse many of the key players in national politics, academic migration studies, and the art world because the conventions of their respective discourses were clearly challenged. The lack of a very kind of representational grasp associated with more official-looking exhibitions and publications made people nervous, as did an experimental sense of play and a certain difficulty in the presentation of the apparently heterogeneous archival materials, activist and academic texts, and contributions by visual artists and cultural practitioners. With *Projekt Migration,* the project exhibition template was taken beyond and above the previous institutional and organizational levels in terms of scope, budget, and project management requirements. In keeping with Marion's political agenda of exhibition making, *Projekt Migration* was defined by collaborative research, discussion, and struggle within and outside the group/network. It created, through the critical framing and the continuation of collaborations with former contexts and individuals, a discursive environment close to earlier mid-scale projects such as *MoneyNations* or *Be Creative!* while also having to moderate, if not reconcile, the demands and expectations of activists, academics, independent researchers, artists, the various institutions involved, and the main commissioning/funding body, the German Federal Cultural Foundation. Coming from a practice that is about challenging (and changing) the conventions of not only exhibition making but of acting within the art and/or academic institution, to engage in a large-scale endeavor such as *Projekt Migration*, conspicuously state-funded and politically charged (considering the German state and its tenacious denial of migration as a constitutive factor of culture and society), the retooling of strategies for negotiating different interests, methodologies, and histories brought to the table became crucial. The benefits of such retooling are not always easy to discern.

Maybe first of all, compared with earlier projects, a different, broader kind of public, as well as spectatorship, was to be reckoned with. An exhibition for once not primarily addressed to professionals and activists from the fields of art, creative industries, and alternative politics, *Projekt Migration* and its makers gestured toward various constituencies from migrant communities and representatives of "civil society" in charge of issues such as migration and interculturality in political milieus. For Marion and her collaborators, it proved difficult but not impossible to shift registers to this extent, to expand not only in scale but also to change the composition of real and potential interlocutors. Yet for everyone involved, *Projekt Migration* remained a singular, one-off experience. Stretching the ethos and practice of the project exhibition to the limits reached between 2002 and 2006 was a major accomplishment, but also hardly sustainable.

New Institutionalism and Educational Utopia
In the aftermath of this both appreciated and criticized translation of the project exhibition into greater institutional dimensions, Marion—after having worked for 10 years at Zurich institutions such as Shedhalle Zürich and HGKZ, the local art and design school—took a job as a professor at the Academy of Fine Arts Vienna, Vienna in 2006 and departed for her next exhibitionary adventure. *In the Desert of Modernity: Colonial Planning and After* was to be realized in 2008 with and at Haus der Kulturen der Welt (HKW) in Berlin. HKW is the one large institution that has made itself known in past years for exploiting and consolidating the project exhibition template like no one else, despite having entered the New Institutionalism paradigm of internalized institutional critique in the cultural sphere rather late. Again, the ethos of transnational and transdisciplinary research and curating was put to a test in a context largely funded by the

German Federal Ministry of Foreign Affairs.[22] HKW certainly had an interest in fostering practices of this kind, but the ideological framework provided by the state institution, in its preparation for self-transformation, had to be reckoned with by the curatorial team (in this case, Marion, the architectural historian Tom Avermaete, and the sociologist Serhat Karakayali).[23]

In the Desert of Modernity embodied a presumably new mode of knowledge production, of artistic research that was about to define new standards in exhibition making at HKW.[24] However, the relationship between a large cultural institution starting to assimilate various non-standard models of curating and organizing events, exhibitions, and long-term research endeavors and a team of researchers looking for an opportunity to organize their research differently was only one level of potential contestation. Bringing different backgrounds and methodologies to the table, the three curators themselves had to internally negotiate a common ground for collaboration. Between a political understanding of the making of exhibitions as projects based on processes, the militant practice of migrants' activism, and the specific academic cultures of German sociology or Dutch/Flemish architectural history, no pre-established harmony was to be expected.

Working toward inversions of center/periphery topologies in modernist urbanism and architecture by emphasizing the role

22 Among the academic and para-academic partners were the Academy of Fine Arts Vienna, Vienna, the architectural faculty of Delft University of Technology, Delft, Casamémoire in Casablanca, CPKC (Center for Post-Colonial Knowledge and Culture, Berlin), and École Supérieure d'Architecture de Casablanca, Casablanca.

23 Many thanks to art historian Sven Lütticken for pointing out gaps in the argument here and elsewhere in the text.

24 *In the Desert of Modernity* set the tone for a series of exhibitions to come, among them the 2010–2011 *The Potosí Principle: How Can We Sing the Song of the Lord in an Alien Land?* curated by Andreas Siekmann, Alice Creischer, and Max Jorge Hinderer, as well as for artists and cultural producers who have tested the limits of existing cultural institutions and formats of political-discursive exhibition making not unlike Marion in projects such as: *Die Gewalt ist der Rand aller Dinge*, Generali Foundation, Vienna, 2002; *Ex Argentina*, Museum Ludwig, Cologne, 2004; and earlier on with the important 1995 anti-art fair *Messe 2ok. ÖkonoMiese Machen*, Cologne.

of the colony in informing the production of metropolitan urban space inevitably addresses and ultimately questions the very institutional framework in which such investigation takes place. What is of crucial importance, though, is how the address is orchestrated, how the questions are phrased. Hence, any reading of projects such as *In the Desert of Modernity* remains fragmentary if it simply focuses on the documented exhibition or its accompanying publications. Rather, attention is to be guided toward the constitutive social, material, and epistemological processes that precede and transgress the final "products" that, by default, tend to make their production invisible. To a certain extent, Marion's way of *doing* culture and research is an attempt at decentering the very idea of an exhibition, book, symposium. Though these products never fail to be delivered, the undergirding desire of this multi-scalar critical machine[25] is one of not merely acknowledging, but rather celebrating the undocumented energies and exchanges that have gone into its realizations as the prime social and epistemic reasons for any engagement in such activity at all.

An ongoing concern of the project exhibition, understood in the way Marion has conceived it, would thus include the constant reflection on the conditions of its own possibility. A progressive politics of knowledge production in the hybrid, transdisciplinary spaces of New Institutionalism continues to be about avoiding the subsumption of the material processes under the rule of representation, of public relations and the communication of a "theme," as well as being about a struggle for modes of collaboration that go beyond fixed roles and identities, beyond technocratic understandings of transdisciplinarity itself. As it happens, in the various networks and collaborative

25 Many thanks to Brian Kuan Wood for this formulation and further editorial advice throughout.

entities she has been and is a part of, Marion usually acts as the transversal figure that time and again attempts to align the logics of various knowledge milieus, research agendas, styles of thinking, practices of making things public. Her indefatigable quest for hidden, neglected, or repressed histories of transcultural networks, such as the non-aligned movements of the Cold War and the anti-colonial movement of the Tricontinental (among the subjects of recent research for an exhibition project at Tensta konsthall in Stockholm and her PhD in Fine Arts at Lund University in Malmö), is distinctive in its double move of continuously decentering one's own skills and knowledge in the confrontation with ever new histories of transgression and invention, and the ongoing exploration of the genealogies of potentially new subjectivities of transgression and invention to lead to future decenterings.

Implied in the genealogical work of identifying predecessors for desirable changes to come is a concern for the ways knowledge is generated and transmitted in (radical) pedagogies and in the politics (and utopias) of education. The acts of teaching and learning don't necessarily interest Marion as such, though. The pedagogical impulse is less tangible in any overt didactics or great educational schemes. Rather, it can be detected in the ways in which problems and histories are narrated and visualized. Along with the explanatory discourse framing most of her projects, there exist conceptual shortcuts, punchlines, and visual wit that usually receive no comment, if they are noticed at all. Another essay would be needed in order to discuss the sculptural, performative, or filmic work that Marion has produced inside and outside the greater projects for which she is mostly known; to name just a few: her 1995 *Utopia* installation, the 2000–2002 *Oblomov's Corner* lecture performance, the contributions to the *Lapdogs of the Bourgeoisie* exhibitions (2006–2009), the work on shipwrecks at the 2013

Göteborg International Biennal for Contemporary Art, or the mural representing a diagrammatic rendering of educational budgets at the 2012 Tbilisi Triennial.

Of the latter, painted by Bessa K. and herself on the outdoor walls of the Center for Contemporary Art in the Georgian capital, Marion says it refers to political statements in the public sphere and the tradition of socialist murals in Georgia before 1989, yet "it does not say anything directly; it is too abstract; it seems to only speak about itself as nice, handmade, color fields."[26] Such apparent meaninglessness notwithstanding, there are more allusions—to Sol LeWitt's wall drawings or the entire field of data visualization used in politics and science. Moreover, it is claimed that "the work is about the question of how knowledge and public opinions are represented or, better put, abstracted," while its particular craft-like quality (it is painted by hand) is supposedly eloquent with regard to "the relation of knowledge, manual production, and labor duration" and the devaluation of manual labor in cognitive capitalism.[27]

Such emphasis on manual labor and craft is also evident in <reformpause> (2006). Marion had been invited by the directors and students of the art and visual studies department of the University of Lüneburg to conceive and realize, as an individual artist, an artistic research project for Kunstraum, Leuphana University of Lüneburg, the on-campus art space that had been the site of exhibitions and events by several artists and curators working in the vein of second-wave Institutional Critique, such as Andrea Fraser or Christian Philipp Müller. Using the particular campus situation at Lüneburg and the general sense of crisis among students and faculty caused

26 Marion von Osten, "Academic Ambivalences," in *Offside Effect: Academy as Exhibition. 1st Tbilisi Triennial*, ed. Henk Slager (Utrecht: Metropolis M Books, 2013), pp. 4–5.
27 Ibid., p. 5.

Marion von Osten, *Oblomov's Corner*,
2000–2002, lecture-performance and mixed
media installation, installation view Kunsthaus
Dresden, Dresden, photo: Kunsthaus Dresden

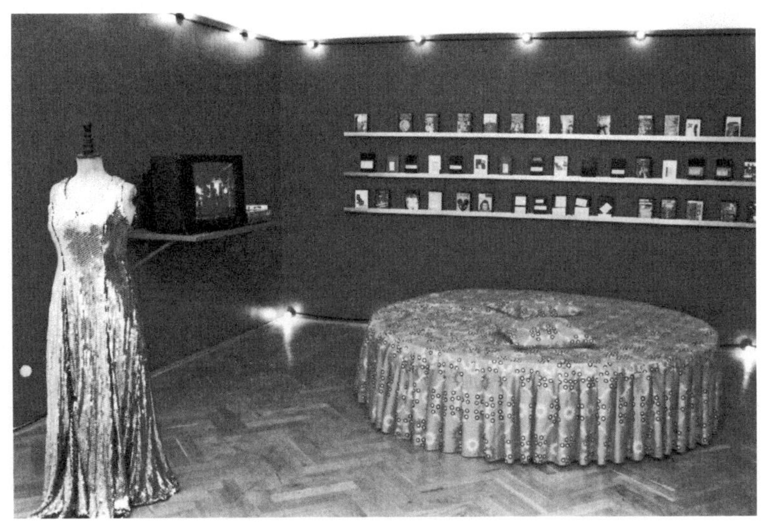

Marion von Osten, *How Do You Shipwreck
in the Harbor?,* 2013, board-mounted
posters, installation view Göteborg
International Biennial for Contemporary Art,
Gothenburg, photo: Marion von Osten

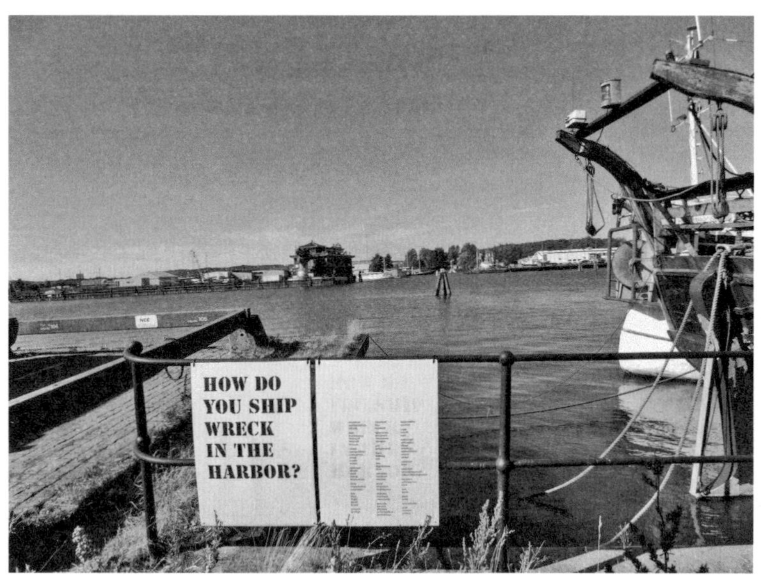

by the Bologna reforms, Marion collaborated with students to research the implications of the current reform and history of university reforms in Germany. Together they produced the poster/newspaper *Plakat* using the template of a legendary workers' and students' newspaper of the same name, first designed and printed by author Peter Grohmann for Daimler-Benz employees in the 1970s, and, with film historian Madeleine Bernstorff, organized a roaming ciné club at the university, in which movies and documentaries on education were screened, including the films of Marion's all-time favorite, Swiss director Daniel Schmid. Finally, she presented an installation in the Kunstraum itself, an abstract model of the arguably most futuristic university campus in West Germany, the Ruhr University in Bochum (RUB) that was opened, while still under construction, in 1965. Architect Helmut Hentrich considered his design for RUB in metaphorical terms: as a harbor in the sea of knowledge, with the buildings as vessels moored at this port. Born in Bochum a year before construction of the first university in the Ruhr area started, Marion built her 2006 model using boards of compressed wood and scantlings placed on a diagrammatic rendering of the university's ground plan, simplifying the architecture to the extent that it could (almost) be used as pieces of furniture, as benches to sit on. This educational complex was demonstratively *built* using simple, makeshift materials while brushing off any aspirations of a de-materialization of art or labor, and it was built by the instigator of <reformpause> herself. The rough, unpolished, handmade work did not stand out from the other activities, interventions, discussions, or publications of the project, but it also did not completely fit in. How serious could it be? How much fun did it draw from the investigations into the dreary pasts and presents of educational reform? The question in the face of the present move of knowledge to more economic and hier-archized forms, as Marion elsewhere states, remains: "Which concepts and models of 'other spaces of knowledge' are productive today for the formation of new subjectivities, alliances and coalitions?"[28] The wooden, DIY reduction of a model campus of the 1960s, filling an art space of a model campus of Bologna in the 2000s, might be exactly the kind of gesture that is needed to proffer the agency that enables us to collectively imagine and eventually activate such "other spaces of knowledge." It is a gesture particularly insofar as it is "a moment of life subtracted from the context of individual biography as well as a moment of art subtracted from the neutrality of aesthetics," and thus, as political philosopher Giorgio Agamben has it, "pure praxis."[29] If the purity of anything, "praxis" included, is something that Marion is barely interested in, her rich body of work is nonetheless composed of gestures that don't stop to delineate the other side of the commodity where labor is redirected and liberated to become situation.

[28] Marion von Osten and Eva Egermann, "Twist and Shout: On Free Universities, Educational Reforms and Twists and Turns Inside and Outside the Art World," in *Curating and the Educational Turn*, Paul O'Neill and Mick Wilson, eds. (London and Amsterdam: Open Editions and de Appel, 2010), p. 279.

[29] Giorgio Agamben, "Marginal Notes on *Commentaries of the Society of Spectacle*," in *Means without End: Notes on Politics*, Vincenzo Binetti and Cesare Casarino, trans. (Minneapolis: University of Minnesota Press, 2000), p. 79.

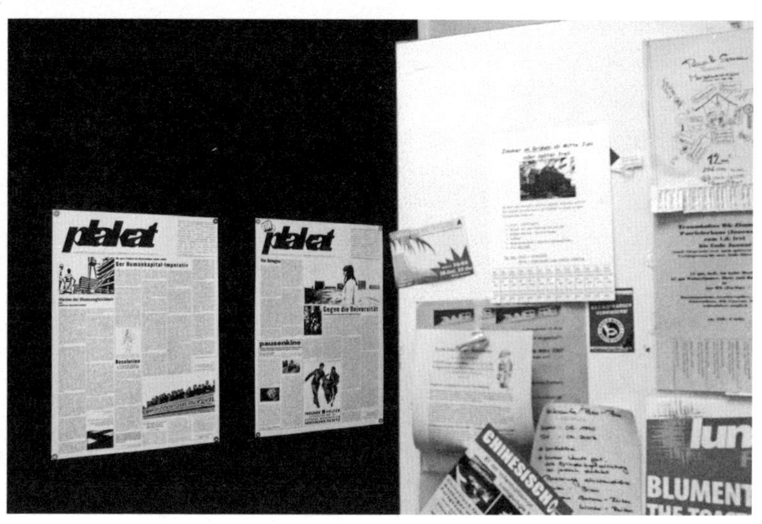

Plakat, 2006, newspaper as part of
<*reformpause*>, 2006, installation, poster,
and intervention, installation view Kunstraum,
Leuphana University of Lüneburg, Lüneburg,
photo: Wege

Marion von Osten, *<reformpause>*, 2006,
installation, poster, and intervention, detail of
installation, installation view Kunstraum,
Leuphana University of Lüneburg, Lüneburg,
photo: Wege

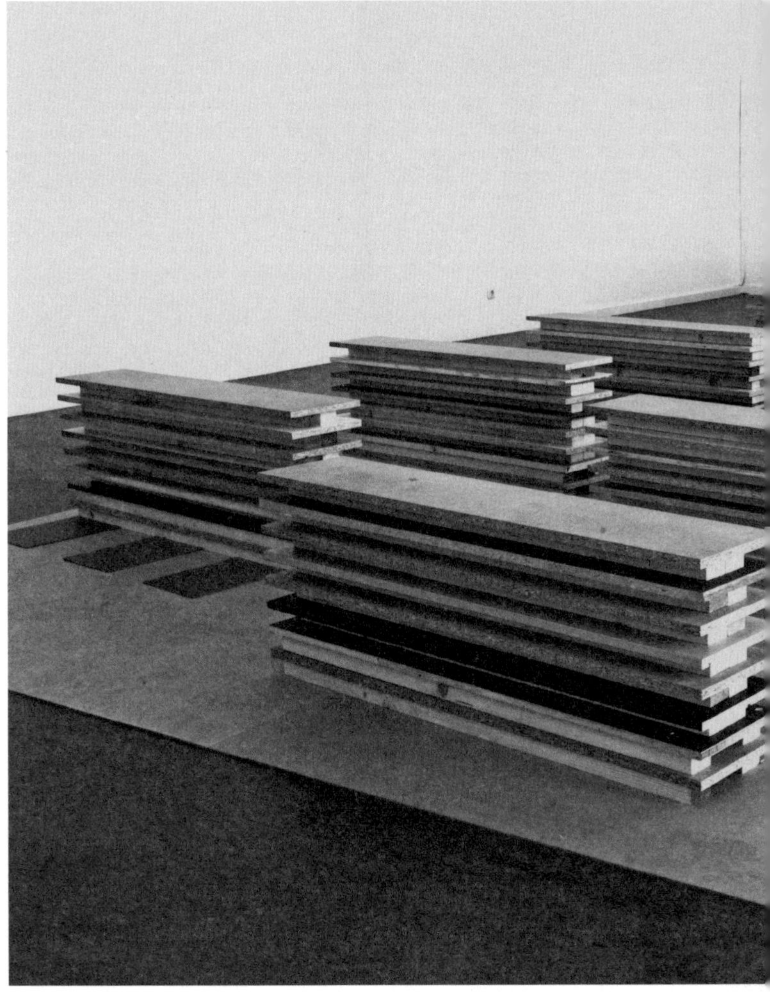

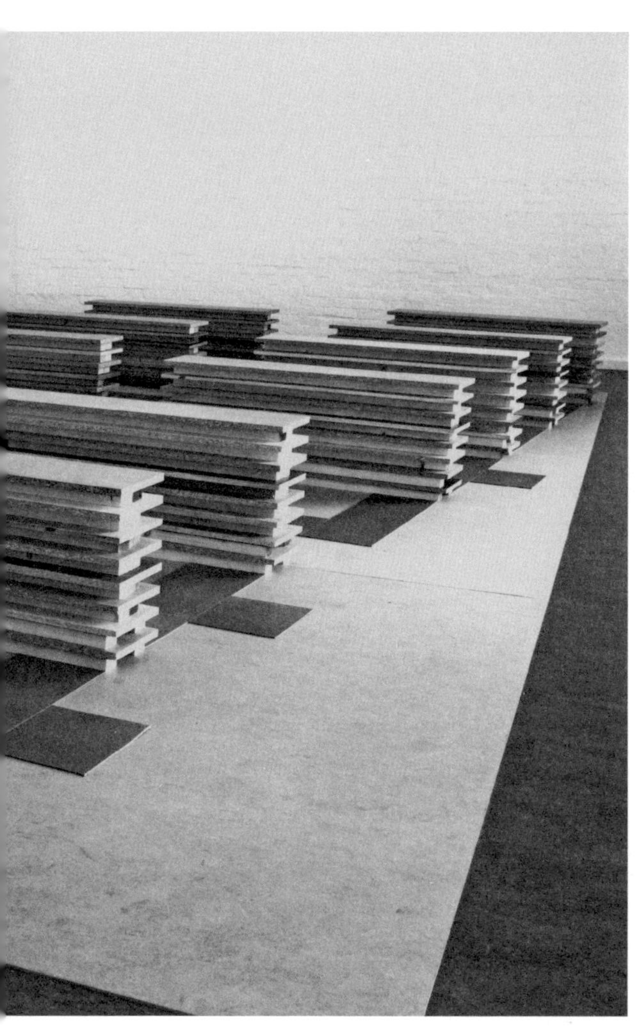

<u>Brian Kuan Wood</u>
The Horses

By studying the body of a horse, giving special attention to its bone structure and the sizes and shapes of its various parts, Bole was able to assess with unfailing accuracy hidden capacities that a lesser judge of horses would have overlooked. His reliability was such that at a horse market a single glance from Bole instantly raised the price of any horse. Not only was Bole able to identify superior horses, the animals themselves responded to his sympathetic appreciation of their quality. When he happened upon a fine horse being used to pull a humble salt cart, the horse gave a long cry, whereupon Bole got down from his own vehicle and wept over the animal's sad fate.[1]

Of all the people I know in Berlin, Marion von Osten is the only one who speaks to me in German, knowing I don't understand German. And I always figured it was because she thought I would eventually understand or already did understand. Not because I speak German, which I don't, but because Marion knows that if you are to understand anything at all ever, well, then you had better get comfortable feeling like an idiot, not knowing what it is you're working with, chucking all macho hopes for mastery out the window. Get ready to be ferociously messy with your curiosity. And you'd better do it fast before they take the object of your curiosity and turn it into a discipline. And discipline you in the process for accidentally stumbling on gunpowder or the microprocessor without even knowing what something like "knowledge capital" is supposed to mean even when it seems to be a matter of life and death when it gets integrated and becomes subject to measurement and scrutiny. Hm, this could actually be quite interesting to pursue further.

[1]   Robert E. Harrist, Jr., "The Legacy of Bole: Physiognomy and Horses in Chinese Painting," *Artibus Asiae* 57, nos. 1/2 (1997), p. 136. The passage continues: "Praising the skill of Bole, a passage in the *Lishi chunqiu* (third century BC) states that 'it is better to have a single Bole than to have ten superior horses.'"

So let's look at what constitutes knowledge capital today. Which particular institutional positions had to be created to produce its actors and protagonists, and which more general structural changes brought about the culture of its particular form of capture and redeployment? How can we identify the mechanism that converts inquiry into the production of life processes into a site of industry and a form of value ripe for exchange? And how is it that this mechanism anticipates such an inquiry by producing its own culture and forms of life that become entangled with my own life and my own concerns until it merges with my very object of study? Wow, this could actually be something to develop into a conference of some kind, don't you think? Or maybe not. Hey, Marion! What are you doing Saturday? Are you going again to Müncheberg?

In the last couple of years, Marion adopted in the Brandenburg area between Berlin and the border to Poland a mare named Lucky, who was going to be slaughtered for being slightly crippled. And she started writing and thinking about equestrian culture. But she also wanted to care for this horse and not think about how the pleasure in caring for Lucky could ever be a means to any other kind of end. It is dangerous to walk directly behind a horse because they can be easily startled and their hind legs are very powerful—Lucky's as well, even though those crippled legs nearly had her executed for not fulfilling the criteria for a horse, which is to support the weight of a human, to be ridden. Lucky was this massive powerful beast that for this simple and stupid reason could not perform the work of being a horse within the equestrian community.

So Marion started to notice how equestrian culture contains an implicit social contract regulating the mutual expectations of human and horse and registering their respective powers and abilities in relation to each other. But interspecies social contracts are more complex than those of human societies, because they have to account for vastly different strengths and weaknesses, as well as the different desires and uses one species has for another. If today's dominant liberal form of human social contract inherited from the likes of the philosophers Thomas Hobbes, John Locke, and Jean-Jacques Rousseau assumes liberty to emerge from some degree of submission to its binding terms, equestrian culture would seem to mock any hope of collective emancipation by casting all of its contingencies in high relief. In the case of horses, we can see it very immediately in the way the contract itself takes the very vivid form of a kind of sadomasochistic system permanently installed into its DNA. The cultural practice of riding involves a whole apparatus of whips and stirrups and leather bits, which are about power—domination and control—just as much as they are a means of communication between the different species. They are the very form of the interspecies contract just as they are a testament to the violence at the very heart of it: abusive riders are common but so are serious human injuries or deaths when dealing with an animal ten times a rider's size. On the other hand, depending on their level of experience and familiarity with a horse, skilled riders are often able to bypass this disciplinary apparatus. Without some (or any) of the armature, "natural dressage," or other new practices of riding without bridle or saddle establish a shared premise between human and horse or even restore the wild bond within the virtuosity of classical dressage. And through muscular acts of micro-communication, the rider asks the horse: Do you want to go this way now? No. Are you sure? OK. Let's go that way. It's a deal. But after that, I want to go this way. OK, agreed. It's not far from the logic of lovemaking. But, even if it appears less coercive, neither is it far from the magic of power.

United States diplomat Richard Holbrooke was known to say often that, while former National Security Advisor and, later, US Secretary of State Henry Kissinger liked to compare diplomacy to chess, for Holbrooke himself diplomacy was more like jazz: "endless variations on a theme."[2] It shouldn't come as a surprise that he held his highest political positions in the 1980s, 1990s, and early 2000s, when many other aspects of life and politics started to bop and swing—in particular with the gradual release of a global market economy that would activate and privilege expressions of internal states of being as structural forces responsible for the functioning of broader geopolitical and economic systems. Even if there was always an affective dimension to high-level negotiations of power, its ethics had to be grounded in a structural play of positions like Kissinger's chess analogy of hawkish men staring each other down over a grid of knights and kings and bishops. But the rise of the so-called informal sector or the privatization of public or state-administered resources made the game very different. It was not only about sliding money and power away from hawkish men in government over to hawkish men in private corporations. They might be master strategists, but if any of them played jazz, no one wanted to hear it. No one was ever supposed to care about his or her internal states of being. Even Holbrooke's idea of jazz as "endless variations on a theme" sounds utterly boring. Some kind of smooth jazz for soft power. But he must have known that many jazz variations are improvised and unpredictable. And that the move toward the private sector would not only make business and commerce structural, but also the politics of life itself: the

2   Stephen Kinzer, "Richard Holbrooke: A Consummate Insider Who Left Us Wanting More," *Huffington Post* (14 December 2010), online at: http://www.huffingtonpost.com/ stephen-kinzer/richard-holbrookes-approach-to-diplomacy_b_796809.html. Also see Metahaven's wonderful essay on soft power: Metahaven, "Brand States: Postmodern Power, Democratic Pluralism, and Design," *e-flux journal,* no. 1 (December 2008), online at: http://www.e-flux.com/ journal/01/68478/brand-states-postmodern-power-democratic-pluralism-and-design/.

vital forces of private administration determined by things like what Foucault termed "conduct," but within intimate relations previously thought to be outside of the domain of economy or even history.

Nobody really doubts that this is a new phase of capitalism moving deeper into the inner functioning of life to mobilize social bonds and solidarities to harvest their value. But few have managed to use it as a starting point for something far more interesting whereby, in the course of going on the prowl for new energies, capital tapped into a vast subaltern ocean of micropolitical jazz improvisers playing social contracts as instruments using only muscular micromovements. In a brilliant essay from 2009, Marion suggested that, in fact, the mobilization of the private has, by one means or another, come into contact with precisely the same sphere of life processes that feminists have identified and tried to politicize for years: the sphere of care labor, of unremunerated domestic or cognitive work, of intimate relations.[3] All the "women's work" that had before been deemed under the threshold of valorization suddenly became integrated into the economy precisely because of its marginal status. But what to do with the fact that, after analyzing and calling for proper recognition of this sphere of work, it was capitalism that was the first to answer the call? After having been considered peripheral to processes of industrialization based in the sweaty masculine space of the factory, the categories of labor traditionally ascribed to women are brought back into the fold not by way of rights but alongside a flood of other hidden and otherwise unregistered immaterial forms of labor that give body and character to the reproduction and reception of information. More specifically, in the 1990s and

3   Marion von Osten, "Irene ist Viele! Or What We Call 'Productive' Forces," *e-flux journal*, no. 8 (September 2009), online at: http://www.e-flux.com/journal/08/61381/irene-ist-viele-or-what-we-call-productive-forces/.

especially the 2000s, the affective solidarities that held people together became the real network that Facebook would need to build—not with wires and servers but through people themselves and their loving bonds.

More than another example of capital's catastrophic ingenuity for subsumption, Marion reminds us that the sphere of affect identified by feminism is no less stable and no less sovereign than when it is being commodified. It is still being accessed precisely for its sovereignty, and the scenario only goes to show how a marginal discourse can reveal such profound weaknesses in the basic structure of a political paradigm that it cannot possibly be considered hegemonic. The dual subsumption of affective and cognitive labor into a supercharged libidinal paradigm of work is in fact an opening to realizing the tepid demands for recognition as a full blown catastrophic enterprise of affective labor in the absence of any kind of sensible calculus by which to ascertain how ethics should work anymore. Terrifying as this may be, the ambiguity and compulsion to improvise one's own political reaction on the fly is not unknown to women, to artists, to migrants, to colonized subjects, to groups who made their way by internalizing the master logic so as to evade it. Put differently: the only way is the punk way.

Before I get too much further, I should explain my particular approach to writing this text on Marion, because it is ultimately a very limited account of a person or practitioner whose seemingly endless range of interests appear to deliberately exceed or evade comprehensive summation as a singular corpus or oeuvre, even as they congeal as artworks; expansive curatorial research projects, such as *In the Desert of Modernity: Colonial Planning and After* (2008–2009) and *Projekt Migration* (2002–2006); and countless essays and books. I only met her in 2009 in Cairo, where artists Shahira Issa and Malak Helmy, as well as writer and curator Nida Ghouse, had organized a conference on urban trajectories in Cairo, where Marion delivered a brilliant lecture on the garden city in colonial town planning. By this time (at least in certain circles), the enormous influence Marion had, especially in the 1990s, on those around her through both her work and the energy of her curiosity and generosity was already clear. More recently, just mentioning the forbidding task of writing this essay on Marion in passing to the artist Pauline Boudry, Pauline recalled with a twinkle in her eye how Marion was the one who first exhibited her work publicly as a curator at Shedhalle Zürich, Zurich in the 1990s. Others explain how formative her projects and discussions with her have been to their own work, and I can certainly testify to that being the case for me as well. To know Marion as a colleague and friend is to repeatedly witness projects—artworks, essays, books, symposia, ideas—appear countless times in the course of a single conversation. And yet, if there is any single thread to be drawn through her seemingly endless ways of working, it is not just a restless autodidactic productivity but really a thorough and ongoing commitment to the transgressive capacities of curiosity itself. Reflecting on this a bit further, I would have to say that the most enduring lesson Marion has given me was this: curiosity itself, if taken all the way, can become a force so powerful that it can never be contained.

It has to be said: Marion was and is a total punk. And punk curiosity is not about some kind of open-ended state-subsidized industrial-contemplation complex, but about forging a weapon of pedagogical dissidence.[4] In the hands of those who once might have been recognizable as more orthodox or old school punks—or old school artists or feminists, for that matter—

4   Thanks to curator Maria Lind for reminding me that Marion is really a pedagogical dissident!

curiosity becomes the energetic thrust for transposing transgressive countercultural capacities or promises onto the structural commitments of institutional or intellectual work. It is actually a canny means of playing the knowledge economy against itself—by constantly moving, by constantly rooting out its inconsistencies and contradictions, by draining its resources into something that it needs from you in order to function but that also overwhelms its governing logic entirely. Punk curiosity maintains its transgressive edge by always exercising its fascination in the craft of the very contradictions that threaten to codify or contain its output. This is how an artist or academic simultaneously embraces and evades exploitation and possibly even reaps concrete and equitable benefits from the perverse generosity of their own production. Everyone knows that punk was perfectly happy to be commodified just as much as commodification was never the primary objective. As with Andy Warhol, the most enduring pleasure would seem to be found in exposing contradictions to the furthest extent imaginable. The pedagogical dissident knows that if we don't start mixing it up and having some fun with this, we will die of boredom. That is how they will really bend us into submission and ultimately kill us.

Marion's writing and thinking helped me to understand how the degree to which institutions—whether social, financial, or artistic—rely on vital forces in order to function makes them at the same time highly vulnerable to those forces and how they are used. Which is to say that exploitation and emancipation have become so simultaneous and coextensive that an entirely new approach to living a good life becomes not only necessary for survival, but also invested with a new plasticity. Likewise, institutional work becomes reactivated as a potent means of drilling into precisely these same contradictions with the resources and authority to access them as historical processes.

This is at the heart of Marion's exhibition *In the Desert of Modernity: Colonial Planning and After* (curated together with Tom Avermaete and Serhat Karakayali) and its accompanying book *Colonial Modern: Aesthetics of the Past, Rebellions for the Future* (2010), which has exhaustively researched the often roundabout ways modernist architecture was imposed, absorbed, and metabolized by both colonial and decolonial projects alike. But what is remarkable about the project's staunch focus on case studies from architectural history and colonial town planning is how they serve to articulate a much larger and far more ominous reality of the modern condition in general—one for which the export of modern architecture serves as a kind of indexical sculptural artifact. At times when the project betrays its true focus, it becomes clear that the actual site of inquiry, as well as the sentiment driving the project, is more concerned with a much broader universalization of both colonial and colonized positions alike in a way that resists reduction to geographical divisions of global north and global south. While historical research often necessarily deals in the currency of this division, the radicality of the project's proposition shows through most clearly at the moments when it emphasizes that, for instance, urban master plans in North Africa were used as advanced prototypes for planning projects to be realized to their full extent in European and North American cities, which is to say that those western capitals that are the greatest beneficiaries of the colonial project also enjoy the most refined forms of colonial governmentality and violence. No one really escapes the colonial project, least of all its beneficiaries. For those who were subjected to its experiments, meanwhile, the synthetic forms of modernity also doubled as signals of progress that could be used in struggles for emancipation.

Likewise, the neglect that accompanied colonial experiments created pockets in which, for instance, an informal vernacular architecture could grow within and around the edges of colonial master plans. Here also, coercive centralized power is taken as only the starting point for the de facto anarchism of self-built improvised structures that took the imposed grid of western modernity and converted it into something else entirely precisely at the merging point or conflation between subjugation and emancipation. While there is a healthy bit of skepticism when western (and, often especially, German) researchers choose to study the global south as such, it has to be said that when considered alongside Marion's other projects, the real strength of character behind her methodology in confronting colonial history comes in her attempt to understand her own political formation not as a master but as the object of an updated contemporary strain of a more cutting-edge colonial planning. This of course reflects a deeply feminist investment connected to queer and subaltern discourses that assume the self to be an ethical speaking position as well as a recording device by which to read politics from the inside—by way of the imprints and trace materials it deposits in the body, the psyche, the language. Insofar as the colonization of life cannot possibly be total, after the point where power exhausts itself, one can find very surprising things starting to happen.

When Marion started going to Müncheberg to look after Lucky the horse, I was a little worried that she was going off-grid. She explained how the demands of work were becoming too much and too toxic. The contradictions and stresses of a certain paradigm of precarious labor's charismatic competency that previously served as inspiration and input had become either unspeakable in its brutality or simply too dull to bother mentioning. The art world seemed at this particular moment to be eating its own tail more than ever. The demands were becoming absurd. Meanwhile, the landscape in the area around Müncheberg is quite beautiful—together with the horses it looked like Marion might have been making an escapist move towards bucolic nineteenth-century retro-fantasia. That's perfectly understandable, I must have thought. And if it makes her happy, she deserves it. At the same time, I was myself coming out of a brutal separation and in a very delicate emotional state, so she must have thought that a day in the countryside would do me some good. But when I met Lucky, I realized that I had in fact been invited to a very elaborate and intricately devised healing process whose administration had actually been delegated to a horse. And what a trio we were that day: all crippled versions of ourselves trying to compare our various debilitating defeats at the hands of institutions of study, of birth, of marriage, of race, species, gender, and so forth. And yet for some reason, I hadn't felt so calm and so complete in a long time.

Over the past few years, Marion often mentions the "good life" when running up against insufficiencies in the emancipatory political discourses that have fueled so much progressive sentiment in the past. Debates on precarious labor might gleefully unearth every intricate detail of the newest technology of exploitation, but rarely find the means to address how a good life can be attained, e.g., how wealth should be redistributed and by whom and for whom.[5] Furthermore, there is the problem of wealth itself having morphed and expanded its character—many forms of symbolic capital now do translate into material wealth (except for when they don't). If many emancipatory projects of the past appear spectral or malformed today, upon closer inspection they are often not very different from how they were formulated in their own time. Social programs were always vague and insufficient. The Arab Spring reminds us of

5   Just one example was in an exchange we had in *Mousse Magazine*: Marion von Osten and Brian Kuan Wood, "Problems of Endless Fruit," *Mousse Magazine*, no. 37 (March 2013), pp. 216–218.

the French Revolution: whether or not demands were met, the situation afterwards became catastrophic. It seems that the good life was always escaping through the side door at the moment it was most needed. But where did it go? How does it keep evading our grasp?

I wonder whether Marion's repeated visits to Müncheberg had something to do with trying to locate that good life. The philosopher Reza Negarestani has recently remarked that, in spite of being in dire need of an update, Plato's notion of the good life is probably one of the most dangerous and original ideas ever put forward in philosophy.[6] As Plato's *Republic* repeatedly makes clear, the good life—and the *good* in general—is synonymous with virtue but crucially not with merely happiness or desire. Desire encourages people to want more than they have, which leads them to steal from others, to acquire debts, to exacerbate contradictions in the narrow pursuit of self-interest. It is only through the principle and the pursuit of virtue that the good can be realized and maintained in harmony with the material realities and conflicting desires of the city, of other people, of the world. All fine and well, but here we run into the reason Plato's notion of the good is so sorely hurting for an update: today such platitudinous moral absolutism appears hopelessly out of touch with our times. But if our times are characterized mainly by the universalization of extreme contingency—by volatile markets, precarious employment, social upheavals, mass displacement—then what makes the question of virtue or its criteria so profoundly unfashionable may be precisely what makes it necessary. After a half-century or more of Deleuzian desiring-machines, network euphoria, and free market ideologies constantly getting robbed of the object of political, social, or economic desire (Wall Street in 2008, Iraq in 2003 and onward, Tahrir in 2011, Paris in 1968), the "I want" or the "we

6   In personal correspondence.

want" of desire has proven to be an inadequate teleological
spine for realizing anything more than the emancipation and
reproduction of a teenage wasteland of dashed hopes built
over an event-obsessed garbage dump of only the most pre-
dictable oedipal dad-beheadings. Looking back, it almost
seems that the question of virtue has been deliberately suppressed to clear a path for a new order in which judgment is
postponed to the network so as to shield armchair liberals
from taking any position that would jeopardize their sources
of income or sense of goodwill towards all humanity.

At the same time, it becomes clear that the abstraction of good
global cultural and military-economic partnerships are subject
to the finiteness of mineral availability, of cultural understanding,
of computing capacity, and the capacity to absorb the contradictions and abstractions of finance. Many of the new materialist
or posthuman strains of thinking are in fact trying to reconstitute
the limits to desire as a material stress on the unlimited capacity
of the desiring appetites of our humanistic economy. These
abstractions now serve to affirm the need for hegemonic limits
that crucially cannot be traced back to the modernist, colonial,
or totalitarian programs that sought to systematize conduct for
the sake of control in the name of some kind of Enlightenment
rationality or twisted humanistic determinism. Today the material
or structural conditions providing the support for human systems
are what crucially restrain humans from devouring everything
around them, including themselves. With this teenage wasteland
scenario in mind, one wonders whether it might be possible
to return to the question of how human conduct should or can
only be organized to realize its own desires—not as another
chain of desires expressed as abstractions but in reality.
What, after all, was the good life ever supposed to be if not
a codification of behavior in accordance with a wealth of real
contingencies?

Like any horse, Lucky shits a lot. Marion had to clean up after her when she would do her business in the stables. Flies like to try and get at the fluid around horses' eyes, which is irritating for the horse and a risk of infection. So Lucky had a large, black face mask made of netting that had to be attached to her each time she went outside. Lucky was actually a quite withdrawn and fearful horse, which Marion attributed to her having been overridden or abused by a previous owner. She was scared of humans and even cowered in a corner when left alone with me. When Marion came back with Lucky's food, she was surprised and remarked that Lucky trusted me. How strange: this enormous beast ten times my size and body mass, scared of me. And what a sublime privilege to gain her trust.

In seventh-century China, there lived a man who went by the name Bole, who has since stood as the main figure of Chinese antiquity to gain an extraordinarily deep understanding of horses and their physiognomy. But as Robert E. Harrist writes, "the original discourse of horse physiognomy was not that of simple veterinary practice: the horse's body was a site where understanding of the cosmos, and of natural forces and processes, were mapped and articulated."[7] Bole would assess the horse's body not only for its functional health but would more crucially read it according to its qualities as reflections of a larger cosmic order: a corporeal moral order.[8] No wonder that, like Plato (who lived only some 300 years after Bole), the moral compass found in horse physiognomy pointed not only to human conduct and temperament but also to statecraft and political organization:

[7] Harrist, "The Legacy of Bole," p. 136.

[8] Harrist quotes a text on horse physiognomy dated to the second century BC found at Mawangdui in Hunan Province in 1973: "What Bole physiognomized were the horses of a superior man. Yin and yang abided by the plumb line, and curved and straight were exactly even." And in a later passage: "The four areas of flesh were exactly in measure. The square bones were in accord with the [carpenter's] square and the round bones with the compass." The body of an ideal horse also is said to be in accord with heavenly forms: "[The eye of the horse is like] a moon coming out above; it is a half [moon] and not yet bright," p. 137.

A horse's head is king; it should be square. The eyes are the prime ministers; they should be radiant. The spine is the general; it should be strong. The belly and chest are the city walls; they should be extended. The four legs are the local officials; they should be long.[9]

So where was the good life to be found in the horses' stables in Müncheberg that day with Marion? In the train on the way back, we ran into her friend from the stables who was a retired Berlin advertising executive. I remembered him sitting in a lawn chair with his massive stallion. Making conversation, I mentioned how it could be nice to go riding sometime, and his expression went grim. Marion later explained to me that he was part of a group of people at the stables who don't believe in riding horses. For them, horses are to be admired as part of a kind of distanced contemplation of a pastoral scene—a triumph cleansed of the violence of domestication in which an enclosed animal is to be respected in all its original power and wildness. Some people just don't get it. But for Marion, together with the horses, all of these equestrians were themselves part of a much larger theater of different actors trying to find their part at the edges of what we understand to be a social contract. As an exit from the strictures of human society, the scene I encountered with Marion in Müncheberg was an experiment in developing real forms of interspecies conduct out of the historical violence of conquest or domestication or simply the more immediate fact that horses and people are vastly different creatures that can do things that the other can't. At this edge, politics becomes about how the universe can only function. Any good life in any society, human or cosmic, resolves itself with that very universal order.[10]

[9] Quoted from the *Qimin yaoshu* in Harrist, p. 138.
[10] In fact, one of the reasons Marion invited me to visit Müncheberg was actually because only a month or so earlier, shortly after she had adopted her, Lucky had given birth to a young foal.

But who can interpret this order? Who is receptive enough to feel its boundaries and restraints, the stirrups and bits and saddles and bridles and all the hardware of power bearing down on a beast ten times more powerful than oneself? Only someone with an even more ferocious curiosity.

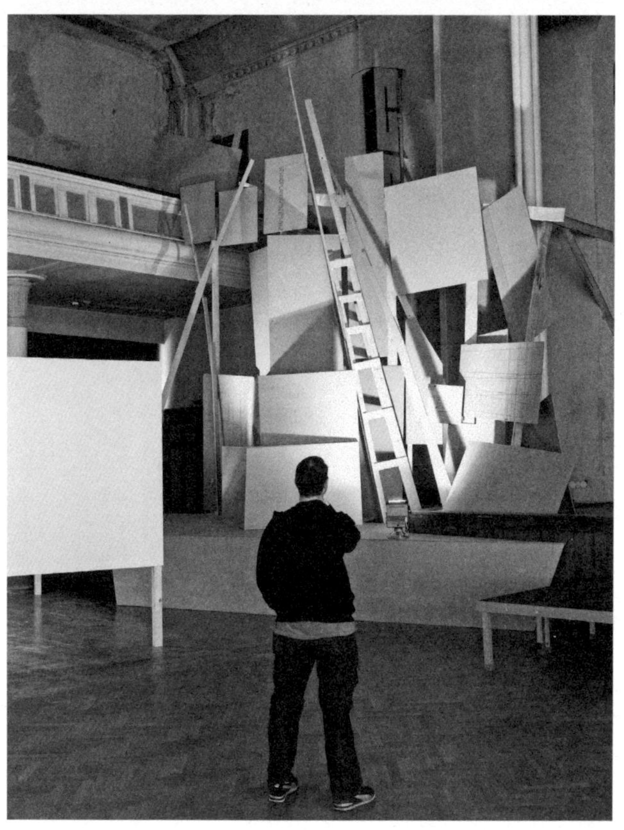

Simone Hain, Marion von Osten, Christiane
Post, Karin Rebbert, Katja Reichard, Peter
Spillmann, and Axel John Wieder, *Insert 3*,
2004, reconstruction of stage design for
Velimir Khlebnikov's *Zangezi* (1923) by
Vladimir Tatlin, installation view *Insert 1–4:
Common Property*, 6th Werkleitz Biennale,
Halle, photo: courtesy of the artists

Simone Hain, Marion von Osten, Christiane Post, Karin Rebbert, Katja Reichard, Peter Spillmann, and Axel John Wieder, *Insert 2*, 2004, reconstruction of *Raum der Gegenwart* by László Moholy-Nagy (1930), installation view *Insert 1–4: Common Property*, 6th Werkleitz Biennale, Halle, photo: courtesy of the artists

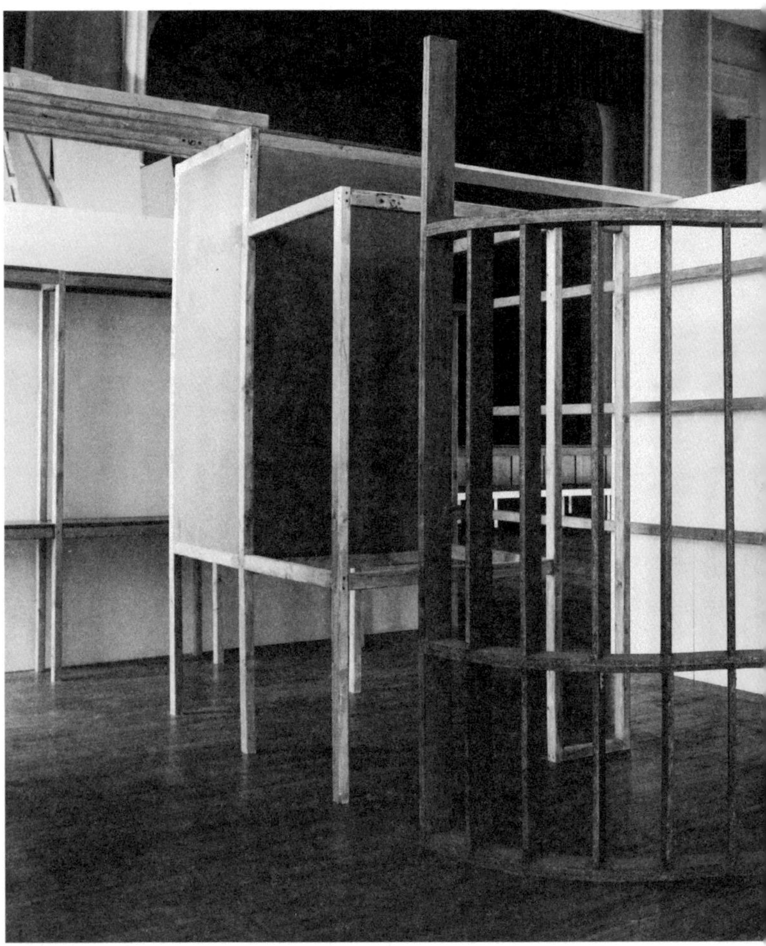

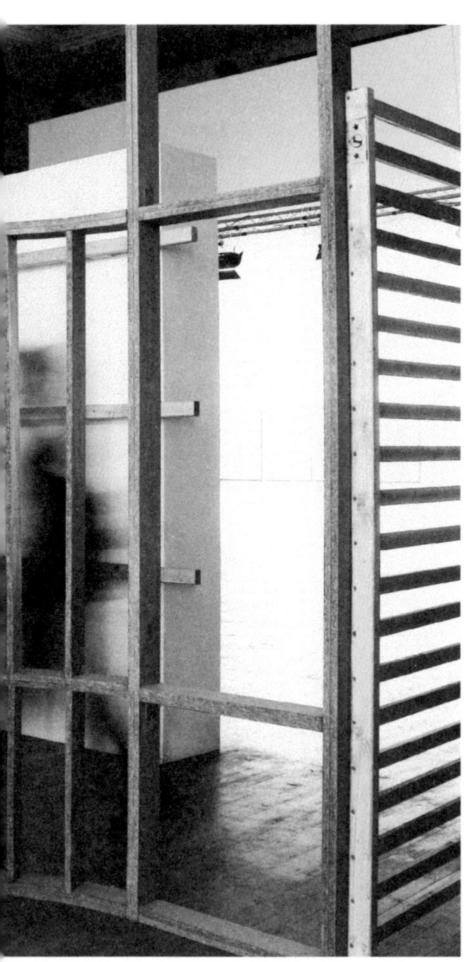

Isabell Lorey

Becoming Common: Precarization as Political Constituting (A Revision)

This text was first published in June 2010 in the "In Search of the Postcapitalist Self" special issue of *e-flux journal*, no. 17, edited by Marion von Osten. This version has been slightly revised. The passages on kleines postfordistisches Drama (kpD) and the terminology of the precarious have been expanded. It is translated from German by Aileen Derieg and reprinted here with permission of the author and *e-flux journal*.

Political-Cultural Queerings

The discourse on precarization that has emerged in the last two decades, primarily in Europe, rests on extremely complex understandings of social insecurity and its productivity. The various strands of this discourse have been brought together time and again in the movement of the European precarious, organized as EuroMayDay since the early 2000s.[1] This trans-national movement has thematized precarious working and living conditions as the starting point for political struggles and has sought possibilities for political action in neoliberal condi-tions. Key to EuroMayDay are not only the alliances between non-migrant and migrant precarious people and the ways in which, under its auspices, new forms of political struggles have been tested and new perspectives on precarization developed; also—and this is striking in relation to other social movements—it is how EuroMayDay has queered the seemingly disparate fields of the cultural and the political time and again.

1   Since the early 2000s, on 1 May, the traditional International Workers' Day, EuroMayDay parades have taken place in over 20 European cities with up to 150,000 participants to call attention to the precari-zation of living and working conditions. The activists come from the most diverse social positionings. While the parades of this transnational network are but one event, they are organized alongside other activities, surveys, and publications throughout the year. EuroMayDay involves new forms of organizing and consciousness raising about different modes of precarization and collective knowledge production. See also http://www.euromayday.org; the multilingual European Institute for Progressive Cultural Policies (eipcp) web journal *transversal: precariat* (2004), online at: http://transversal. at/transversal/0704; *transversal: militant research* (2006), online at: http://transversal. at/transversal/0406; *Mute Volume 2.0— Precarious Reader* (2005), online at: http:// metamute.org/en/Precarious-Reader; and Gerald Raunig, *A Thousand Machines: A Concise Philosophy of the Machine as a Social Movement*, trans. Aileen Derieg (Los Angeles: Semiotext(e), 2010).

Conversations concerning both the (partly subversive) knowledge of the precarious and the search for what is common (in order to enable political constituting[2]) have conspicuously taken place more often in art institutions than in social, political, or even university contexts.

In 2003–2004, for example, the research, exhibition, and event project *Atelier Europa*, initiated by Marion von Osten and Angela McRobbie in the Kunstverein München, Munich, brought theorists and artists together to exchange ideas about precarious living and working conditions, and possible resistance to them.[3] The project focused on the increasing number and variety of forms of precarization not only in the field of cultural production, but also in social fields, especially the caregiving and reproductive work still largely assigned to women.[4] The feminist activist group from Madrid, Precarias a la deriva, provided an important contribution in this respect.[5]

Another example from 2004: on the day before 1 May, activists from Indymedia groups from all over Spain met via the invitation of MACBA (Museu d'Art Contemporani de Barcelona), Barcelona to conduct an intensive debate about their media activism practices. On 1 May, they not only took part in the

2   From the Latin word *constituo*; see also Gerald Raunig, "Instituent Practices, No. 2: Institutional Critique, Constituent Power, and the Persistence of Instituting," trans. Aileen Derieg, in *Art and Contemporary Critical Practice: Reinventing Institutional Critique*, Gerald Raunig and Gene Ray, eds. (London: MayFlyBooks, 2009), pp. 173–186.

3   See http://www.ateliereuropa.com.

4   The practices and discourses of the Intermittents du Spectacle in France have been very influential. See Global Project/ Coordination des Intermittents et Précaires d'Ile de France, "Spectacle Inside the State and Out. Social Rights and the Appropriation of Public Spaces: The Battles of the French Intermittents," trans. Aileen Derieg, *transversal: precariat* (2004), online at: http://transversal. at/transversal/0704/intermittents/en; and Antonella Corsani and Maurizio Lazzarato, *Intermittents et Précaires* (Paris: Éditions Amsterdam, 2008).

5   See Precarias a la Deriva, "A drift through the circuits of feminized precarious work" (2004), online at: http://transversal.at/ transversal/0704/precarias1/en; and Precarias a la deriva, *Was ist dein Streik? Militante Streifzüge durch die Kreisläufe der Prekarität*, trans. Birgit Mennel and Stefan Nowotny (Vienna: transversal texts, 2014).

EuroMayDay demonstration but also carried the problematization of precarious working conditions back to MACBA. It became possible to articulate a critique of the ambivalent role of art institutions: on the one hand, institutions in the art field are the sites of critical discussions about neoliberal transformation processes; on the other, such institutions are important players in the game of cognitive capitalism and increasing precarization tendencies.[6]

As a third example, in January 2005 the international Klartext! Conference, "The Status of the Political in Contemporary Art and Culture," took place in Berlin in the Künstlerhaus Bethanien and the Volksbühne am Rosa-Luxemburg-Platz.[7] Many of those invited were also activists in the transnational EuroMayDay network, and met the day before the conference in Berlin. They brought the current problematics of precarization to the conference (and were able to have their travel costs reimbursed).

Beyond these examples, theoretical analyses of precarization linked to activist practices (such as in the context of the EuroMayDay network) have been increasingly carried out

6   See Raunig, *A Thousand Machines;* Bojana Kunst, *Artist at Work: Proximity of Art and Capitalism* (Winchester: Zero Books, 2015); and Gigi Argyropoulou and Hypatia Vourloumis, eds., "On Institutions," Special Issue, *Performance Research*, vol. 20, no. 4 (2015).

7   Organized by Marina Sorbello and Antje Weitzel. See also the conference "Another Relationality (second part). On a cure in times of divest poetry/On poetry in incurable times," organized by Marcelo Expósito and Jorge Ribalta in cooperation with the eipcp at MACBA in Barcelona (2006), online at: http://marceloexposito.net/pdf/exposito_otrarelacionalidad_en.pdf; and *WORK TO DO! Self-organisation in precarious working conditions—An exhibition project in 3 chapters*, organized by Sønke Gau and Katharina Schlieben, Shedhalle Zürich, Zurich (2007–2008). In the context of education, see, among others, Chto delat?/ What is to be done? and Street University in St. Petersburg, online at: http://www.streetuniver.narod.ru/index_e.htm; Edu-factory, online at: http://www.edu-factory.org/edu15/; free/slow university in Warsaw, online at: http://www.wuw-warsaw.pl/oprojekcie.php?lang=eng; Radical Education Collective in Ljubljana, online at: http://radical.temp.si/; and Universidad Nomada in Spain, online at: http://www.universidadnomada.net.

in online journals conjoining art, political theory, and activism, such as *Mute Magazine* and *transversal*—many years before precarity/precarization became a major theme in institutionalized social science research.[8]

Normalizing and Governing Differences
Precarization is by no means a phenomenon that first affects social groups imagined to be at the margins before moving to the center to affect the so-called middle class—those who have previously been secured in their integration in the capitalist production regime and therefore able to fortify and improve their social position. A model of this kind, based on a precarious margin and a threatened center, does not do justice to the remodeling and dismantling of social security systems in Europe. It is a development that has long since reached the so-called center with the massive reduction of permanent employment contracts and the increase in temporary jobs often calling for a high degree of mobility, with or without minimal social security benefits such as health insurance, paid holidays, or pensions.

In the context of such changes, precarization can be seen as a neoliberal instrument of governing.[9] Neoliberal societies are now governed internally through social insecurity, which means balancing out a minimum of social security. Social insecurity is not a phenomenon that only applies to certain groups in society. Precarization is currently in a process of normalization, and thus picks up from social insecurities that were already a subject of complaint before Fordism without being identical to them. The Fordist social welfare state reveals itself as a historical exception and not at all as a norm from which precarious

8   See footnote 2.
9   See Isabell Lorey, *State of Insecurity: Government of the Precarious*, trans. Aileen Derieg (London: Verso, 2015).

working conditions can be understood as a deviation or an anomaly.[10]

The art of governing currently consists of balancing a maximum of precarization, which probably cannot be exactly calculated, with minimum safeguarding to ensure that the minimum is secured at this threshold. Normalized precarization does not mean equality in insecurity. For reasons of self-preservation, neoliberal logic wants no reduction, no end to inequality, because it necessarily toys with hierarchized differences and governs on the basis of them. This governmental logic does not primarily focus on regulating fixed identitarian differences. It only regulates the "absolute poverty" that could prevent individuals from being competitive.[11]

If we understand precarization in this sense, as the normalization and governing of differences in insecurity, then it becomes less useful to construct group-related divisions of precarization, as divisions into "luxury precarity" and "impoverished precarity" ultimately reproduce neoliberal dynamics of competitiveness among different degrees of precarization.

Debates Over New Political Practices

So as not to further individualize and separate the manifold precarious, in the past decades critical discourses and resistant practices in the context of precarization have repeatedly concentrated on what the precarious have in common. This kind of search for the common starts from differences and does not end in sameness, but is instead accompanied by permanent debates about what counts as the common.

10   Angela Mitropoulos, "Precari-Us?," *transversal: precariat* (2005), online at: http://transversal.at/transversal/0704/mitropoulos/en; and Brett Neilson and Ned Rossiter, "Precarity as a Political Concept, or, Fordism as Exception," *Theory, Culture & Society*, vol. 25, nos. 7–8 (2008), pp. 51–72.

11   Maurizio Lazzarato, *Le gouvernement des inégalités: Critique de l'insécurité néolibérale* (Paris: Éditions Amsterdam, 2008).

The theoretical reflections on and the social movements about precarization largely make use of poststructuralist and post-operaist thinking, thus searching at the same time for practices outside the realm of traditional politics of representation. These politics, in which representation is primarily understood as a standing-in-for, are not only evident in parliamentary democracies, but also in leftist political notions of an identitarian collective subject who should be able to articulate demands (representationally) with one voice, as necessary for political practices. Yet when it is a matter of searching for the common in the various forms of precarization, then identitarian, subject-oriented politics are obviously not suitable because they hinder the search for what is common in difference.[12]

In addition, particularly among leftists, one has to be reminded that expressions of solidarity with the mostly migrant "others" not only leave one's "own" position unreflected, but also victimize the "poor others" and deny them their capacity for political action. Contrary to stagnating identity categories, which distinguish between precarious creatives on the one hand and the excluded precarious on the other (the white "lower class," migrants, or illegalized persons), alliances have been constituted within the framework of EuroMayDay that cross over class and status: among precarious cultural producers, knowledge workers, migrant organizations, initiatives of the unemployed, organizations of illegalized persons, and also unions. Thus the topic of repeated debates concerns how modes of refiguring the subject, and thus identitarian logics, can be deconstructed to find a new language of politics capable of widening the field of political possibilities.

[12] See also Antonio Negri, "Logic and Theory of Inquiry: Militant praxis as subject and as episteme," Nate Holdren and Arianna Bove, trans., *transversal: militant research* (2003), online at: http://transversal.at/transversal/0406/negri/en.

When precarization, as an instrument of governing that tends to become normal, surpasses specific groups and classes, social and political struggles should not assume separating and hierarchizing differentiations. Without negating the different extents of precarization, they should look specifically for what they have in common in the midst of normalization.

Productivity That Cannot Be Completely Economicized

There is an important presupposition for both a political and a theoretical perspective of the common: the new figure of work based on communication, knowledge, creativity, and affect is by no means exclusively productive for a new phase of capitalist accumulation.[13] The economicization of the social, the confluence of work and life, the demand to involve the whole person in immaterial and affective work—in other words, the capitalization of modes of subjectivation—are not total, comprehensive, nor wholly determined. There are always surpluses, possibilities for articulation, and potentialities for resistance. Modes of subjectivation are not completely absorbed into the normative state or into economic interpellations of flexibility, mobility, and affective and creative labor. In insecure, flexibilized, and discontinuous working and living conditions, subjectivations arise that do not wholly correspond to a neoliberal logic of exploitation, that also resist and refuse. "Precarization thus

13 See Maurizio Lazzarato, "Immaterial Labor," in *Radical Thought in Italy: A Potential Politic*s, Michael Hardt and Paolo Virno, eds. (Minneapolis: University of Minnesota Press, 1996), pp. 133–148; and Michael Hardt and Antonio Negri, *Empire* (Cambridge, MA: Harvard University Press, 2000). The terms immaterial and affective labor have been repeatedly criticized, especially from feminisms, because they describe labor from the perspective of capitalist accumulation and insufficiently reflect on non-work, care work, the production of the social, etc. See the folder on the exhibition *Atelier Europa*, supplement to the *Drucksache. Zeitschrift des Kunstvereins München*, no. 4, 2004. See also http://www.kunstverein-muenchen.de/de/programm/publikationen/2004/atelier-europa; Precarias a la Deriva, "Adrift through the circuits"; and George Caffentzis and Silvia Federici, "Notes on the edu-factory and the cognitive capitalism," *transversal: knowledge production and its discontents* (2007), online at: http://transversal.at/transversal/0809/caffentzisfederici/en.

symbolizes a contested field: a field in which the attempt to start a new cycle of exploitation also meets desires and subjective behaviors which express the refusal of the old, so-called fordist regime of labor and the search for another, better, we can even say flexible life."[14] Processes of precarization are a contested social terrain, on which the struggles of the workers and the desires for other forms of living and working are articulated. These processes are not only productive in the sense of economic exploitation. In post-Fordist, precarious production conditions, new forms of living and new social relationships are constantly being developed and invented, and processes of precarization are also productive in this sense.[15]

The forms of work that are primarily based on communication and affect, on exchange with others, cannot be entirely measured, as these activities transgress the terms required by Fordist industrial labor.[16] What is unforeseen, contingent, and, also in this sense, precarious, emerges at many moments in the process of precarization. And an inherent aspect of this precarization is the capacity of refusal, and hence it recomposes work, life, and sociality in a way that cannot be thus, not immediately, not so quickly, and perhaps not even at all economicized. In these kinds of recompositions, interruptions occur in the processes of normalization; that is, in the continuity of exploitability. In this sense, the assemblage of meanings of precarization in the discourses associated with the EuroMayDay does not have an exclusively negative connotation, but also

14 Frassanito-Network, "Precarious, Precarization, Precariat? Impacts, traps and challenges of a complex term and its relationship to migration" (2005), online at: http://precariousunderstanding.blogsome. com/2007/01/05/precarious-precarization-precariat/#more-44.
15 See Michael Hardt and Antonio Negri, *Commonwealth* (Cambridge, MA: Belknap Press of Harvard University Press, 2009).
16 Ibid.

always holds the potential for common refusals, the potential of exodus, and of constituting.[17]

The Knowledge of the Precarious

Productive interruptions—the foldings of the precarious into the potentiality of common constituting—cannot simply be stated theoretically, of course, but must instead be found and invented in social and political confrontations. What was needed in the early 2000s (and is still needed today) was knowledge about different forms of precarization and the practices of refusal and subversion newly emerging in them. Many militant investigations were carried out—for instance in cultural and artistic contexts (such as that of kpD[18]) or in various social contexts (such as by Precarias a la deriva)—in order to bring together the different strands of knowledge about the precarious. The practice of militant research, including that pursued as co-research, ties into the worker (self-)surveys, as conducted primarily in the 1970s in conjunction with Italian *operaismo*. Conditions of domination and exploitation were to be investigated by those affected, that is, by the experts themselves, with their specific knowledges of subversive practices, and thus made articulable. The most effective militant research, however, was carried out in the 1970s in the consciousness-raising groups of the women's movement.

17   On exodus and constituting, see Paolo Virno, "Virtuosity and Revolution," trans. Ed Emory (1994/2003), online at: http://www.makeworlds.org/node/34; Isabell Lorey, "Attempt to Think the Plebeian: Exodus and Constituting as Critique," trans. Aileen Derieg, in *Art and Contemporary Critical Practice: Reinventing Institutional Critique*, Gerald Raunig and Gene Ray, eds. (London: MayFlyBooks, 2009), pp. 131–139, online at: http://transversal.at/transversal/0808/lorey/en; and Isabell Lorey, "Critique and Category: On the restriction of political practice through recent theorems of intersectionality, interdependence and critical whiteness studies," trans. Mary O'Neill, *transversal: critique* (2008), online at: http://transversal.at/transversal/0806/lorey/en.

18   kpD is the abbreviation for the feminist research and activist group kleines postfordistisches Drama (small post-Fordist drama) based in Berlin. kpD are Brigitta Kuster, Marion von Osten, Katja Reichard, and the author.

Consciousness-raising women's groups aimed to focus on the self-awareness that women have about their own oppression, in order to promote a political reinterpretation of their own life and establish bases for its transformation. . . 'Consciousness-raising was seen as both a method for arriving at the truth and a means for action and organizing.'[19]

All these kinds of mutual surveys are "the basis for a political intervention," according to Marta Malo de Molina from Precarias a la deriva. The practice of militant research seeks to initiate interest, emancipation, debates, social struggles, and to amplify movements of searching for better ways of living and working. "The underground, and frequently invisible, trajectory of every-day life uneasiness and insubordinations"[20] is to be explored so that the capacity, the *potentia* of the precarious can compose a constituent power.[21]

Using militant research makes it possible to understand what is already common in precarization and, at the same time, what becoming common means in an extended present (and not just in the future). In the common knowledge of conditions of oppression and exploitation, and in individual practices of sabotage and refusal, a common practice of complicity can unfold, a mutual, common abundance that is neither measurable nor able to be economized.[22] Whereas precarization

19 Marta Malo de Molina, "Common notions, part 1: workers-inquiry, co-research, consciousness-raising," *transversal: militant research* (2004), online at: http://transversal.at/transversal/0406/malo/en. Malo de Molina refers to Kathi Sarachild, "Consciousness-Raising: A Radical Weapon," in *Feminist Revolution*, ed. Redstockings (New York: Random House, 1978), pp. 144–150.
20 Ibid.
21 See Antonio Negri and Michael Hardt, *Labor of Dionysus: A Critique of the State-Form* (Minneapolis: University of Minnesota Press, 1994), and Antonio Negri, *Insurgencies: Constituent Power and the Modern State*, trans. Maurizia Boscagli (Minneapolis: University of Minnesota Press, 1999).
22 See Valentina Desideri and Stefano Harney, "Fate work: A conversation," *ephemera: theory & politics in organization*, vol. 13, no. 1 (2013), pp. 159–176.

makes it impossible to plan and work for an imaginary future, in the shared, extended present the question of how we want to live with one another in the midst of the abundance of precariousness becomes more and more urgent.

kpD—A Small Post-Fordist Drama

But how to become common in the present, starting from different forms of precarization? In late 2003, kpD conducted militant interviews with cultural producers in Berlin—including with the members of the collective ourselves—about everyday life, desires, and perspectives on a working day that was seen as being as flexible as possible and largely autonomous.
We used the term "cultural producers" for practices traversing different fields: theory production, design, political and cultural self-organization, forms of collaboration, paid and unpaid jobs, informal and formal economies, temporary alliances, project-related work, and living.[23]

We talked with people who not only worked with cultural products but also co-produced discourses and critiques of society and capitalism. This provided a view of the relationships between the precarization of working and living conditions of the interviewees and the recalcitrance about culture and knowledge production. We wanted to find out, on the basis of five questions, how individual experiences could make a process of becoming common possible. Our questions were: How would you describe your work life? What do you like about it, and what should change? When and why does it all become too much, and what do you do then? What do you consider a "good life"? Should cultural producers, as role models for society, join with other social movements to work toward new forms of globalization?

23 kpD, "Precarization of Cultural Producers and the Missing 'Good Life,'" trans. Aileen Derieg, *transversal: militant research* (2005), online at: http://transversal.at/transversal/0406/kpd/en.

These questions were inspired by the survey action conducted by Fronte della Gioventù Lavoratrice and Potere Operaio in early 1967 in Mirafiori called "Fiat is our university," which asked about, among other topics, what people imagined as a "good life" and about organizing. In our research, however, we did not really get answers to these two questions. We heard a great deal about individual practices of work and everyday life, about being stressed, feeling overwhelmed, and about individual strategies of refusal. What all the interviewees had in common was that they suffered from a lack of time and continuity. What interested us, though, in terms of a politicization of cultural producers, were strategies of refusal, ideas and desires for a societal "good life" with many others. Yet what was too much for the individuals, what was excessive, could only be experienced as a lack. In response to abundance in the present's becoming-common, to questions of politicization and organizing, we hardly got answers.

After evaluating the audio interviews, we produced the film project *Kamera läuft!* (Rolling!) (2004) From various interviews, we constructed texts that were performed by actors in a fictive casting setting.[24] Because of the unsatisfactory responses to the questions about organizing the precarious and living a

24 In creating the film *Kamera läuft!* (2004, 30 min.), the fictional casting setting allowed separating "the individual statements from the specific people who made them, and yet made it possible to imagine them as a specific performative relationship to the self: on a production set somewhere between a casting stage, a chill-out lounge, and a bar, our questions about self marketing and the associated techniques of the self obtained a certain trenchancy, on the one hand, and, on the other, a second reality in which they could be renegotiated. The film set represents not only the place of performance and staging but is at the same time always a place where the immediate working conditions are being negotiated, with all the associated potential for conflict" (kpD, "Rolling! A Small Post-Fordist Drama," in *WHW: Collective Creativity/Kollektive Kreativität*, catalogue for the exhibition at Kunsthalle Fridericianum, Kassel [2005], p. 331). This was the first exhibition in which the film was shown without a discussion with kpD (supplemented by footage shot in the casting setting). We showed the first part of a rough cut of the film, with us present, in conjunction with the exhibition and workshop project *Atelier Europa* at the Kunstverein München, Munich, 2004.

good life together, for us the militant research was not finished with the film. We could not simply leave it for circulation in a (progressive) cultural field because for us it was less an artistic work and more of an instrument in a process of becoming common. We were concerned that showing the film in an art institution would have a depoliticizing effect. The functions of art institutions are highly ambivalent in neoliberal capitalism. As philosopher and performance art theorist Bojana Kunst writes, art production is "in an interesting relationship with the functioning of contemporary capitalism which structures all pores of social life: the criticism and the provocativeness of art seem to be a part of the exploitation of human powers."[25] Several members of kpD therefore traveled in different con-stellations for years with the film to various places in Europe and used it at events in conjunction with EuroMayDay, in self-organized contexts of the unemployed, at universities, and also in art institutions as a means to discuss with the respective audiences the questions of a "good life" and of organizing the precarious. We wanted to trigger and impel a viral process of becoming common. In the meantime, the film now travels "alone," frequently also outside of Europe, especially to Latin America, and is used by others as an instrument for provoking discus-sions about common precarization and, with that, about social and political organizing.

The precarious have no common identity, but common experiences. Precarization, according to kpD, can be understood beyond the economic dimension as a manifold experience emerging from a non-functioning identitar[ian] ascription/appeal and its associated disambiguations, which nevertheless materialize in subjecti[vation] conditions in certain ways. . . Various professional, status-related,

25 Kunst, *Artist at Work*, p. 1.

kleines postfordistisches Drama (Brigitta
Kuster, Isabell Lorey, Marion von Osten, and
Katja Reichard), *Kamera läuft!*, 2004, film
stills, courtesy kleines postfordistisches
Drama

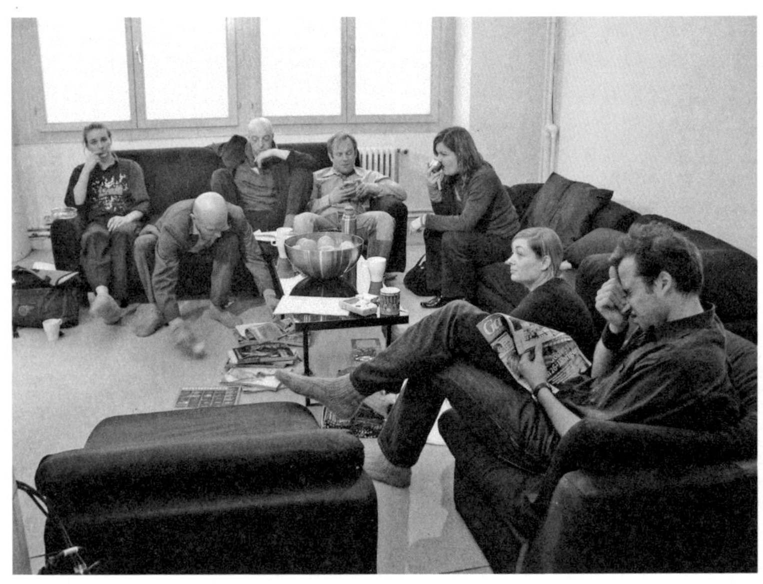

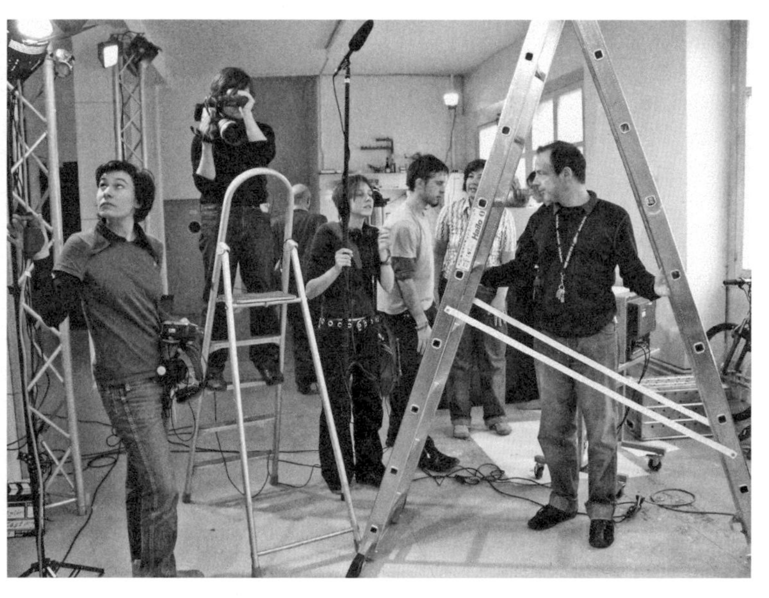

gendered, sexual and ethnicizing positions, which are so-cially very contradictory, frequently have to be taken at the same time or one after another.[26]

Precarization refers to the very laborious practice of queering multiple positions and appeals at the same time and one after another.[27] Taken this way, precarization also indicates the impossibility of disambiguation, the impossibility of an identitarian standstill, the experience of dealing with simultaneous multiplicities, with the heterogeneity of ascriptions and interpellations.

A Process of Constituting Instead of an Ontological Constitution of the Common

To be able to imagine this becoming-common as political agency and not a concept of the common as a socio-ontological constitution,[28] I would like to focus on a concept by political philosopher and activist Antonio Negri that has been somewhat forgotten, namely, the concept of *constituent power*.[29] In making demands for political and social rights, it can certainly be necessary to (strategically) refer to an ontologically grounded common, the common that strives for equality in the sense of equal opportunities in difference. But the common I am speaking about derives not from equality, but from differences; from multiplicity. This common is something that must emerge, something that has to be put together. There is no community that emerges here, no totalizing association or disambiguation, but rather a com-position fleeing from notions of community.[30]

26 kpD, "Precarization of Cultural Producers."

27 See also Renate Lorenz and Brigitta Kuster, *Sexuell arbeiten: Eine queere Perspektive auf Arbeit und prekäres Leben* (Berlin: b_books, 2007).

28 See Hardt and Negri, *Commonwealth*.

29 See Negri, *Insurgencies*.

30 See Isabell Lorey, "Constituent Immunisation: Paths Towards the Common," *Open! Platform for Art, Culture & the Public Domain* (2015), online at: http://www.onlineopen.org/constituent-immunisation.

Constituting, the emergence of a constituent power, is not without conflicts, and is therefore political in a fundamental sense. Confrontations—in the sense of taking apart and taking sides behind different fronts—are expressions of refusals and resistances, on the basis of which a constituent power is able to emerge. Without conflicts, without social struggles, constituent power remains a set of merely latent individual potentialities.

Precariousness and Precarity

With this background, let us return to the topic of precarization and link the discussion with some relevant ideas from political philosopher Judith Butler. She has suggested a socio-ontological concept of precariousness,[31] of existential vulnerability, which can be productively considered together with political theorist Michael Hardt and Negri's socio-ontological concept of the common.

Butler conceives the general precariousness of life, the vulnerability of the body, not simply as a threat or a danger from which protection is absolutely needed. To her, precariousness distinguishes that which makes up life in general—human as well as non-human. Butler formulates an ontology that can only be understood as embedded in social and political conditions. Vulnerability becomes extensive at birth because initial survival already depends on social networks, on sociality and labor.[32]

To say that life is precarious thus means pointing out that it does not exist independently and autonomously. Life requires social support and political and economic conditions that enable it to

31 Judith Butler, *Precarious Life: The Powers of Mourning and Violence* (London: Verso, 2004); see also Lorey, *State of Insecurity*.

32 Judith Butler, "Introduction: Precarious Life, Grievable Life," in *Frames of War: When Is Life Grievable?* (London: Verso, 2009), pp. 1–32. Butler's ideas refer not only to the existential significance of reproductive work, but precariousness also underlines the radical replaceability of every life.

continue in order for that life to be livable. An "ontology of individualism"[33] is not capable of recognizing the precariousness of life. According to Butler, a social ontology of precariousness calls exactly this individualism into question: "We are. . . social beings from the start, dependent on what is outside ourselves, on others, on institutions, and on sustained and sustainable environments, and so are, in this sense, precarious."[34]

The conditions that enable life are, at the same time, exactly those that keep it precarious. For this reason, as Butler argues, focus must be put on the political decisions and social practices under which some lives are protected and others are not. Butler calls the social and material insecurities arising from these kinds of decisions and practices *precarity*.

This notion of precarity can be understood as a functional effect of the political and legal regulations that are supposed to provide protection from general precariousness. It arises from certain conditions of domination, which have been legitimized in hegemonic western political thinking since state theorist Thomas Hobbes as protection from precariousness, and are at the same time based on the precarity of all those who are constructed as other and alien. Precarity, as a functional effect of specific security systems, is not limited to a national political phenomenon, but extends to global scale. Referring to political theorist Achille Mbembe, Butler states that *precarity* "is at once a material and a perceptual issue, since those whose lives are not 'regarded' as potentially grievable, and hence valuable, are made to bear the burden of starvation, underemployment, legal disenfranchisement, and differential exposure to violence and death."[35]

33 Ibid., p. 19.
34 Ibid., p. 23.
35 Ibid., p. 25.

Precarity—or in my terms: precarization—as an effect of specific conditions of domination means, on the one hand—as Butler makes clear—that this is not the socio-ontological concept of precariousness, but rather a political concept. Yet, on the other hand, precarity is therefore not to be understood as determining, but, on the contrary—although Butler does not make this sufficiently clear—as decidedly productive: in its productivity as an instrument of governing and a condition of economic exploitation, and also as a productive, always also incalculable, and potentially empowering subjectivation.[36]

Even though she does not imagine the political agency of singularities in the context of precarity, Butler supplies an extremely important argument in regard to how precariousness and precarity are interwoven: the fact that precarity is expanding instead of being minimized means—and this is Butler's political focus—that the generally shared vulnerability of life—precariousness—is not recognized, and cannot therefore function as a starting point for politics. For this reason, Butler calls especially on leftist politics to recognize shared precariousness, and to orientate normative obligations of equality and universal rights toward this.[37] Unlike socio-ontological precariousness, political precarity crosses all categories of identity and cannot be contained within them.

In my book *State of Insecurity: Government of the Precarious*, I have attempted to differentiate this unclear mixing of the terms precariousness and precarity in Butler's passages (above) into three dimensions of the precarious with my understanding of

36 Elsewhere, I have called this manifold productivity "governmental precarization": Lorey, "Prekarisierung als Verunsicherung und Entsetzen: Immunisierung, Normalisierung und neue Furcht erregende Subjektivierungsweisen," in *Prekarisierung zwischen Anomie und Normalisierung*, Alexandra Manske and Katharina Pühl, eds. (Münster: Westfälisches Dampfboot, 2010), pp. 48–81; for the actualization of these thoughts, see Lorey, *State of Insecurity*.
37 See Butler, *Frames of War*.

productive precarization. My use of precariousness continues to be largely inspired by Butler's term. I use precarity as a category of ordering, which designates structural societal conditions of inequality, the effects of political, social, legal, and economic compensations of precariousness. The dynamics of modes of governing and the concomitant subjectivations and practices of self-conduct are covered by the term governmental precarization. Understanding precarization as governmental makes it possible to problematize the complex interactions between an instrument of governing and the conditions of economic exploitation, and modes of subjectivation in their ambivalence between subjugation and self-empowerment.

The point of this more precise terminology is not to posit a politically understood process of becoming common against a socio-ontological common like precariousness.[38] Precariousness does not refer to a lack, but rather to a social abundance, to connectedness with others, which in the present consists in all dynamics, which cannot be referred to, however, as immutable and closed commonality. Although mutual, commonly shared precariousness is placed in hierarchy and devalued in favor of masculinist ideas of autonomy and superiority, and because it is privatized and feminized together with care and reproductive work, in the ambivalence between subjugation and the self-empowerment of governmental precarization, the process of becoming common is possible: with militant research and consciousness-raising practices, with other forms of knowledge production, and with new political practices based on mutual connectedness.[39] Individuals, then, no longer compose as already existing parts like in a mosaic. It is much

38 See Lorey, "Constituent Immunisation."
39 See Isabell Lorey, "Autonomy and Precarization," trans. Aileen Derieg, in *Mobile Autonomy: Exercises in Artists' Self-Organization*, Nico Dockx and Pascal Gielen, eds. (Amsterdam: Valiz, 2015), pp. 39–52.

more interesting to start from connectedness, rather than from an identitarian idea of participation, and to actualize and newly constitute connectedness again and again. Becoming common emerges from current constitutings that suspend place and time, and which produce new socialities and economies in an untimely now-time.[40]

The European movements of the precarious and the theoretical discourses interwoven with them have been able to perceive what is in common through precarization—unreasonable demands as well as opportunities. Even if it appears as though at least the EuroMayDay movement's time has passed, it is important to remember it not only as the context from which new forms of the political have emerged, but also in which important assemblages have been composed, setting in motion a process of becoming common. Even if these compositions dissolve again, their experiences and knowledge will remain. To me it seems most interesting to find that the processes of constituting continue to generate further interruptions and unforeseeable breaks elsewhere.

As in 2009 in the universities, as from 2011 on in the many occupied places and sites, to be continued. . .

40 See Isabell Lorey, "Presentist Democracy: Exodus and Tiger's Leap," trans. Aileen Derieg, *transversal texts* (2014), online at: http://transversal.at/blog/Presentist-Democracy.

Pauline Boudry, Rachel Mader, Marion von Osten, and Michael Zinganel, *Sex & Space: Space. Gender. Economy*, 1996, film studio, exhibition and site for workshops and discussions, installation view Shedhalle Zürich, Zurich, source: Archiv Shedhalle Zürich

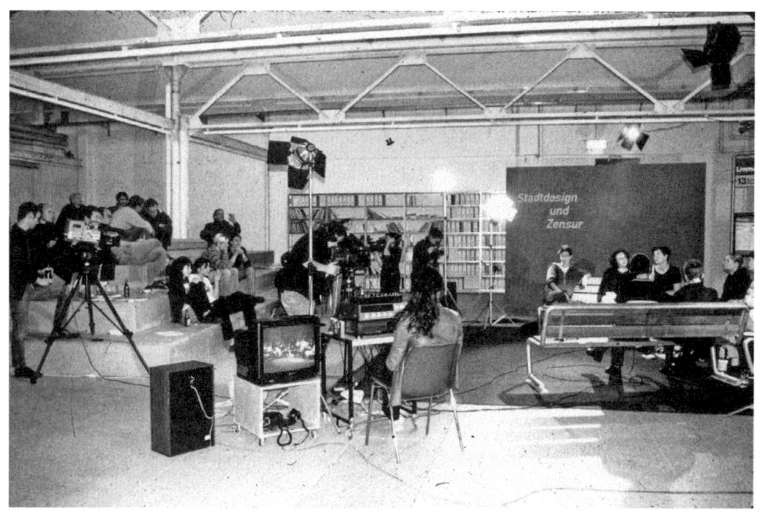

Booklet for *Sex & Space II: Space, Gender, Economy*, 1997, research and exhibition project, Forum Stadtpark, Graz, design: Labor k3000

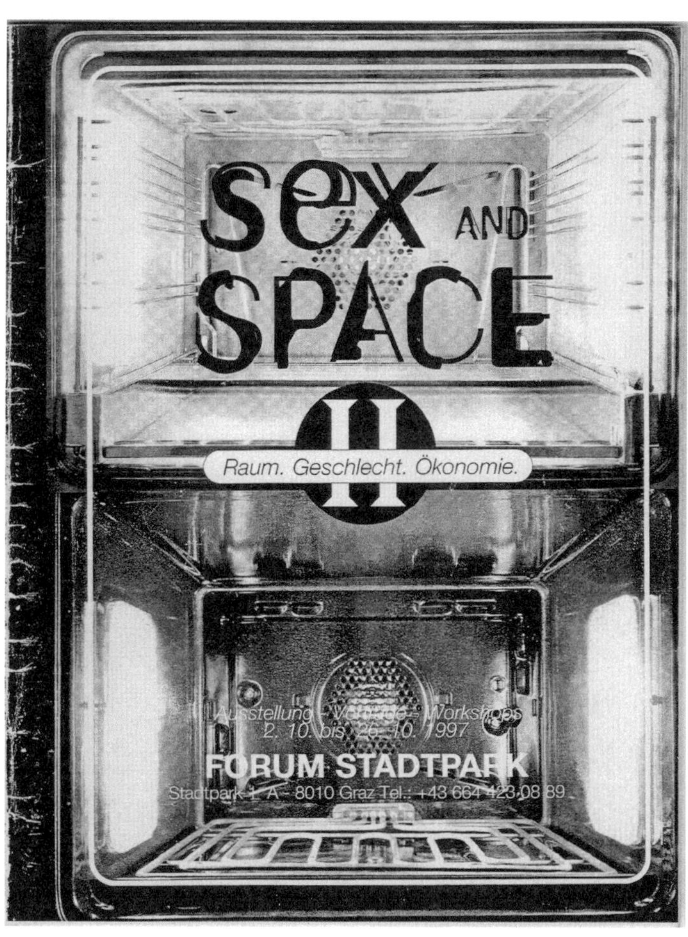

Angela McRobbie

Notes on Cultural Production: Marion von Osten, Art, and the Birmingham Contemporary Cultural Studies Tradition

<u>Inside and Outside the Classroom</u>
A defining feature of Marion von Osten's work is that she translates, updates, and relocates some of the characteristics of the Birmingham School of British cultural studies, most significantly from the perspective of a feminist artist and pedagogue. She does this primarily in the German-speaking world of art and design universities, where critical theory and the overwhelming influence of German philosopher Theodor Adorno and his critics have held the key position within the radical university sector as it engages with social life, media institutions, and the public sphere. Von Osten has been a key feminist figure in bringing a different understanding of popular culture not just to the art academy but also to informal spaces that are not so clearly structured. She moves in and out of the academy, favoring less tightly defined environments, not hampered by the new rules and obligations of the neoliberal university with its audits, assessments, benchmarking, and entrepreneurial culture.

Elsewhere I have argued that radical pedagogy in its most open form was a defining feature of the life-work of Stuart Hall, which was then extended in and through the Birmingham School and later at the Open University. With this in mind, I want to identify the kind of work we associate with von Osten.[1] If the notes below give the impression that von Osten's specific artworks are somewhat submerged by or entangled with the topics under consideration, this also is deliberate because most of my encounters with her have taken place in the context of the seminar room, lecture theater, arts center, workshop, and, occasionally, the traditional gallery. These interactions have been dynamic and fruitful. Von Osten is a feminist artist-pedagogue, someone who prefers process and socially

[1] See Angela McRobbie, "Stuart Hall: Art and the Politics of Black Cultural Production," *South Atlantic Quarterly*, vol. 115, no. 4 (2016), pp. 665–683.

engaged practice as part of an attempt to refuse the individual-izing tropes of our current modes of governmentality as they apply to art and culture. That is to say, she has consistently sidestepped the calls of the new neoliberal modes of female success in favor of a more embedded practice, one that is nevertheless theoretically informed and far removed from the previously allocated spaces for women within community arts. Indeed, the concept of art itself does not always figure so boldly in this kind of practice. Rather the purpose is to generate a wider milieu of feminist cultural production. One of von Osten's key achievements has been to bring to bear on the traditional art school curriculum a whole different body of work. To reform the element of what was art history and then became liberal studies against great opposition, and then eventually to bring cultural studies to the table, has been a defining feature of her projects.

In the context of the German, Swiss, or Austrian academy, where there is little or no tradition of cultural studies outside the *Kulturwissenschaft* approach and where everywhere the shadow of Adorno looms large, von Osten had to look to British cultural studies, and there she found of course a dy-namic and oppositional idea of working class culture as some-thing of value, something that deserved proper sociological analysis, something that had given rise to such important crea-tive formations and movements. The very idea of attaching this body of work—studies of motorbike culture, girls' magazines, mods and their scooters, etc.—to the more carefully guarded boundaries of the art academy was a bold and hazardous undertaking. One knows from hearing von Osten speak at conferences and events how much this task was both exciting and exhausting. Although the battle to open the curriculum to contemporary cultural studies was also a fraught endeavor in the United Kingdom, such efforts were mostly directed toward the establishment of media and cultural studies departments within or alongside existing sociology or English literature departments and not so much in the art school. There is a whole tale to be told about the history of these undertakings, but, suffice to say, former polytechnics (now called the new universities) proved more open to these proposals than older traditional and more elite universities. This latter group instead carefully attached a modest cultural studies element onto their existing provisions, e.g., modern languages with a cultural studies component.

However, in the last decade, there have been further changes in this landscape, with more and more emphasis on professional media and communications training rather than on the fine details of cultural theory. The discipline of cultural studies is often squeezed into a very busy curriculum as a result of current governmental emphasis on employability. Von Osten enters these changes in the increasingly international space of the art school and its opening out—albeit perhaps reluctantly— first to cultural studies and then, more recently, as it is pushed to embrace a curriculum that includes business studies and management.

Here, though, I will limit my reflections to the more specific contours of British cultural studies and offer two formative moments in my own engagement with what von Osten has been doing over several decades: first, her focus on feminist subcultural theory, and second, her contribution to the politics of cultural production. In her work at Shedhalle Zürich, Zurich, von Osten approached subculture as a kind of informal education. Trained in a more sclerotic tradition of the German art school system with all the rigidities it preserved and protected, von Osten looked to the subcultural practices of music-making, punk styles, and fanzine production as forms of cultural intervention that merited the kinds of analyses provided at that time by post-graduate students within the Birmingham Centre for Contemporary Cultural Studies (CCCS) under Hall's directorship. However, what has come to be consolidated as subcultural theory has had a lifecycle in the UK different from its place or reception in Germany. Arguably, in Germany and Austria, this body of work—the objects and texts, as well as the newer permutations of subculture—has been less denuded by the predatory forces of commercial youth-culture-driven capitalism than in the UK. One could suggest that the life cycle of subculture follows a very different pathway in German-speaking worlds, where it has found the means to preserve a more political element.

Let me expand on this point as it has implications for what we might describe as a feminist inter-generational subcultural practice. The Birmingham work initially understood subcultures within a mediated class model of British society. From the mid-1950s, the working classes were managed, overseen, and pacified by the allure of consumer culture and the social contract, which, as Hall has argued, was a way of subduing the power of trade unions by reducing class antagonisms in favor of wage bargaining.[2] Forced to relocate to the new housing schemes when the traditional extended family forms of living were demolished in working class communities, such as Bethnal Green in East London, the working classes took on a new aura of respectability and quietude, even though the jobs they performed in the Fordist factory lines were repetitive, unrewarding, and offered little in the way of training and upward mobility. This post-war "settlement" was internally disrupted, however, by the explosion of the younger generation. These were not students pulled into the anti-war movements of the

2   See Stuart Hall and Tony Jefferson, eds., *Resistance Through Rituals: Youth* *Subcultures in Post-War Britain* (London: Routledge, 1978).

times; instead, the urban subcultures that emerged in the UK from the mid-1960s on took place within leisure spaces unvisited—indeed, possibly unknown—by their middle-class counterparts. The CCCS argument was broadly that these were spectacular expressions of underlying class revolt waged in symbolic terms through a process of subverting or repurposing various, often ordinary and familiar artifacts. In addition, the whole panoply of activities had an anti-elitist and collective potential. If working class culture in the oppositional sense, as described magisterially by historian E. P. Thompson, had long since lain dormant, it was suddenly resurrected in this pop-culture mode. What Hall, et al., argue is that these vivid expressions—scattered across the landscape of the UK media and giving rise to any number of moral panics—disturbed the peace of the social contract and hence came as a warning that an unruly working class could once again threaten the always precarious social stability arrived at thanks to consumer culture: the car, house, and holiday abroad. Hall has argued in turn that there were indeed displaced or sublimated forms of class discontent. The young generation played out the internalized grievances of the parent culture, and so there was a line of connection between young and old. British media theorist Dick Hebdige has extended this account to bring into play the impact of black migrant youth culture as a backdrop for the white, working class youngsters to invent their own badges of cultural identity in music, in fashion and style, and in language and argot.[3]

So what was the fate of this British writing that could be summarized under the label of "resistance through rituals"? The imaginative and inventive—indeed, spectacular—elements of youth subcultures had an immense audio-visual impact on the

[3] See Dick Hebdige, *Subculture: The Meaning of Style* (London: Routledge, 1979).

urban environment, while the sociologists of the Birmingham School provided a strong academic discourse that gave weight and substance to these often ephemeral activities. Some elements of subcultural theory, Hebdige's work in particular, found a much bigger readership far beyond the academy. Likewise, the commercialization of subculture was rapid, unrelenting, and indeed a forerunner for what eventually became known as the creative economy. At the same time, the art schools in effect professionalized youth culture as a result of the eventual canonization of the Birmingham CCCS in curricula. Alongside this transformation, ethnographer Sarah Thornton's famous 1995 book *Club Cultures*[4] theorizes and in many ways legitimates this very process. What Thornton has seen (*pace* sociologist Pierre Bourdieu) is that subcultures themselves generated their own hierarchies of taste, and these also generated forms of subcultural capital. Contra what she saw as a romanticized Birmingham model, subcultures were, it seemed, just as willing and able as any other social group to trade in the values that had been accrued, especially in regard to the high value of insider knowledge, which appeared to come from the underground. In addition, Thornton argues that there was a logic to protecting this status of the underground precisely because it could be capitalized on. She challenges the assumption that these were, in some symbolic sense, anti-capitalist formations and instead finds within them the building blocks for all kinds of micro-enterprises. This, in a sense, poured cold water over the seemingly inflated meanings ascribed to subcultures by the Birmingham School. Thornton was proved right in that subcultures came within a decade to be one of the most valued sources for innovation and ideas in the creative economy.

4   Sarah Thornton, *Club Cultures: Music, Media and Subcultural Capital* (Cambridge: Polity Press, 1995).

This is what I mean by its professionalization in the art school, where, from the point at which young people from working class backgrounds eventually made it into a degree course on arts, graphic design, fashion, and media arts, etc., with the help of cultural studies and subcultural theory, they were in many ways able to then turn this kind of repertoire into a more polished career than the likes of Hebdige could ever imagine. Since then, subculture has provided a huge archive for all sorts of brands to plunder in the hope of gaining greater credibility, particularly in the desire to reach new youth markets. This process can be seen at work especially within the big luxury fashion brands, which find new ideas by commissioning youth culture research, as author Naomi Klein shows so vividly in her book *No Logo*.[5] In addition, having a store of subcultural knowledge can nowadays be a stronger currency in the job market and in interviews than the traditional forms of cultural capital described by Bourdieu, as it shows the applicant to be in touch.

In contrast, it has been more possible in German-speaking countries to hold on to and extend further the anti-capitalist elements of subculture, especially through appending queer politics with youth and moving the activities into the various spaces of art events, club scenes, and feminist-queer magazines like *Missy*. Arguably, this is the trope that von Osten's work has pursued, where she has applied the ethos of the indies to see things to fruition. To see subculture as redundant and merely a tool of contemporary neoliberalism is to overlook the kind of life it has for young people, especially sexual minorities for whom distinctive musical forms, hair styles, and bodily markings permit the possibility of escaping the grip of normative

5   Naomi Klein, *No Logo: Taking Aim At The Brand Bullies* (New York: Picador, 2000).

heterosexual everyday life. In this way, subcultures become a space for new cultural politics. Or to be more precise, in particular locations, youth cultural repertoires have continued to generate a constellation of signs and other markers of symbolic opposition or protest, which function with audiences and flowers in an openly dialogic or antiphonal way. This is the kind of activity that von Osten was drawn to and in effect has implemented in the kinds of curatorial work she has embarked upon since the early 1990s; that is to say, from feminist punk subcultural activity she developed a sense of DIY aesthetics and of informal learning in gallery spaces that no longer carried the elitist connotations of high art. This topic has been a regular point of conversation between von Osten and myself since 2000, as she has described her own intellectual formation in these "Birmingham" terms. It shows von Osten to be an artist-theorist looking to agency and change rather than to uncovering further the forces of subjugation.

Most of von Osten's work takes the curatorial/collectivist form of a visual and written series of statements, as well as videos and short films that are shown in art spaces, inviting audiences to engage with the work. The mode of address is pedagogic without being directive or dogmatic. There are traces of past feminist art projects in her work, but the overall effect is of the value of subcultures for initiating new kinds of address that disavow the exclusions of high art. Von Osten has confirmed and clarified an aesthetic strategy that draws on the subcultural repertoire, thereby saving it from mere absorption into the world of brands and consumer culture. However, youth subcultures do belong to youth, and as one gets older, other strategies for cultural engagement become necessary, even if they continue to bear this imprint. Von Osten's subsequent work shows as close a parallel to British cultural studies as before. Following the work of Paul Gilroy and Hall, and then extending out to the

Marion von Osten, spatial arrangement for
Atelier Europa: A Small Post-Fordist Drama,
2004, research and exhibition project,
installation view Kunstverein München,
Munich, photo: Dorothee Richter

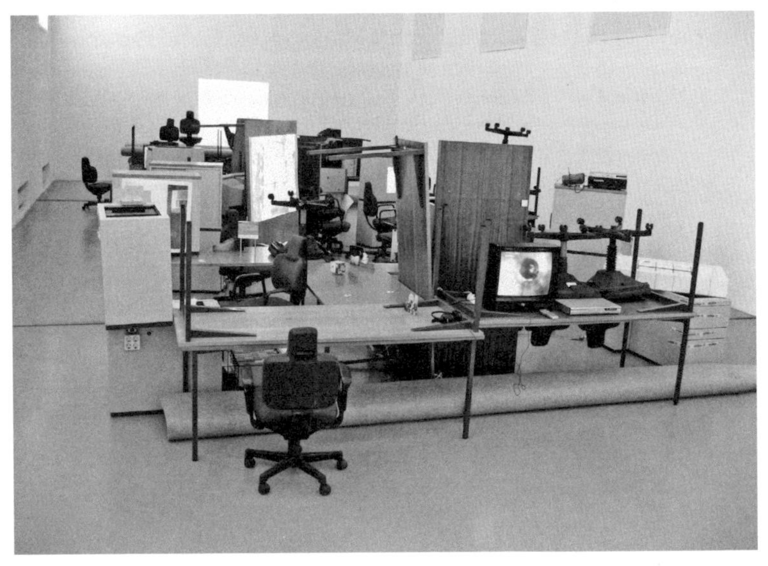

whole field of postcolonial studies as well as migration studies, von Osten has continued with and developed further the cultural methodology of art as visual research, which can be seen in the earlier phase. Her curatorial-editorial role has resulted in some exceptional undertakings: *In the Desert of Modernity: Colonial Planning and After* (2008–2009) and of course *Projekt Migration* (2002–2006).

However, I want to continue with the intellectual common ground I am most familiar with in regard to von Osten. Let us say that one of the things she has developed is the now established relation between radical artistic practice and the social theories that have emerged around post-Fordism. How exactly did this come into being? I would propose one line of connection is as follows: We became familiar with the wider significance of post-Fordist techniques of production from the debates that Hall and journalist Martin Jacques inaugurated during the administration of Margaret Thatcher under the label of New Times.[6] Here we were shown how working class tastes had been opened out to the more differentiated and dazzling world of consumer culture made available by post-Fordist processes of customization and the rise of design. "Everybody can now have their own distinctive identities" is what it seemed people were told, with the effect that class began to fade as a rallying point, to be replaced by so many other splintered or fragmented marks of belonging. Young heterosexual women increasingly looked to consumer culture for a sense of their own identity and achievement. These processes, as Hall has pointed out, meant that the left could no longer rely on stable ideas of class but had to take cognizance of more fluid or multiple identities, including those of "new ethnicities." The outcome of the New Times work was to prompt the left to take into account some

[6]   See Stuart Hall and Martin Jacques, *New Times: The Changing Face of Politics* *in the 1990s* (London: Lawrence & Wishart, 1989).

seemingly irreversible changes, such that failure to do so could only result in even more support for Thatcher, who of course valorized the end of class and the diminishing role of trade unions. Hall was not so much endorsing the new consumer culture with its ability to tap into popular desires, as he was attempting to develop a new politics of articulation, such that gender, race, and sexuality would no longer be seen by what remained of the Marxist left as secondary to class in the field of anti-capitalist politics. Popular culture was of course woven into this politics of articulation; Hall observed the (perhaps compensatory) pleasures young black people got from style and fashion as well as from various music genres, all of which were part and parcel of consumer culture. However, what was missing from this perspective (or what was rather less prominent) was the empirical question of who were the producers of post-Fordist culture? Who were the designers and musicians and graphic artists who, as sociologists Scott Lash and John Urry have argued, were now the architects of the "economy of signs and space"?[7] Of course, the question might also have been asked: "Who were the people in the factories across the world who produced the goods in some sort of factory environment equipped with the technology to ensure just-in-time systems, and which could adapt to the demands of the electronic point of sale machines installed in shops across the western world?" Attention from the mid-1990s into the early 2000s was, however, directed toward these new cadres of design professionals or, indeed, artists and the conditions of their labor. The *Atelier Europa* project in 2003–2004 took up this theme as its key topic on the grounds that von Osten had already assembled a group of artists and social theorists from Austria, France, Germany, and the UK who were engaged in thinking through the consequences of the rise of a new type of

[7] Scott Lash and John Urry, *Economies of Signs and Space* (London: Sage, 1994).

mostly freelance or insecure temporary worker. The group was paradoxically devoted to their creative work but increasingly aware that this very dynamic was what was being relied upon by the state, employers, and policymakers increasingly concerned with rationalizing both labor markets and the cost of welfare, especially welfare in work in the form of various securities and forms of social insurance such as maternity pay, sickness wages, and paid holidays. Their awareness of the conditions of their own labor and, indeed, their desire to theorize it really formed one of many initiatives for the new politics of creative labor often described as the politics of precarity.

While there has been an enormous literature stemming from philosophers Michael Hardt and Antonio Negri's rereading of Marx's *Grundrisse,* which in turn permitted a less defeatist understanding of the fate of the European left from the late 1970s onwards, this has remained an analysis relatively inattentive to gender and to precisely the kind of politics of articulation argued for by Hall. However, it does have the value of emphasizing the possibility, even in the face of intractable forces, of political agency and activism. In contrast to the masculinist trope of the (post)*operaismo* writers, von Osten's role here has been substantial for her investment in the idea of a feminist postcapitalist subjectivity. Once again we see von Osten's commitment to acknowledging struggles even if they remain at the margins of mainstream political life.[8] If my own recent work has been given over to the dynamics of subject formation within the creativity *dispositif* with all the dire consequences this has for sociality, von Osten has looked to the more emancipatory ensemble of relations that can be envisaged. She sees this possibility not as a nostalgic re-rendering of

8   Marion von Osten, "In Search of the Postcapitalist Self," *e-flux journal*, no. 17 (June 2010), online at: http://www.e-flux. com/journal/17/67350/editorial-in-search-of-the-postcapitalist-self/.

feminist community, but as supporting forms of cultural production that enable producers to work in this direction of envisaging alternative worlds. The enactment of these dilemmas in the creative work itself, and in the various milieus in which they are performed and presented, advances this possibility further. To sum up, throughout von Osten's work, there is a forward-looking imagination that records and documents often overlooked aspects of popular struggle, some of which could be understood as subcultural. Informed by contemporary social and cultural theory, highly aware of the powers of biopolitics that organize our subjectivities around pleasures, desires, and satisfactions, in this case couched at the level of creative work, von Osten nevertheless sees feminist agency as capable of breaking through and out of these regulated subjectivities.

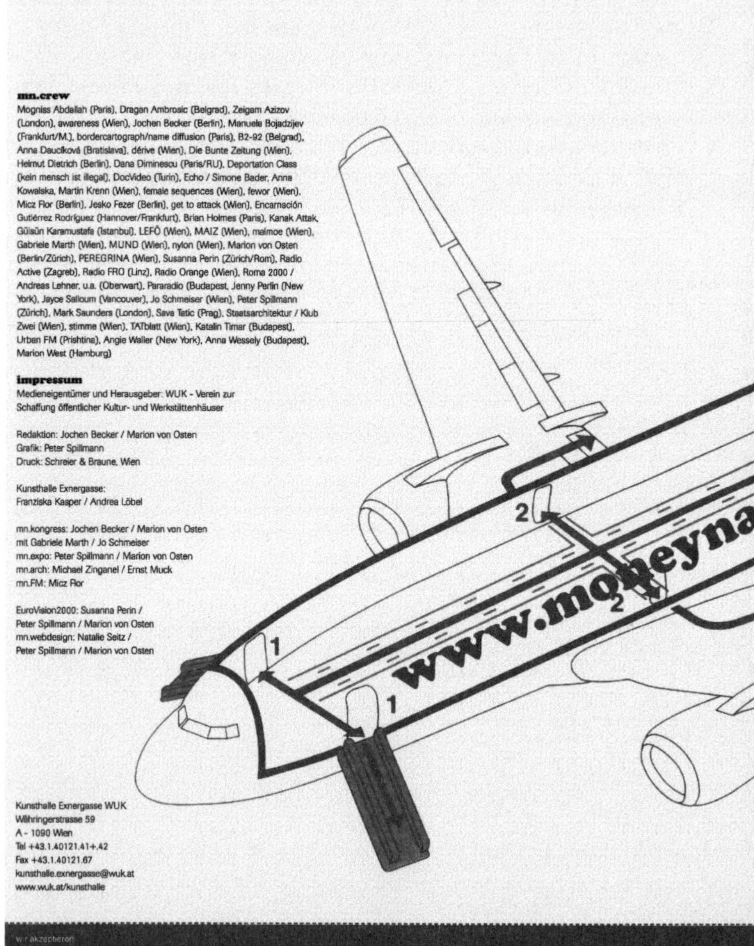

mn.crew

Mogniss Abdallah (Paris), Dragan Ambrosic (Belgrad), Zeigam Azizov (London), awareness (Wien), Jochen Becker (Berlin), Manuela Bojadzijev (Frankfurt/M.), bordercartograph/name diffusion (Paris), B2-92 (Belgrad), Anna Daucíková (Bratislava), dérive (Wien), Die Bunte Zeitung (Wien), Helmut Dietrich (Berlin), Dana Diminescu (Paris/RU), Deportation Class (kein mensch ist illegal), DocVideo (Turin), Echo / Simone Bader, Anna Kowalska, Martin Krenn (Wien), female sequences (Wien), fewor (Wien), Micz Flor (Berlin), Jesko Fezer (Berlin), get to attack (Wien), Encarnación Gutiérrez Rodríguez (Hannover/Frankfurt), Brian Holmes (Paris), Kanak Attak, Gülsün Karamustafa (Istanbul), LEFÖ (Wien), MAIZ (Wien), malmoe (Wien), Gabriele Marth (Wien), MUND (Wien), nylon (Wien), Marion von Osten (Berlin/Zürich), PEREGRINA (Wien), Susanna Perin (Zürich/Rom), Radio Active (Zagreb), Radio FRO (Linz), Radio Orange (Wien), Roma 2000 / Andreas Lehner, u.a. (Oberwart), Pararadio (Budapest, Jenny Perlin (New York), Jayce Salloum (Vancouver), Jo Schmeiser (Wien), Peter Spillmann (Zürich), Mark Saunders (London), Sava Tatic (Prag), Staatsarchitektur / Klub Zwei (Wien), stimme (Wien), TATblatt (Wien), Katalin Timar (Budapest), Urban FM (Prishtina), Angie Waller (New York), Anna Wessely (Budapest), Marion West (Hamburg)

impressum

Medieneigentümer und Herausgeber: WUK - Verein zur Schaffung öffentlicher Kultur- und Werkstättenhäuser

Redaktion: Jochen Becker / Marion von Osten
Grafik: Peter Spillmann
Druck: Schreier & Braune, Wien

Kunsthalle Exnergasse:
Franziska Kasper / Andrea Löbel

mn.kongress: Jochen Becker / Marion von Osten
mit Gabriele Marth / Jo Schmeiser
mn.expo: Peter Spillmann / Marion von Osten
mn.arch: Michael Zinganel / Ernst Muck
mn.FM: Micz Flor

EuroVision2000: Susanna Perin /
Peter Spillmann / Marion von Osten
mn.webdesign: Natalie Seitz /
Peter Spillmann / Marion von Osten

Kunsthalle Exnergasse WUK
Währingerstrasse 59
A - 1090 Wien
Tel +43.1.40121.41+.42
Fax +43.1.40121.67
kunsthalle.exnergasse@wuk.at
www.wuk.at/kunsthalle

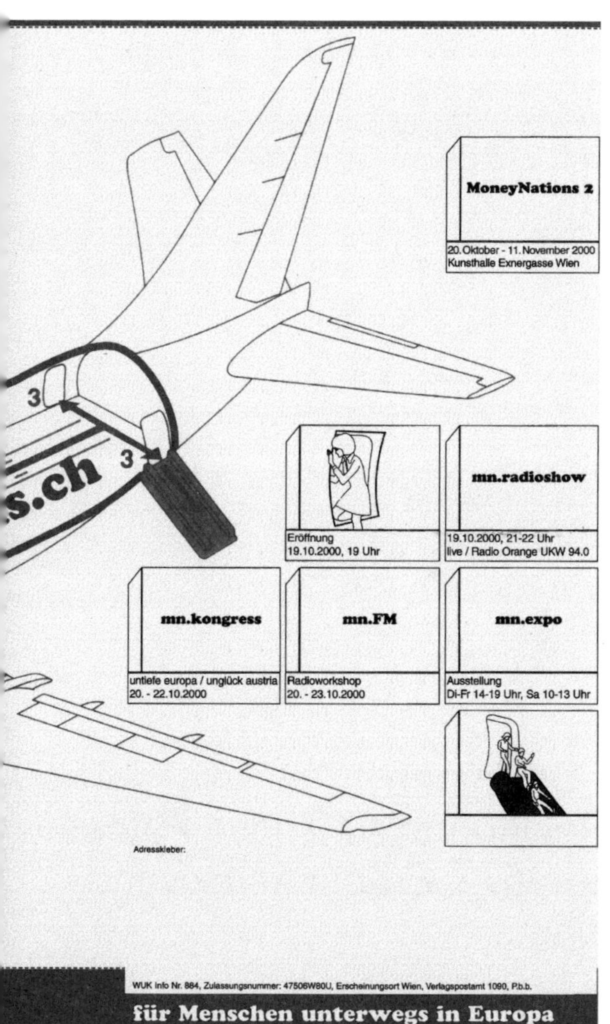

WUK Info Nr. 884, Zulassungsnummer: 47506W80U, Erscheinungsort Wien, Verlagspostamt 1090, P.b.b.

für Menschen unterwegs in Europa

Peter Spillmann

Our Relation to All These Places Is Operative: Practices Beyond Curating

<u>Prologue</u>

How can you best write about a shared practice? By conducting a conversation about it, mutually questioning one another (or letting others ask the questions), by trying to describe what each generally does, how decisions are made, how tasks are distributed, who does what better? This form of description seems less suitable to me for the kind of practice that Marion von Osten and I have carried out together for over twenty years. Therefore, I have decided to give an account of/from various projects from the perspective of a narrator. This is something for which there has hardly been an opportunity thus far, because when the projects have been presented, the focus has always been on considerations of content and concept, on formal decisions, and, mostly, on reflections on the concrete reasons for the projects. An essential moment of our practice, which could perhaps be generally outlined as continually acting and communicating in ever new, given situations and constellations, hardly comes into view in those kinds of presentations. Along with the idea that a text should be entertaining, which is not to be underestimated, I understand narrating here as a strategy for giving the many parallel impressions, experiences, and encounters accompanying the project work a significance that they deserve in this kind of practice. The following accounts relate to moments/episodes from our work in three different project contexts before and around the year 2000. In retrospect, this period proves to be the phase in which we developed and established a specific way of working with and in our projects, which continues up to the present. In conclusion, I will attempt to name the most important characteristics or features of our shared practice more specifically again, thus also sketching several connections in content and form to a number of further projects.

<u>Labor k3000</u>
With the opening of the k3000 space,[1] we were under the pressure of time. As part of the framework program for the exhibition *MoneyNations*[2] in Shedhalle Zürich (1998),[3] the workshop titled "Double Check the Information" was supposed to take place at the end of October 1998 in the rooms into which we had only just moved. Yet on the evening before the workshop, we were still busy transporting furniture and setting up workplaces.

The initiative for founding k3000 arose from the need to close the self-organized art space Kombirama,[4] which we had run for one year as a temporary project. This newly formed group included, in addition to Marion and myself, art historian and curator Sylvia Kafehsy, video specialist Davide Legittimo, sound artist Marcus Maeder, graphic designer Enea Marieni-Gómez, artist and cultural producer Susanna Perin, journalist Lilian Räber, publisher Georg Rutishauser, activist Patric Schatzmann, graphic designer Natalie Seitz, web programmer Michael Vögeli, and artist Tim Zulauf. In the 1990s, there were numerous self-organized projects and spaces in Zurich that all experimented with diverse artistic and social formats, endeavoring to set themselves apart from established institutions. Debates about content often revolved around the question of the power of definition over one's own practice, about who defines what art is. What predominated at a wholly practical level was mostly competition for suitable and affordable spaces. The specific reason for tensions between a more alternative and self-organized local art scene and art-market-oriented high art institutions was provided by a new gallery and museum complex that had formed in Zurich in the late 1980s, first as temporary in an old dyeing factory at the periphery of the city then moving into the

1   See http://www.k3000.ch/labor/.
2   See http://www.moneynations.net/.
3   See http://www.shedhalle.ch.
4   See http://www.kombirama.ch.

Löwenbräu grounds in 1996; before they were located in the middle of a former workers' quarter marked by migration and alternative lifestyles.

The board of Shedhalle Zürich (of which I was a member from 1992 to 2000) made the decision to at the time pursue a decidedly political program as a statement in favor of critical artistic practice and against "auteur" art. Personal contacts between Kombirama and the Shedhalle team, marked by common interests, had already led to close collaboration with the project *SUPERmarkt: money, market, gender politics* (1998) and the event series *Die aktuelle Wirtschaftswoche* (The Current Economic Week) (1997)—both of which were attempts to bash neoliberalism with artistic formats. What exactly k3000, the successor project to Kombirama, was supposed to be had been discussed in many long meetings for over a year. The central concern was to share a production infrastructure and to jointly operate a project space with workplaces for graphic design, sound, and video editing. The focus was not to be on curating events but rather on the exchange of know-how, collaboration on projects, and, linked with that, an intensive engagement with various strategies and formats for implementing content. So k3000 was not to be another art space. We wanted to counter the imperatives of distribution and self-representation, which were dominant then in our view, with the principle of production. k3000 became real in fall 1998, when renting a floor in a commercial building that was built in the 1950s was offered to us under favorable conditions. The area was much too large for our purposes, however, and twenty more people had to be found within weeks to move in with us. k3000 thus turned into a studio community, and we moved into a somewhat large room in one corner of the floor and began to call ourselves Labor k3000.

The occasion for the workshop "Double Check the Information" was the dramatic conflict in ex-Yugoslavia. In 1998, the situation escalated around Kosovo, where the UÇK (the Kosovo Liberation Army) increasingly undertook armed actions against the Serbian police. How is war, how is a crisis represented? Is a media-artistic practice an appropriate strategy for intervening in processes of forming public opinion? Through contact with exiled communities of people from former Yugoslavia, we learned of the media's central role in the nationalistically aggravated conflicts. Numerous initiatives had arisen inside and outside of Yugoslavia, which actively used the then little known Internet to broadcast and exchange independent news across the borders newly erected with nationalist arguments. We invited media activists from various projects to the workshop: Marica Bender from Radio Zid in Sarajevo, artist Berta Jottar from New York, Drazen Pantic and Mina Vuletić from Radio B92 headquartered in Belgrade, Marko Peljhan from LJUDMILA in Ljubljana, Oliver Sertić from Attack! in Zagreb, Jeta Xharra from Media Project—Pristina in Pristina, and the filmmaker Želimir Žilnik from Novi Sad. The media initiative Ex-Jugoslawien, a non-governmental organization (NGO) in Zurich founded by exiles, took care of visas and co-financed travel and accommodation costs. The plan for the workshop comprised various rounds of discussions and four public presentations, but this plan was already abandoned by the first day and replaced with a kind of ongoing joint negotiation about what should happen next. For four days, Labor k3000's space, which had only just been completely furnished, thus became a turbulent point of intersection of very different artistic, political, and personal interests and urgencies, colliding directly with one another in many of the presentations and discussions.

Xharra represented a group from Pristina that had organized media workshops for women until the conflict openly broke out.

Participants in these workshops attempted to take a stand
against the patriarchal rhetoric of war and violence until their
activity became too dangerous. Later, as someone familiar with
the local situation, she also accompanied a team of BBC jour-
nalists shooting a documentary film about the various parties
of the conflicts. Xharra told us about how the freedom fighters
were advised by the television team to paint themselves black
and carry branches as camouflage so they would look more
authentic. Through her, we also found out that the central
headquarters of the UÇK were located nearby our location
in an apartment on Hohlstrasse and that Hashim Thaçi, their
leader and the 2016 President Elect of the Republic of Kosovo,
studied at the University of Zurich. Today Xharra hosts a populist TV show on Kosovo TV, *Jeta në Kosovë* (Life in Kosovo).

Žilnik brought along several of his films, including older productions that we watched during long film nights. In the film
Tito po drugi put medju Srbima (Tito Among the Serbs for the
Second Time) from 1993, he accompanied an actor through
the streets of Belgrade with a camera. The figure—so similar
to Josip Broz Tito, the first president of Yugoslavia, in clothing,
gestures, and speech as to be easily mistaken—waves, greets,
and approaches people. Many react with amusement; others
use the opportunity to express their opinions at last or to talk
about their hopes and fears. The figure of Tito becomes a
catalyst, and the happening turns into a precise analysis of a
social mood. Žilnik's docu-fictional practice and his complex
perspective on the developments in Yugoslavia provided
the most important impulses of the workshop. He recounted
observations, for example, of how the nationalistic fallout was
reflected in the image politics of everyday life and in public
media, and how national languages were constructed out
of different Slavic dialects. Žilnik also took Labor k3000's
production credo seriously and proposed starting a new

project together. In the end, there was only enough time for
a few impressions from the surroundings, the Langstrasse
quarter heavily influenced by immigration, and several brief
interviews with refugees who had come to Switzerland from
different crisis regions of ex-Yugoslavia and then were con-
fronted with populist media reports and the political advances
of the right-wing-nationalist Swiss People's Party calling for
more restrictive asylum policies.

As founders of Labor k3000, we already found ourselves in
quite an ambivalent position during the first days of the project.
The invited protagonists had made extensive use of the opportunity to exchange and newly network among themselves.
The occasion met great interest in various politically engaged
scenes and even reached a certain public of political activists
and culture-oriented, socially committed citizens. We had
imagined the workshop more as an opportunity to develop
and establish a common activist practice. And we periodically
endeavored to introduce Labor k3000 and our plans for it as
well. These half-hearted endeavors to include our own concerns, however, remained an unessential bracket in light of the
topicality and urgency of the ongoing events, and so we found
ourselves in the old role of organizers again. Following this
experience, we turned over directing the operation of further
public events to the entirety of the renters of the floor and
transferred the events to the foyer. Labor k3000 was then
exclusively our production site. Subsequently and in cooperation
with different teams, graphic designs, videos, and websites
were made for almost all following projects and exhibitions.
The fact that we were able to carry out media productions
entirely by ourselves also helped maintain the autonomy of
our own practice in many collaborations with institutions.

<u>On the Road in Europe</u>

In preparation for *MoneyNations* (1997–2001), in the summer of 1998 Marion and I took a four-week trip that was to crucially influence our further work. The first stopping point was Istanbul, where we were in contact with the artist Gülsün Karamustafa. Conversations about her work and the political situation in Turkey in the 1980s and 1990s filled the evenings. We learned from her about the major changes in Turkey after opening its borders to Eastern Europe and Russia. She guided us through the Laleli quarter, which was marked by countless companies producing textiles for the Georgian and Russian markets. She had noticed that mostly women traveled as traders, buying clothing for small sums and taking it, packed in large bags, across the Black Sea by ferry or by bus to Georgia or Russia. It was not unusual, as Karamustafa discovered, for the women to earn with prostitution the initial capital they needed to start trading. From this, Karamustafa developed the work *Objects of Desire* for the exhibition *MoneyNations*. In a long-term performance at a specially built market stand, she sold colorful clothing and home textiles, toys, and all kinds of bric-a-brac, goods with a value of $100 (US) that she had brought from Istanbul in a large travel bag.

No official numbers are known regarding the effective volumes of the "suitcase trades." The performance on site gave us a glimpse of how dynamic and relevant this economy was for those participating in it. The shopping area in Laleli covered several blocks. Large commercial buildings with exhibition halls on six floors, in which all kinds of textiles were presented, alternated with cheap hotels. The shoppers' bags were piled high in front of the stores. The textiles were produced right around the corner. Young women, crowded together at sewing machines, sat in brightly lit cellars. There were mountains of fabric scraps on the street. In front of the entrances to the sewing factories, there were men who eyed us suspiciously. The encounter with a completely different economic reality of sweatshops, suitcase trade, and informal trade was to become a central theme of the trip and various later projects, such as *Fashion is Work* (1999).

Our further destinations on the *MoneyNations* research trip were Sofia and Bucharest. Because the border in the northwestern part of Turkey had been closed due to political tensions, we were not able to continue the journey as planned. At the train station in Istanbul, we were advised to choose a tourist route instead and take a ferry from a Turkish seaside resort to a Greek holiday island. So we set out by bus from Istanbul via İzmir to Kuşadası. From there, excursion boats traveled daily to the nearby Greek island of Samos, which is linked with the mainland by a ferry to Thessaloniki. The daily train connections to Bulgaria consisted of three dilapidated wagons of the Greek railway. At the border train station, we were finally the only passengers left. Behind the small train station, a wedding party sat eating at a long table in a meadow. In the wagon, it had meanwhile become uncomfortably hot. After a little over an hour, the conductor brought our passports back to us, and the train went on. Just before the border, in the middle of a forest, it stopped again. Some twenty young women with suitcases and bags boarded the train, and the compartments filled up. Several men were standing outside by the train and gave the girls instructions to sit down. Then the journey continued across the border to Bulgaria. During the journey from Sofia to Bucharest, between Ruse and Giurgiu, the trip crossed a steel bridge over the Danube, which forms the border between Bulgaria and Romania. At one point before entering the train station on the Romanian side, the train was taken through a disinfection facility. Border guards, placed at regular intervals along the tracks, waved at passengers standing by the open windows and grinned as they watched the passengers' reactions to being hit by streams of disinfectant liquid without warning. The precariousness of the travel connections, the neglected wagons, the lack of information, the waiting in the heat, and finally the suspicion that we might be bringing in dangerous diseases all seemed an absurd farce to us at that moment.

We had planned to travel back to Istanbul from Bucharest at the end of our trip. The border to Turkey was opened again in the meantime, but tickets for the direct night train to Istanbul were already sold out for the next two months. The closable train compartments were used for the informal transport of goods and were therefore only available through the black market. So, in the end, we traveled back to Zurich by way of Budapest and Vienna. The border as a site of staging difference and state sovereignty and as a reason for multiple tactical maneuvers, deals, and practices of becoming invisible became a central actor in the journey and an important component of our own experiential knowledge.

Our journey was not a research trip in the classical sense, with a clear query and a specific field to be investigated. Instead, we were motivated more by the idea of being on site ourselves, to get our own picture, independent of the conventional media reports, of a situation familiar to us. We were surprised by the extent to which the new circumstances and resultant conflicts were depicted in every place in the space and became readable.

Following the experiences in Istanbul, we let ourselves be guided to the hot spots of transformation in Sofia and Bucharest as well. In both cities, we met people affiliated with art and political activism. We had contacted some of them beforehand; others were introduced to us on site. In Sofia, we had intensive conversations with the then-young artists Luchezar Boyadjiev and Kalin Serapionov; artist Nedko Solakov, who was well

known in Bulgaria at that time and quite controversial due
to his connections with the Communist regime; and with the
curator Iara Boubnova. In Bucharest, we talked for a long time
with the artist Lia Perjovschi. We recorded many of the conversations on video but, in the end, were never able to make use
of the material.

The conversations revolved around an exchange of experiences. How and where had the ideologies of the Cold War
had an impact in the Ruhr region of Germany, where Marion
grew up? What were the effects in Switzerland, where I come
from? And which images of Eastern Europe were conveyed to
us? What was really happening in Sofia, Istanbul, and Bucharest
at the same time? Which perspectives did people take in each,
in a critical milieu, in relation to local situations and the position
of the west? How was art discussed, and which music was
listened to, and were there perhaps common reference systems (like ideas, images, theories, certain artists) referred to
independently on both sides of the border? We also talked
about art and which artists had recently become complicit in
the hegemonic art system of the west. Sometimes we argued
heatedly about how allegedly important it was to make a
name for oneself with the "right" art, in this context marked
by discourses of the west. For the *MoneyNations* exhibition in
Shedhalle, Boyadjiev and Serapionov produced work together,
which was new for them at the time, focusing on a specific
place and theme, namely the gentrification processes in Sofia.
Perjovschi had for some time been collecting snapshots of the
many odd encounters she had had together with her husband,
artist Dan Perjovschi, when curators from the west briefly
stopped by their studio during a jet-setting tour of Eastern
Europe and had two or three works shown to them. This resulted
in *Studio Guests* for *MoneyNations*, an installation with a number of folders full of photos.

Marion von Osten, Nathalie Seitz, and Peter
Spillmann, *MoneyNations@access*, 1998,
exhibition, installation view Shedhalle Zürich,
Zurich, photo: Nadine Podwika, source:
Archiv Shedhalle Zürich

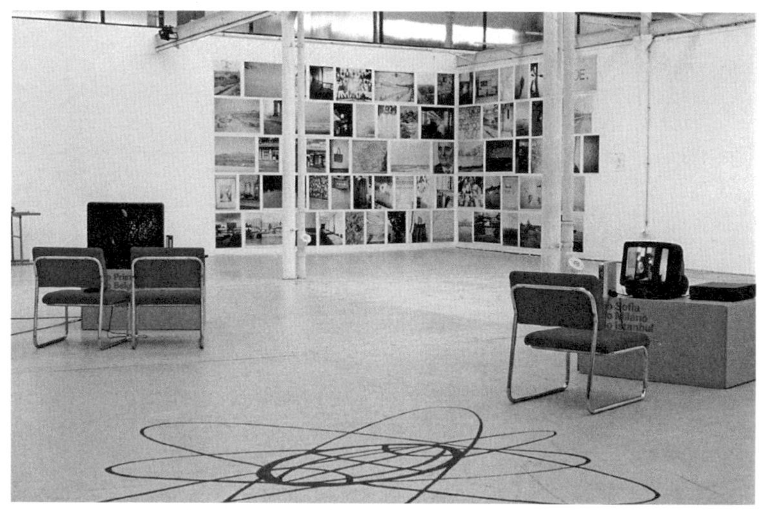

Gülsün Karamustafa, *Objects of Desire*,
1998, mixed media installation, installation
view *MoneyNations@access*, Shedhalle
Zürich, Zurich, photo: Nadine Podwika,
source: Archiv Shedhalle Zürich

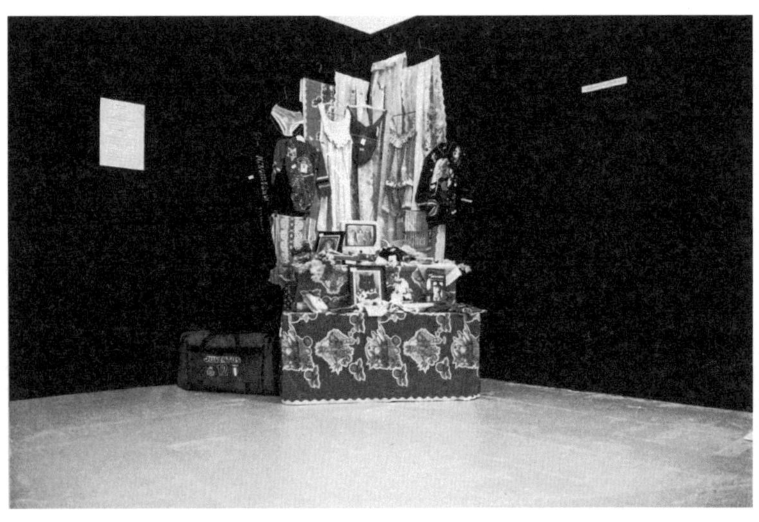

In this open exchange, touching on various personal and social topics such as art, the role of women, personal economic circumstances, and more, we soon realized that the then current changes we had learned to describe and criticize in the 1990s in Germany and Switzerland as effects of new neoliberal politics were closely linked with the dramatic, brutally capitalistic upheavals in the countries of the former Eastern Bloc, which are even mutually conditional and thus allow us to essentially recognize the outlines of a future "new Europe."

The new border regime on the one hand and the practices of migration on the other were researched again in more depth between 2002 and 2006 in conjunction with *Projekt Migration* in the research group Transit Migration (made up of academics in the fields of sociology, political theory, and anthropology, such as Rutvica Andrijasevic, Manuela Bojadžijev, Sabine Hess, Serhat Karakayali, Efthimia Panagiotidis, Regina Römhild, and Vassilis Tsianos), partly in the same region along the Turkish-Greek border of the European Union. In cooperation with Labor k3000, this resulted in the mapping project *MigMap*[5] for the *Projekt Migration* exhibition at the Kölnischer Kunstverein and several other venues in Cologne in 2005–2006. *MigMap* was an attempt to find a representation for the new European migration regime that was so hard to grasp, and additionally to develop a research space, which was to provide insight for Transit Migration's field research.

On the gradually fading Hi8 tapes left over from our research trip and now housed in the Labor k3000 archive, and in between long conversation sequences and journeys through various cities, I recently found several scenes we filmed in Bucharest. We pursued the idea of making a film about the

5   See http://www.transitmigration.org/migmap/.

machinations of the international investors and real estate developers who were swarming within the city at that time and promoting luxury construction projects on gigantic signs on every corner construction site with cheap computer visualizations. We spent one night in a hotel with the promising name Helvetia, whose address we had seen in an investor magazine lying around a train. The hotel was located at the edge of an overgrown park and had recently been elaborately renovated and catapulted into the luxury category through the use of lots of marble. In our room, we found a whole stack of other brochures advertising construction projects, spas, shopping malls, luxury villas, media parks, everything that was happening in the late 1990s, and they were obviously all still searching for investors. The price for one night seemed outrageous to us— the trip was privately financed—and so we decided to at least use the opportunity and the ambience to make something: a small film. The spontaneously developed plot had real estate developers and investors from the west meeting in the secure territory of a five-star business hotel, and from there they would divide up the post-Communist city and its businesses among themselves. The hotel, with its discreet suites, elegant restaurant, and conference rooms equipped with modern communication infrastructure, was indeed frequented by all kinds of financiers, consultants, experts, and correspondents (namely from the Reuters agency). They all used the exterritorial hub, insulated from everyday life and in keeping with western standards, to enforce the new capitalist order in the country. In the few staged situations we shot, the following actions can be recognized: knocking, opening the door, greeting, a discreet discussion between a businessman and businesswoman in a room, handing over a file, shaking hands. And in a second series of takes: a businessman with a wheeled suitcase leaves the elevator, a key and credit card on a desk, the reception desk, the businessman leaves the hotel, the businessman gets into a taxi. The discussion scene, shot several times, always ends in laughter. We were not able to succeed at all in slipping into the role of serious businesspeople. On the way to the reception desk, my rather impractical trolley suitcase got caught in the seam of a carpet, exposing a rubber mat underneath it, which a uniformed hotel employee discreetly covered up again. Leaving the hotel, we heard a helicopter and machine gun fire. The camera, first focused on me, panned with some delay to the park. Later, the taxi driver explained that it was an exercise of the elite troop of the police that was conducted in the park because Roma people often stayed there. We were simply shocked. Nothing ever came of the film.

A *EuroVision2000* Experience

The project *EuroVision2000* (2000–2001)[6] was created following *MoneyNations*, again against the backdrop of a tightening European border and migration regime. By the end of the 1990s, the discourses about a "new" European identity, neoliberal politics, and economically argued "competitiveness" had produced not only conflicts and social inequalities in the EU states but also increasingly had state-political consequences. These included the tightening of asylum laws, the introduction of new apparatuses of control such as the Schengen Information System (SIS), and an accentuation of/emphasis on security discourses. The significance of reporting on television and in the press was substantial in this process. "Border crossings" became media events, whereas critical analyses that questioned the predominance of the capitalistically organized societies of the "west" hardly still found a public. Structurally, the project *EuroVision2000* was a continuation of the network of correspondents that had developed with *MoneyNations*, for which we had already called on filmmakers and artists to send us

6   See http://www.eurovision2000.net.

video clips of current events and ongoing debates in their surroundings. The opportunity to realize *EuroVision2000* arose
in 1999 during my studio scholarship in Prague through a
contact to local net activists. Prague was one of nine European
cities named as a Capital of Culture for the year 2000, and the
net activist project venue Café9 was organized from there. The
nine cities were to be connected via live streaming through the
Internet. Our idea of a network of correspondents around the
themes of new border and migration policies and the effects of
globalization fit well with this in terms of both form and content.
We started another call, and in the end, the archive comprised
a good thirty longer and shorter contributions in the three
"sections" of "globalization," "New Europe," and "migration
policies."

The public events were the most productive. Together with
local partners, we managed to initiate events in three cities:
Marion in Brussels, Susanna in Bologna, and me in Prague.
The event in Prague took place shortly before the demonstrations of the anti-globalization movement during the World
Trade Organization (WTO) summit in fall of 2000. Already in
summer, at one of the first preparation meetings on site, our
paths crossed with those of young global activists who were
equipped with the latest mobile phones and laptops and
searching for efficient media infrastructures and Internet
connections. The battle against globalization was carried out
through media. Our project, on the other hand, aimed more for
dialogue. We wanted to communicate with a generation of older
critical intellectuals from Prague about terms and strategies of
the "political" and to exchange ideas about local developments, e.g., in terms of gentrification in Berlin and Prague.
In the context of the anti-globalization movement, however,
the concepts of activist practices following the models of
the movement in the United States were hardly critically

questioned. Many of the activists who had traveled to Prague from the US and Western Europe who came by to see us were obviously convinced that "political" means the same thing everywhere, and they had little awareness of specific conditions, such as those in Prague, where public manifestations had a special significance due to experiences from the history of the Prague Spring of 1968 and the Velvet Revolution of 1989.

The *EuroVision2000* events in Prague took place from 7 to 14 September 2000 at Roxy, an alternative cultural center. Its high, circular, windowless room had served as a kitchen for a renowned Jewish restaurant before World War II. A simple spatial setting—a circle with chairs, a scaffolding element with various presentation devices, and construction lamps—formed the framework. The program structure provided for five days of various open forums on the themes of "The New Europe?," "Transformations and Transitions," "Media Effects," and "Globalization." The result was a richly contrasting mixture of screenings of experimental films from the 1970s, accounts of experiences with the events and conflicts in the ongoing rebuilding of Prague, readings, discussions, and video screenings. Sometimes two presentations even ran parallel. In the discussions, the skeptically distanced attitude of many older intellectuals collided with the missionary zeal of young global activists. We endeavored to bring in critical perspectives on neoliberalism and the time's politics of representation, while in the next room new symbolic formats of political practice were rehearsed, slapstick puppets of the head of the World Bank were built, and rebel clowning workshops were held.

The event in Brussels, which took place from 22 to 24 September 2000, also revealed various fault lines and conflicts. Here Café9 was part of the representative information center of what was titled *Brussels 2000*. A lounge interior had been especially designed for the new glass pavilion. Orange, plastic, and technology dominated the space. Some of the local actors we had wanted to work with boycotted the activities of *Brussels 2000*. In light of the many major investment projects that threatened the alternative character of the district directly behind the Gare du Midi rail station, "Capital of Culture" symbolically stood for displacement, and the organizers of *Brussels 2000* never distanced themselves from that. The discussions organized together with the Strasbourg cultural association Syndicat Potentiel about the precarious conditions of cultural producers took place in the then occupied Office for Employment/Office national de l'emploi in the district of Saint Josse. The title of the event was "Hegemony of Labor, the Disparition of Activity." In the representative headquarters of *Brussels 2000*, together with artist Marion Baruch, the group Sans Papiers Antwerp, and various actors from Paris and Brussels, Marion von Osten organized an event on the ongoing regularization campaign (Papers for Everybody—Civil Rights for All!). For the sections "No Neoliberalism" and "Zero Tolerance," videos from the network were shown on two other days.

The project *EuroVision2000* was not about depicting a social phenomenon or representing a certain discourse or debate. Instead, we attempted to further extend the network that had emerged with *MoneyNations*, to open up new spaces for political debates, and to form temporary communities through shared interests. We used the video collection to incite parallel discussions in the three different social contexts. Aesthetic criteria for selecting the contributions played no role. The project was open for all kinds of contributions, as long as they evinced a reflected relationship with representation and a critical leftist stance, regardless of whether it was a film by professionals or someone who had just made their first video.

This approach of putting the perspectives of those affected in the center instead of producing our own representations as video makers or artists is something Marion and I later developed in various projects, such as in *This Was Tomorrow!* (2008),[7] regarding the strategies of housing construction projects from the 1950s to the 1980s, in which residents of such high-rise developments from different cities participated with their own videos. Since then, we have also used the strategy of developing content in a network of correspondents for a number of projects, most recently with *Tricontinentale.net.*[8] Here, via a publication platform launched in 2015, the Tricontinental movement of the 1960s is reflected upon retrospectively in collaboration with a network of correspondents. The role that visual artists, designers, authors, and musicians have played in it is to be especially investigated.

What Kind of Practice Is It, Actually?
The collaboration between Marion and myself started with an agreement on various subjects and shared views. We were united, not least of all by our discontent with the institutional embrace (becoming more and more evident since the 1990s) of self-organized, critical, and subcultural scenes and the derisive criticism of economic models of explanation and description that was increasingly seeping into social discourses in the spread of neoliberal ideology in the 1990s. A further starting point was mutual interest in space and spatiality, which goes back to the time of our studies in the 1980s. In our artistic practices, we have each extensively explored formal, creative, social, and content-related dimensions of spaces. We have used studios in old industrial sites and engaged in self-organized contexts. Social encounters, intense discussions of ideas, and the cultivation of counter-public spheres thus became

7   See http://www.this-was-tomorrow.net.   8   See http://tricontinentale.net.

central motifs. The practice of enabling new networks of
critical cultural producers, who bring together their experiences
and skills with regard to the hidden urgencies of the globalization process from the most diverse contexts, was thus a collaboration from the beginning. It is a strategic, context-specific
practice. The projects arise in relation to people, places, events,
and networks. A critical reflection on the context, such as the
analysis of power relations and constellations of interest, forms
the basis for decisions about perspectives and thematic em-
phases. People and networks co-determine the procedure,
and specific places are decisive for the choice of formats and
communication strategies. The form of practice must be newly
reconstituted and recomposed again and again in relation to
each occasion. In this way, it follows the tradition of site-specific
art that has become increasingly differentiated since the 1960s.
In line with what was, in the 1990s, an expanded perspective
of site specificity, in our projects we queried the conditions of
institutions, conventions of representation and education, and
strategically recomposed themes anew. The way in which a
project comes about, the course of research, the roles of those
involved, expectations and specifications from participating
institutions—these are all factors that influence the orientation
of the subject matter as well as the choice of communication
formats and strategies. Therefore, our practice is also multi-
sided. It is composed of very different intellectual, conceptual,
design, and practical abilities, which are ultimately all equally
important for a project. They include various concrete activities:
furnishing and designing spaces, drafting and building displays
or furniture, writing texts, graphic design, scenography, camera
work, audio or video editing, installing technical equipment,
organizing and coordinating production processes, hosting,
conveying the content, etc. The projects are constituted through
alliances of people and develop in collaborations. The cooperation consists of mutually informing one another, as well as

openly exchanging knowledge and ideas. Building on this or arising from it, joint productions or actions emerge. This is a practice that refers to the Italian *operaismo* workerist approaches and collective models of the 1970s. It turned out that interim use, temporary solutions, or periods of upheaval in institutions often offered the best preconditions for working in an open approach and in transdisciplinary networks with experimental themes. This form of practice has to roam around, always needs new challenges, niches, lacunae, and blind spots that can be discovered, recognized, and temporarily occupied.

The central questions for us have been about what artistic practice could look like beyond authorship and which political and social significance could be attributed to it. In various projects, we have used terms like context, platform, and network, and we have often discussed our own roles and possible institutional formats. Do we see ourselves more as researchers or service providers? Are we really curators? Do we need more stable structures—those of an institute, for example, or a kind of educational institution? The floor in Zurich that we inhabited with Labor k3000 provided a concrete reason to intensively and critically engage with the neoliberal concept of the creative industry and for the new social challenges for subjects to be constantly creative and act in a self-entrepreneurial way. Productions like *Fashion is Work* or *Schöneggstrasse 5* (2002) relate directly to experiences in our own production environment and deal with the precarious circumstances of creative freelancers. When an opportunity arose in conjunction with Marion's position at the Zurich University of the Arts in Zurich to develop a symposium and an exhibition in the Museum für Gestaltung, it was possible to transfer this self-reflective approach to an institutional critique focus. The exhibition *Be Creative! The Creative Imperative* was done in 2002–2003 in a collaboration among various students from Zurich and Leipzig, staff members from Academy of Fine Arts, Leipzig, Labor k3000, and external consultants sociologist Ulrich Bröckling and art historian and writer Tom Holert. The design of the exhibition space was intended to evoke a young company in the creative industry. At the different work islands and the lounge zones in between them, the material was gathered in a joint research and production process and the resultant leaflets, posters, and videos were displayed. Experiences from our own practice and its framework conditions were also both the starting point and the subject matter for *Atelier Europa* (2003–2004)[9] and the film *Kamera läuft!* (Rolling!) (2004) that was realized for it. The productions were carried out in close collaboration with Labor k3000 and other people from the floor. The *Atelier Europa* exhibition display—office furnishings prepared for moving—in the main space of the Kunstverein München can also be read as a commentary on our own situation.

Epilogue
When *EuroVision2000* was invited to the Videonale 2001 in Bonn, we had an opportunity to present the project again retrospectively. For this, we chose the format of a lecture-performance and imitated a kind of news show. We reported on the various themes of the project and showed about 10 excerpts from videos by various makers that were all part of the *EuroVision2000* collection while commenting critically on our own practice. Live spoken sequences and projected sequences alternated. VHS cassettes were inserted in the playing devices before the eyes of the audience. Minor mishaps, breaks, and embarrassments were planned for. Following reports from the studios in Bologna, Brussels, and Prague, toward the end of the program we switched to an activist camouflaged with a black face mask. She stood in front of a chroma-keyed background,

[9]   See http://www.ateliereuropa.com.

where a peacefully grazing pony could be seen. By way of
explanation: the masked speakers of the Zapatistas often
appeared in news broadcasts at that time with horses in the
background, although it was never clear whether western television stations purposely tried to put the Zapatista movement
in an archaic light in this way or whether it was a tactic of the
guerrilla fighters to depict their agility and mobility.

> *Speaker in the Studio: We have now gone live to our activist
> out in the field. Can you hear me?*
>
> *Activist: Yes, I hear you. Hello.*
>
> *Speaker in the Studio: It seems to work. I hope the connec-
> tion is stable. Can you explain the extent to which your
> producer-network sees itself as a political project since
> it was actually initiated in the cultural field?*
>
> *Activist: Culture and the knowledge about cultural pro-
> cesses, such as lifestyles and their significance for consumer
> behavior, are a central resources for advanced information-
> capitalism. At the same time, the transfer and the generation
> of information are not only market products but also regulate
> the financial market, the organization of production and
> distribution—in other words, the whole of management. So
> as long as the means of the production and distribution of
> information are in the hands of those who only use them to
> consolidate their power, no political and no cultural utopia
> can be successful. If we do not design and try out alternative
> structures of information and distribution, which break
> through and reform those that have existed until now, then
> cultural utopias cannot be anything more than a product of
> what already exists.*

This was already formulated—to come back to your question—by the first video collectives of the 1970s. If you read magazines like Radical Software, *which already belonged to the tradition of community videos or operative video with their call for an alternative television movement in the 1970s and which came from the micro-political and autonomous, social and political movements, then you can see that many of the ideas we presume today had already been anticipated there: the criticism of standardized formats, the rejection of journalistic representative positions, etc.*

Speaker in the Studio: What is the relationship between globalization dynamics and these mediatization and informatization processes?

Activist: The globalization process is a new process of ordering and hierarchization. Its course is characterized by being contradictory and discontinuous. To depict these discontinuities or to make them comparable and exchangeable, that is one of the things we aim for in the project EuroVision2000; *for example, the international distribution of labor, which is based on racist and sexist conditions of inequality and which repeatedly confirms and thus newly produces these conditions at the same time. In a sense, I would tend to speak of a recolonization today rather than globalization.*

Speaker in the Studio: At the same time, though, it is due to exactly these dynamics that resistance is also forming.

Activist: Yes, access to the new communication technologies also makes new forms of political action and mobilization campaigns possible. Indymedia, for example, follows the operative video approach. On the other hand, it cannot be a matter of simply holding on to the old concept of a counter-public sphere.

For EuroVision2000, *it is not a question of pitting video practices against one another, whether they are documentary videos, clips, or artistic narratives, especially when they are not made as a speaking-about but rather as speaking-from a certain engaged or pertinent position. We resist talking about media-specific aesthetics but instead attempt to focus on singular strategies and narratives, self-representation, and collaboration, where amateurs can also become pro-ducers, not only so-called professionals. The videos can be used in political contexts, as discussion input for anti-racist, anti-capitalist events, for TV evenings with friends at home, as agitprop for the* sans-papiers, *as exhibition contributions, such as in the project* MoneyNations, *etc. Our relationship to all these different spaces is an operative one. We broad-cast wherever we are given an opportunity, however, not through traditional channels. What is central are the political intention and the audience that is addressed since we pursue a political aim with cultural strategies.*

Speaker in the Studio: Many thanks for your explanations and goodbye.

Activist: Goodbye.

Labor k3000, *MigMap*, 2005, online project and digital print on paper, courtesy Labor k3000

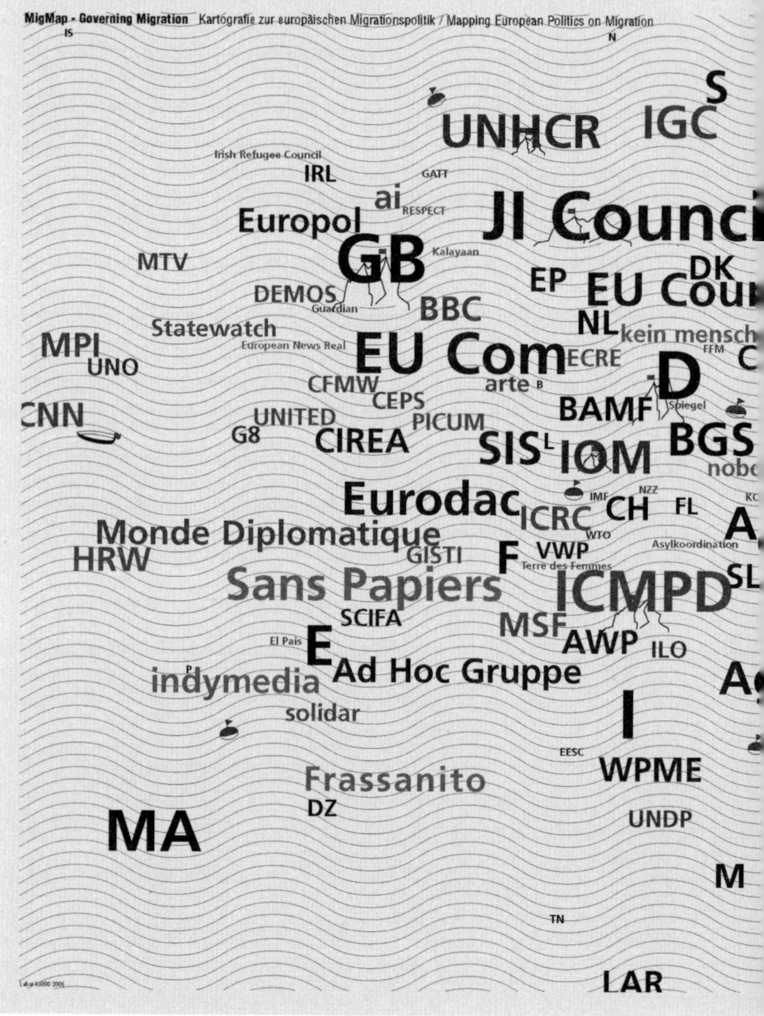

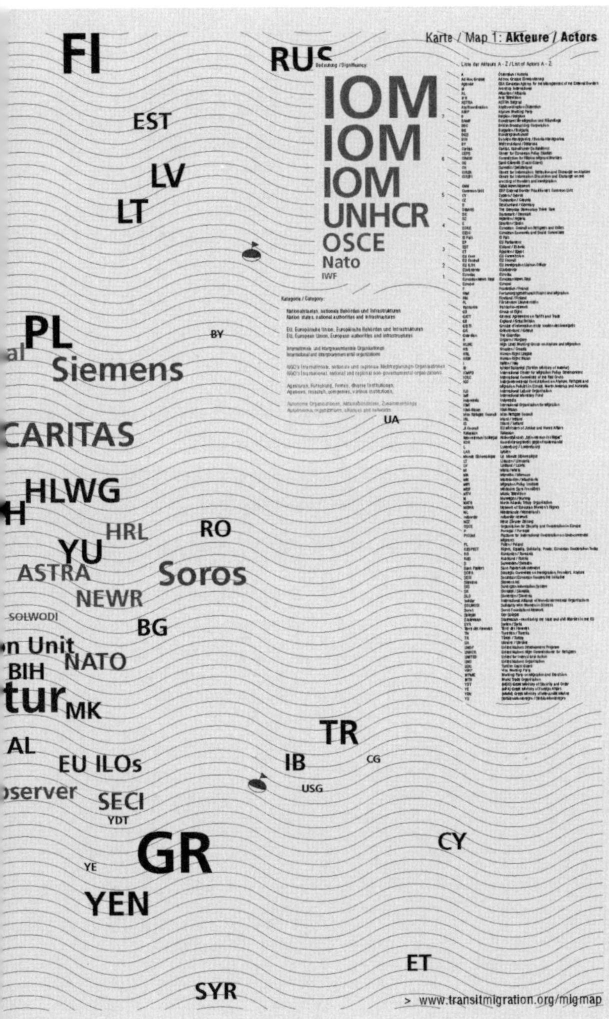

Karte / Map 1: Akteure / Actors
FI
RUS
Bedeutung / Significancy
EST
LV
LT
IOM
IOM
IOM
UNHCR
OSCE
Nato
IWF
Liste der Akteure A - Z / List of Actors A - Z.
Kategorie / Category:
Nationalstaaten, nationale Behörden und Infrastrukturen
Nation states, national authorities and infrastructures
EU, Europäische Union, Europäische Behörden und Infrastrukturen
EU, European Union, European authorities and infrastructures
Internationale und intergouvernmentale Organisationen
International and intergovernmental organizations
NGO's Internationale, nationale und regionale Nichtregierungs-Organisationen
NGO's International, national and regional non-governmental organizations
Agenturen, Forschung, Firmen, diverse Institutionen,
Agencies, research, companies, various institutions,
Autonome Organisationen, Aktionsbündnisse, Zusammenhänge
Autonomous organizations, alliances and networks
PL
al
Siemens
BY
CARITAS
UA
HLWG
H
HRL
RO
YU
ASTRA
Soros
NEWR
SOLWODI
BG
n Unit
NATO
BIH
tur
MK
AL
TR
EU ILOs
IB
CG
observer
USG
SECI
YDT
GR
CY
YE
YEN
ET
SYR
> www.transitmigration.org/migmap

Labor k3000, *MigMap*, 2005, online project
and digital print on paper, courtesy Labor
k3000

MigMap - Governing Migration Kartografie zur europäischen Migrationspolitik / Mapping European Politics on Migration
ILLEGAL MIGRATION
(ILLEGALE EINWANDERUNG)
Rassismus
Organisierte Kriminalität
Organized Criminality
SMUGGLING
Menschenrechte
ASYLUM
GR
Ad Hoc Gruppe
ILO
EURO MAYDAY
Fremdarbeiter
Schwarzarbeit
Sans Papiers
Papiere für alle!
Sans Papiers
Universal Embassy
Recht auf Legalisierung
Gegen illegale Beschäftigung
DEMOS
Transit Servei
Migration Management
MFI
IGC
EU
FFM
ICMPD
EU
PICUM
RESPECT
Kalayaan
NATO
SUS
Agenfor
Regional Protection Area
I
GB
Safe Haven
Schleuser / Schlepper
Best Practice
One Chance Rule
BOITA
Border Management
Caritas
Extraterritoriale Lager
Sicherer Zufluchtsort
SMUGGLING
Good Governance
ICRC
SOS
Virtuelle Grenze
CIREFI
Kein Mensch ist illegal
Focal Route
Autonomie der Migration
Lost Souls
Prasanito
Kanak Attak
CEREA
Random Route
no border
Pro Asyl
Eurodac
BAMP
Deportation Class
FIB
The Voice
Hier geblieben!
Abschiebeautomonie
No Lager
Sichere Drittstaaten Regelung
Karawane
D
Absaugefilter
Human Right Watch
ECRE
ASYLUM
UNHCR
(ASYL)
Labor k3000 2005

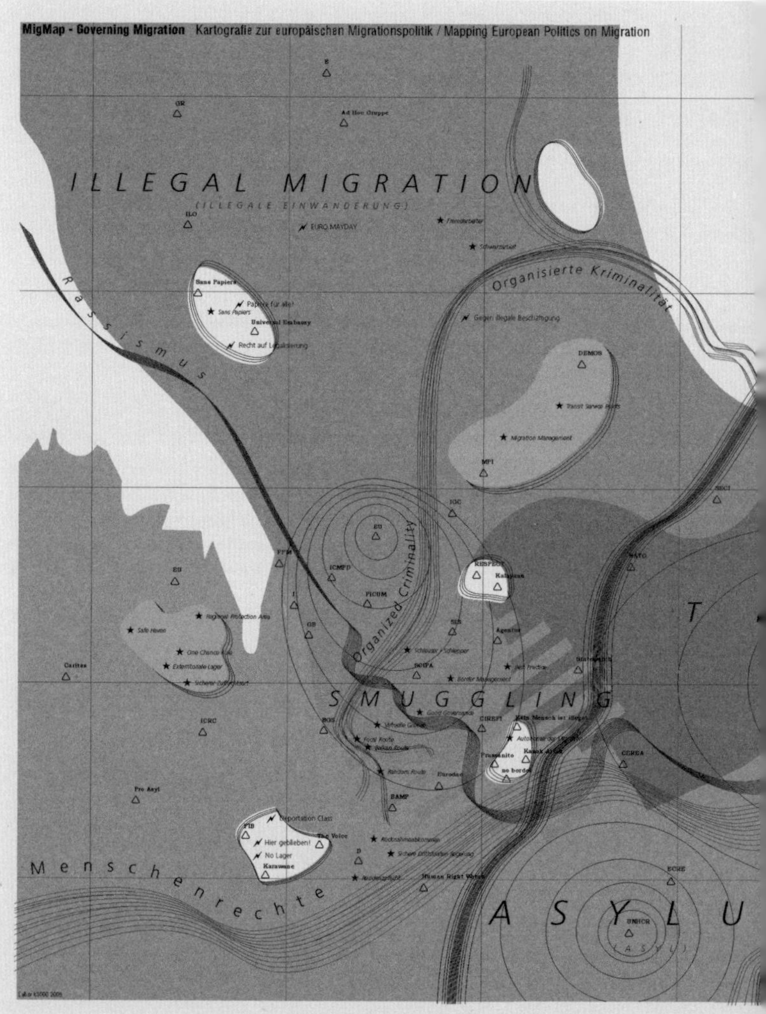

216

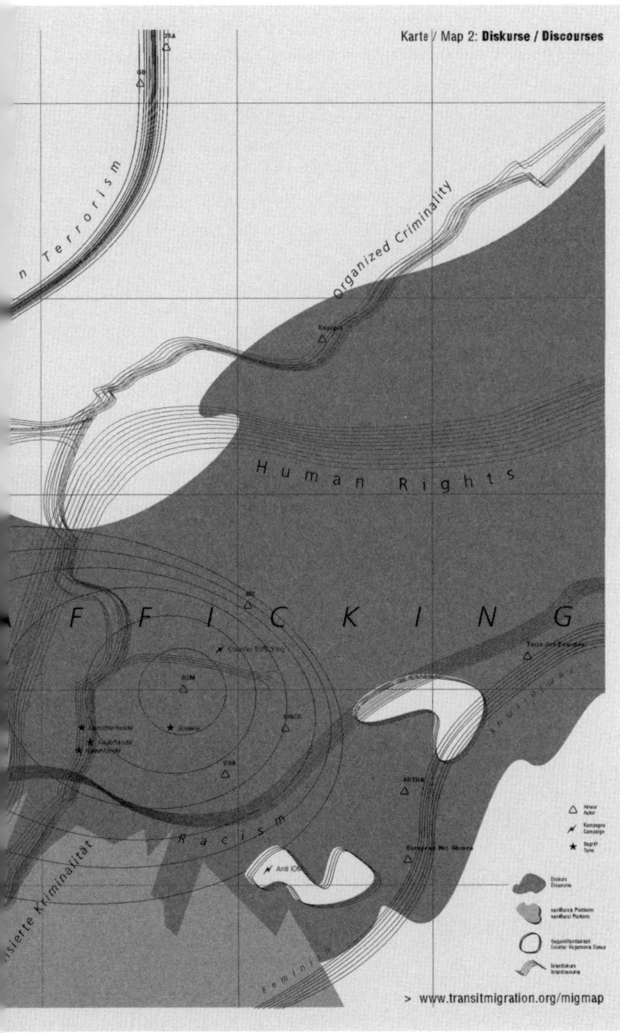
USA
GB
n Terrorism
Organized Criminality
Hotspot
Human Rights
F F I C K I N G
BIT
Counter Trafficking
Terre des Femmes
IOM
Unsichtbar
OSCE
Menschenhandel
Sklaverei
Kinderhandel
Frauenhandel
USA
ASTRA
Racism
Bulgarian Net Women
Anti IOM
Akteur
Actor
Kampagne
Campaign
Begriff
Term
Diskurs
Discourse
neoliberale Plattform
neoliberal Platform
Gegenöffentlichkeit
Counter Hegemonic Space
Interdiskurs
Interdiscourse
...sierte Kriminalität
...isierte Kriminalität
Feminism
> www.transitmigration.org/migmap

Marina Vishmidt

Beneath the Atelier, the Desert:
Critique, Institutional and
Infrastructural

There has always been a resonant paradox at the heart of institutional critique, which can be framed in Kantian terms: exposing the transcendental conditions of institutional critique amplifies rather than undermines its claims. If western art institutions can be seen as plenipotentiaries of a contested—or embattled—Enlightenment legacy (depending how you look at it), then the artistic strategy of institutional critique was fated from the start to slot into the master's toolbox, however fervently it has been avowed to be the most serious, if not the only, political implement that artists have at their disposal.[1] As with philosopher Immanuel Kant's project, it has aimed to clarify the legitimate bounds of critique, but in this case, the bounds have been drawn around the type of critique artists could, in good faith, level at the institution of art, while also embodying it professionally, socially, psychically, and economically. This soldered artists and institutions together in an increasingly half-hearted *tableau vivant* of autonomy, a reconciled *realpolitik* not all that different from the kind that anointed liberal democracy as the least-worst form of government still standing after everything else had ostensibly been tried.

If this schema appears somewhat on the reductive side, this may be because the libidinal economy of institutional critique has had a number of other facets to show. Author Franz Kafka's "A Report to an Academy" evokes that aspect of institutional critique that entails dressing up in the master's clothes as an affront to the master's society.[2] The mode here would owe less to constructive criticism and more to the apotropaic vaudeville of director Jean Rouch's short film *Les maîtres fous* (The Mad Masters) (1995), with its plebeian cultists possessed by the

1   Andrea Fraser, "From the Critical Institutions to the Institution of Critique," *Artforum*, vol. 44, no. 1 (September 2005), pp. 278–283.

2   Franz Kafka, "A Report to an Academy," in *Franz Kafka: The Complete Stories*, ed. Nahum N. Glazer (New York: Shockhen Books, 1983), pp. 250–263.

spirits of the French colonial administration and trade. Here
we could think about the address of such modes of critique
to institutions that have traversed but could not be contained
within the institution of art—institutions such as white supremacy,
patriarchy, capitalism—and how the art institution could be
repurposed to put these institutionalized exclusions on view,
if not redress them. Such an expanded notion of "institution"
would reflect the expansive, sociologically and psychoanalyti-
cally inflected sense of "institution" deployed by, for example,
performance artist Andrea Fraser—a complex of social relations
and practices acting to reproduce itself and its conditions of
existence in a hierarchically structured society.[3] It is then such
a widened definition of institutional critique we can employ
retrospectively to analyze the relationships between activist
practices in and out of the "art world" in the restless period the
term usually encompasses: from the late 1960s to the early
1990s. Troubling the historical parameters of "first-" and "sec-
ond-generation" institutional critique, with the solidified division into an era that emphasized fixed (artist Michael Asher) or
variable capital (Fraser), we find collective and individual practices sometimes in alliance with campaigns led by organizations like the Women's Liberation Art Group, the Art Workers'
Coalition, or the American Indian Movement—artists Jimmie
Durham, David Hammons, Adrian Piper, the Guerrilla Girls,
VALIE EXPORT, William Pope.L. . . The radicalizations and
individuations enacted in these historical instances may surface
in the work of more recent generations of artists, if often man-
neristically. But their key significance was in laying a track

3   Apposite here could also be philosopher
Louis Althusser's concept of the "institutional
state apparatus" as one that operates to
reproduce a society's conditions of
production, in line with his reading of social
reproduction as the reproduction of the
conditions of production that can be situated
with "relative autonomy" from the direct sites
of economic production. See Louis Althusser,
"Ideology and Ideological State Apparatuses:
(Notes towards an Investigation)," in *Lenin
and Philosophy and Other Essays*, trans. Ben
Brewster (New York: Monthly Review Press,
1971), pp. 127–186.

between the critique of institutions and critique of infrastructures; that is, not simply the formal but the material conditions that located the institution in an expanded field of structural violence. The extra-murality of this tendency was taken up in later iterations as a call to build or at least model institutions, whether in the temporary sociality of the project, the erratic durability of the project space, or the ambient resource economies of the research cluster. The question of what would thereby constitute the "formal" and the "material" could perhaps be displaced to consider it rather more a matter of whether these institution-critical practices situated themselves principally in an immanent or a transversal relation to the spaces of artistic exhibition and discourse. The materiality of the art institution would, for example, form the center of Asher's excavation projects,[4] and the disturbance of its architectural layers would be a means of exposing other social and symbolic parameters of its existence, yet it would be the physical fabric that stayed at the core of these implications. A similar framing would apply to Fraser, for whom the protocols and economies of the mainstream field of art would be the substance and subject of critique, with the wider social conditions for its existence as a backdrop to be disclosed by implication. The Art Workers' Coalition[5] could be considered as mediating the immanent and the transversal with its campaigns addressing systemic social inequality in the representational spaces of art. The

Marina Vishmidt Beneath the Atelier, the Desert: Critique, Institutional and Infrastructural

4   One of the oft-cited examples would be the intervention at Galleria Toselli in Milan in 1973, where Asher sandblasted many years of layers of white paint off the wall, reuniting the brick with the concrete of the floor. Asher wrote, "the withdrawal of the white paint, in this case, became the objectification of the work." See Anne Rorimer, "Michael Asher: Context as Content," *InterReview* (2004), online at: http://www.mit.edu/~allanmc/asher1.pdf.

5   The Art Workers' Coalition formed in New York in 1969 with a list of demands presented to the Museum of Modern Art. See Lucy Lippard, "The Art Workers' Coalition: Not a History," in *Get the Message? A Decade of Art for Social Change* (New York: E. P. Dutton, 1984), pp. 10–20.

contemporary group We Are Here,[6] on the other hand, could be seen as more transversal insofar as the institution of art is but a subset, as well as an occasional platform for a systemic critique of border regimes and white supremacy as functional institutions reproducing European society via a normalized coercion of exclusion. However, the formal/material, immanent/transversal style of analysis should not signify a desire to perpetuate dualities that divide trained artists from activist groups, especially if both are viewed as "users" of art institutions. Rather, the question is where the institution of art is situated in the different approaches to institutional critique —is it exemplary but contingent, or is it a principal focus often hypertrophied into the only valid site of dissidence for those who would inscribe their activities in the space of art? Here I argue that the difference is not always clear, but that it is the former tendency (or focus) that allows us to more clearly track a shift—perhaps rather a *drift*, since the shift is not historical but one that can be observed as temporally concentrated in the wake of the exhaustion of other strategies—from an institutional to an infrastructural critique. "Infrastructure," like "institution," is used here in a moderately flexible way but chiefly to signal a view of the art institution as a site of resources—material and symbolic—and that calls for an opportunist deployment for the sake of furthering all sorts of projects rather than the loyal criticism attendant on "institutional critique" in its established version. In this light, the construction of institutions may be, at the same time, a practice of institutional and infrastructural critique, depending on whether the institution is mainly intended to critically reassess or renew working conditions and visibility in the space of art or has other ambitions.

6   We Are Here is an organization of refugees who have united in Amsterdam to bring their collective struggle in the Netherlands into public discussion. Consisting of some 200 immigrants from approximately fifteen countries, their search for asylum has failed, and yet for a variety of reasons they cannot be sent back to their countries of origin. See http://wijzijnhier.org.

The late 1990s and early 2000s saw the development of critical discourses in sociology and politics around the "project" and "precarity" as cardinal terms of the deregulated work patterns and cultural habitus of an educated, self-motivated stratum in the interstices between artistic, service, and skilled labor. Endowed with a readymade unity by neo-Marxian argot such as "creative class," the "cognitariat," or, more dystopically, the "precariat," this was in reality a de-classed group with eclectic skill sets and whose forms of life often reflected a historically novel (at least in Western Europe and North America) middle-class experience of the poorly waged and unstable conditions that had usually been the preserve of the working classes, especially the feminized and racialized segments. Diagnosed by sociologists Luc Boltanski and Ève Chiapello as the children of a bohemian dissidence more interested in individual rebellion than social transformation (which the authors called "artistic critique")[7] and apostrophized by art critic and activist Brian Holmes as bearers of the "flexible personality,"[8] this was a community that sustained the contradictions of a "double freedom"[9] rendered poignant by the horizon of creative self-expression and independent cultural dynamics that drove it forward. Everywhere could be observed the formation of

[7]   See Luc Boltanski and Ève Chiapello, *The New Spirit of Capitalism*, trans. Gregory Elliott (London: Verso, 2005).

[8]   Brian Holmes, "The Flexible Personality: For a New Cultural Critique," *transversal* (2002), online at: http://eipcp.net/transversal/1106/holmes/en.

[9]   Marx defined double freedom as the historically unprecedented condition of the waged worker in capitalism—the freedom from customary ties (i.e., free to sell his or her labor) and free of means of production (i.e., free to starve). In terms of "creative labor," we can locate a proposition in Immanuel Kant's *Critique of Judgment* (1790) that seems to point to a notion of double freedom for the "free artist": free from wage labor but, akin to the free laborer, also free from the means of production, of having anything to sell more than a personal capacity: "Fine art must be free art in a double sense: it must be free in the sense of not being a mercenary occupation and hence a kind of labor, whose magnitude can be judged, exacted, or paid for according to a determinate standard; but fine art must also be free in the sense that, though the mind is occupying itself, yet it feels satisfied and aroused (independently of any pay) without looking to some other purpose." Immanuel Kant, *Critique of Judgment*, trans. Werner S. Pluhar (Indianapolis, IL: Hackett Publishing Company, 1987), p. 190.

bohemians attendant on still relatively affordable property prices
and still relatively functional social safety nets, not to mention
significantly lower personal debt burdens than today. Berlin
was still Berlin then (if already steeped in Wall-era nostalgia),
but so were Munich, Cologne, Zurich. . . just to name the sites
where our narrative unfolds. These were all sites where the
early 1990s had seen institutional critique folded into the
"non-productive attitude" (artist Josef Strau),[10] the cultivation
of persona and community over professional ambition.
Approximately a decade later, however, small-time entrepre-
neurship was overtly on the agenda, and the contradictions
of autonomy were emerging with ruthless clarity. The mainte-
nance of free-form community space and centers of autonomous
social life as moments of infrastructural critique was vying with
the more mimetic forms native to institutional critique, which
adapted but also reproduced models of enterprise closer to
market and state, such as the gallery, club, boutique, and nuclear family. Nonetheless, compared to the austere strictures
of the present, the field still seemed relatively open both for
experiment and indictment, a phase when the occupation of
institutional platforms still seemed to have critical traction. Or
it did for transversal art-activist projects that had a looser commitment to finding or making critical space in the institution
of art, identifying more with the pedagogy and conviviality of
subcultures. This allowed them to avoid the always-incipient
academicism of an institutional critique that had, by the late
1990s (or, to listen to its critical supporters, from the very
beginning), threatened to become a mode of regulation for
the institution.[11]

10   See Josef Strau, "The Non-productive
Attitude," in *Make Your Own Life: Artists In &
Out of Cologne,* ed. Bennett Simpson
(Philadelphia, PA: Institute of Contemporary
Art, University of Pennsylvania, 2006), online
at: https://s3.amazonaws.com/
contemporaryartgroup/files/documents_
file_401.pdf.
11   Isabelle Graw, "Field Work," *Flash Art,*
vol. 23, no. 155 (November–December
1990), pp. 136–137.

Of the modes canvassed above, such a critique-by-doing seems like the most apposite to Marion von Osten's itinerary as artist, educator, writer, curator, and researcher. A perennial engagement with, as well as a tactical emulation of the tropes of contingency and flexibility as the hallmarks of present-day labor forms one magnetic pole, while the other pole applies these same categories to national borders and coloniality-laden historicisms such as "modernity." From the workers'-inquiry-without-a-workplace scenarios of the group kleines postfordistisches Drama (kpD) (2003–2006) or *Atelier Europa* (2003–2004), to the inquiries into human and financial fluxes in *MoneyNations* (1997–2001) and with *Transit Migration* (2002–2006), or the border-eroding radical journals of colonial modernism showcased in *Action! Painting/Publishing* (2011–2012), von Osten's gamut of activity both puts into play and thematizes a vocational blurring significant for what is here being developed as "infrastructural critique."

The phenomenon of transversally-minded art-activist practices, which take art institutions as a contingent if motivated site of materialization, started to gain ascendancy from the mid-1990s onwards, coincident with a new rollout of institutional critique pursued from within and on behalf of institutions themselves— the "New Institutionalism," which sought to index and respond to the diversification and global expansion of the discursive space and markets for art. This now seems like an ephemeral as well as equivocal moment, whose "turns" retrospectively seem as driven by imperial as by democratizing ambitions, but which also posed one of the last gambits of the bourgeois art institution to refashion itself as a condenser rather than a container of do-it-yourself aspirations and subcultural alliances.[12]

12 See Nina Möntmann, "The Rise and Fall of New Institutionalism: Perspectives on a Possible Future," in *Art and Contemporary Critical Practice: Reinventing Institutional Critique*, Gerald Raunig and Gene Ray, eds. (London: MayFlyBooks, 2009), pp. 155–159, and Nina Möntmann, ed., *Art and Its Institutions: Current Conflicts, Critique and Collaborations* (London: Black Dog Publishing, 2006).

Albeit an unsatisfactory sketch of the broader context for projects like *MoneyNations* or the similarly processual and complex *Ex Argentina* (2004) organized by the artists, curators, and theorists Alice Creischer and Andreas Siekmann,[13] it is enough of a background to highlight what concrete intervention practices like von Osten's were able to be realized here, in the vein of feminist and left-sociological critiques of and from labor.

The domestication of the "critique of institutions" to the "institution of critique" has been memorably portrayed by Fraser as a misreading of the original target of institutional critique as anything less than the total social field—with the vital caveat that this is the total social field as it is encapsulated by art.[14] This analysis recast a purported break between an "objective" (architectural or sociological) institutional critique and the more "subjective" one of the 1990s (focusing on the gendered and racialized margins of the field and the "psychic life" of the institutional ego) into a continuity whose watchword was "total institution."[15] The suggestion that this critique could "ossify" or itself be institutionalized—in other words, become a de-fanged "institution of critique"—was thus deeply misled, according to

13 The project *Ex Argentina* began as an "economy-critical examination of the economic crisis in Argentina and the international lobbies profiting from it." See Alice Creischer and Andreas Siekmann, "Sovereignty of Presence: Real Public Space as Situation," *republicart* (September 2003), online at: http://www.republicart.net/disc/realpublicspaces/creischersiekmann01_en.pdf. These prefigured, equally massive, and multi-site projects like *The Potosí Principle: How Can We Sing the Song of the Lord in an Alien Land?* (2010–2011) take advantage of emancipatory or critical desires within large, national cultural institutions in the European Union and South America.

14 Andrea Fraser, "From the Critique of Institutions to the Institution of Critique," *Artforum,* vol. 44, no. 1 (September 2005), pp. 278–286.

15 Compare to the "total policing" motto of the London Metropolitan Police: "A total war on crime, total care for victims, and total professionalism from our staff. Our objectives are; to cut crime, cut costs, and continue to develop the culture of the organisation. We will achieve this with; humility, integrity and transparency. We will develop making the Met the best police service in the world." See "Total Policing," Metropolitan Police, online at: http://content.met.police.uk/Site/totalpolicing. The aims and questionable punctuation seem hardly dissimilar to those held by all kinds of institutions that do not have crime-fighting as one of their missions, such as art institutions.

Fraser, if it suggested that critique could ever be conducted otherwise or elsewhere than fully inside this field.[16] Yet if we consider art as an institution that is far from self-sufficient, relying both on the separation of waged and unwaged "uncreative" labor and on its constant incorporation materially and symbolically, the imperviousness to an outside seems less than an (enabling) closure for critique and more an alibi for what theorist and activist Denise Ferreira da Silva calls the "onto-epistemological" closure preserving the art field as distinct and autonomous, whatever its representational porosity to practices originating far beyond its channels.[17] When the institution of critique simply (or flatly) becomes coextensive with the institution of art, a Kantian echo chamber of world-historical proportions has truly opened up, possibly designed by architect Frank Gehry. A move to infrastructural critique represents an attempt to mediate some of the closures of this position both discursively and pragmatically, with infrastructure focusing the link between the material and ideological conditions of the institution of art in a way that de-centers rather than affirms it.

Further, if the institution is reproduced in microcosm in every act of artistic authorship, the entanglement in the collective that von Osten has maintained in each of her projects has been a riposte to this irrefragable condition of registering an art practice, helped by the institutional insecurities and robust

Marina Vishmidt Beneath the Atelier, the Desert: Critique, Institutional and Infrastructural

16 An interesting contribution to this debate would be writer Suhail Malik's idea of "anarcho-realism." This is his rubric for the ruling idea in contemporary art that there is a more authentic and critical art somewhere "out there," inasmuch as it functions homeostatically within the field, grounding its idealist and pluralist ideologies. Malik can thus be seen as taking a step beyond Fraser's mid-1990s assessment in that he does pinpoint the institutionality of "escape," but then goes on to call for "institutions of negation." See Malik's series titled "On the Necessity of Art's Exit from Contemporary Art," Artists Space, May–June 2013, online at: http://artistsspace.org/programs/on-the-necessity-of-arts-exit-from-contemporary-art.

17 Denise Ferreira da Silva, "Notes for a Critique of the 'Metaphysics of Race,'" Theory, Culture & Society, vol. 28, no. 1 (January 2011), pp. 138–148.

subcultures of the mid-1990s to early 2000s. The challenge to
the sovereignty of the artist, even when activists or collectives
take that role, transpires ultimately as a challenge to authorship.
This perhaps yields some indication of the limited recognition
of the multivalence of von Osten's practice as curator, organizer,
writer, and artist, as these are often not separated in time or by
project but unfold simultaneously in a practical flouting of the
division of labor that allows such "border-crossing" gestures
to be authored and thus to register. This is a strategy that
amounts to not simply displacing a theoretical or social commodity into an art space but re-performing the social relations
of non-sovereign art contexts in the institution without claiming
authorship in the performance. The art institution rather
becomes a contingent locale for infrastructural critique that
stages or recruits—that siphons capital—from this site of materialization but does not address it directly, thus stemming a
reverse flow of capital back into the institution. Another "onto-
epistemological" frame should interest us here, one that super-
venes the originary exclusion of labor from the site of creative
authorship: the politics of aesthetics wherein the political aspect
of art derives from its capacity to disorder the senses—which
aligns philosopher Jacques Rancière, perhaps unwittingly, with
the classic avant-garde precept of the "derangement of the
senses"—albeit senses that are grounded somewhat in the
social relations that sanction a certain "distribution of the
sensible"[18] in the first place. The contingent occupation of
the institution of art—in all its infra-thin dimensions—signals a
sidestepping of this political claim, one whose valorization of
derangement cannot be sustained outside of the normative
container of the aesthetic. Like artist Pilvi Takala's 2008
work *The Trainee,* in which the artist spent an internship at

18 See Jacques Rancière, *The Politics of
Aesthetics: The Distribution of the Sensible,*
trans. Gabriel Rockhill (London: Continuum
International Publishing Group, 2004).

a financial services company visibly doing "brain work," a.k.a. nothing. Von Osten's projects, such as the knowingly titled group kpD or *Atelier Europa*, have made labor visible where it should be invisible (in the space of art) by displacing the protocols of its inclusion in that space (as found object, as scandal) and to the conditions of production of the artwork as the immediately social ones of co-operative (if fragmented) labor. As projects dwelling in the then not-yet customary zone of indistinction between the curatorial, the artistic, and academic research, they were proleptically *indisciplinary* in a way that could be interpreted as either "too" elusive or "too" fitting in the era of "New Institutionalism"; their clarity of purpose and complexity of orchestration could only have come into focus through the rearview. In other words, it is the retrospection afforded by the stabilization of "social engagement" as a genre and the spectacular staging of the social in the social media-fed works of, for example, artist Ryan Trecartin, that lend the projects described above precision and tentativeness at the same time, which the current horizon may have become too congested and cynical to support. The connection to the "outside" that the projects have, to the sociality and work routines that traverse and exceed the exhibition space—however it is configured or displaced—steps back from making political claims as appended to this act of appearance and thus drains the institution of critique of its heady fragrance. At the same time, the precarity, porosity, and opportunism of this near-beyond can also be seen in sharp relief, a bohemianism of evasion instead of a solidarity of condition. Something rather loose, disparate, pedantic, and effortful can be detected instead, a form of self-directed obstinacy we can recognize from philosopher Oskar Negt and author and filmmaker Alexander Kluge:

A daring hypothesis emerges that partially flies in the face of the bulk of historical empiricism: all this points to the core of labor power's self-will. The need for the confederation and association of producers (as a subjective labor capacity and labor power) does not objectify itself because of the obstinacy of those needs.[19]

What also seems salient in this paradigm is the visibility of a community of practice. The argument that small, dialogic, and reflexive communities could pursue an antagonistic praxis in relation to an ever more autonomized and bureaucratized art world was already being advanced in the mid-1970s as a counter to the gesturality of "institutional critique," a term first coined in 1975 by artist Mel Ramsden in his incisive essay "On Practice" in the first issue of *The Fox*, the journal put out by the New York-based faction of the conceptual artist collaboration Art & Language:

> To dwell perennially on an institutional critique without addressing specific problems within the institutions is to generalize and sloganize. It may also have the unfortunate consequence of affirming that which you set out to criticize. It may even act as a barrier to eventually setting up a community practice (language. . . sociality. . .) which does not just embody a commodity mode of existence.[20]

19 Stewart Martin, "Political Economy of Life: Negt and Kluge's *History and Obstinacy*," *Radical Philosophy*, no. 190 (March–April 2015), p. 32.
20 Mel Ramsden, "On Practice," *The Fox*, vol. 1, no. 1 (1975), p. 69. Notable here is that the introduction of the term is usually attributed to Benjamin H. D. Buchloh's 1990 essay "Conceptual Art 1962–1969: From the Aesthetic of Administration to the Critique of Institutions," in *Conceptual Art: A Critical Anthology*, Alexander Alberro and Blake Stimson, eds. (Cambridge, MA: MIT Press, 1999), p. 528: "In fact an institutional critique became the central focus of all three artists' assaults on the false neutrality of vision that provides the underlying rationale for those institutions." Fraser proposes an alternative provenance in "From a Critique of Institutions to an Institution of Critique," *Artforum*, vol. 44, no. 1 (September 2005), pp. 278–285, in which she claims to have "accidentally" coined it along with her peers in seminar discussions at the Whitney Independent Study Program (ISP) in the 1980s.

While we would need a different lens to analyze the stakes of more recent projects concerned with the dispersal of occidental modernism, the era of production that unfolded for von Osten and her collaborators from roughly the mid-1990s to the mid-2000s can be cognized under the heading of infrastructural critique—infrastructural not because the platform won over the content but because such borders were subject to an inquiry with no terminus in principle. From a present-day vantage, the reflexivity of the research method is fascinatingly tentative as well as obstinate, mobilizing theoretical templates and social scenes as "little dramas" that could eventually travel outwards as refrains and quotidian gestures, never coalescing into a critical legacy or trying to transcend "the creative imperative" (*Be Creative! The Creative Imperative*, 2002–2003) with the pathos of distance or artistic aura—the aura itself built into that imperative as a mystification of the "double freedom" of the cultural worker as a special kind of individual closer to the limitless potential of capital than the hemmed-in dependencies of labor.

Even the notion of tracing an arc that can be articulated in such definitive terms falters when considering the friability of the oeuvre that von Osten enacts as an artist, a confidence in leaving unframed or unauthored, appearing in functions and relations—more akin to an equation than a discrete, accumulative subject. In working to enable certain forms of visibility and collectivity to find themselves in a transversal paradigm, von Osten thereby also actively worked against the exceptionality and romanticism that the watchword "precarity," no less than "creativity," often affirmed, just as did "immaterial labor" slightly later in the sequence of art world political feelings. In this sense, we can rather appreciate von Osten's patient, multiple, and stubborn trajectory in terms of reproductive labor, as she explores in "Irene ist Viele! Or What We Call 'Productive'

Forces" (Irene Is Many!) (2009),[21] wherein a discussion of director Helke Sander's 1978 film *Die allseitig reduzierte Persönlichkeit—Redupers* (All-Around Reduced Personality—Redupers) allows von Osten to outline the institution of art as a site of collective struggle, alongside the distributed (self-) workplace and the family, for labor both idealized and rendered disposable by the gender system, no less than by the small air holes opened up by class belonging and education. Subjectivity is the product and process for a disposable workforce of female freelancers, though nowadays the writing seems to be on the wall for ever-growing segments of the working-age population, condemned to a freedom rapidly moving from double to triple (free of tradition, free of means of re/production, free of a market for one's labor-power).

This situation then opens up a discussion of how the charting of an itinerary from the critique of institutions to critical institutions and infrastructures of critique—in this case, through the prism of two decades of von Osten's exhibition, collaborative, and moving image projects—can account for the drastic shifts precipitated by the global socioeconomic crisis that began unfolding in 2008. If it seems that we don't hear as much about "precarity" in critical discourse, especially in the field of art, it might say as much about the normalization of the circumstances that the term identifies and the widespread adaptation to them as it does about the attenuated shelf life of theory fashions in this field. A poignant example, though not exactly a successful one (perhaps fittingly), is the 2010 film *Eine flexible Frau* by director Tatjana Turanskyj. Fast forward from the era of the chamber tragedies of post-Fordism: here is a survivor of the era of the companionable (if struggling) Berlin bohemian, an

21 Marion von Osten, "Irene ist Viele! Or What We Call 'Productive' Forces," *e-flux journal*, no. 8 (September 2009), online at: http://www.e-flux.com/journal/08/61381/irene-ist-viele-or-what-we-call-productive-forces/.

unemployed architect and lone parent condemned by her gender, obstinacy, and fondness for drink to "drifting" (as the English-language title *The Drifter* has it) outside the bounds of the bourgeois security that has absorbed the majority of her peers. The timeline here could be charted like so: *Redupers* _ kleines postfordistisches Drama _ *Eine flexible Frau*. From a politicized feminist community to a more atomized but genial collective of "cultural producers," to, finally, a woman left in the cold by a gentrified, heteronormative milieu. (An outlier here would be filmmaker Ulrike Ottinger's *Bildnis einer Trinkerin* [Ticket of No Return] [1979], whose view of West Berlin as a lush allegorical landscape to be drunk through is eons away from the more recent film's clipped neurotic realism.) The film's downcast tone is occasionally leavened by the appearance of a male, Marxist feminist tour guide on the fringes of the scene, spouting social reproduction theory on the devaluation of feminized labor while leading bemused groups through parks and waste grounds.

Here we could evoke perhaps theorist Stefano Harney and poet Fred Moten's recent writing on the "logistical," which tracks how the colonial logic of racially coded expropriation is gradually being expanded across space and class to route around subjectivity and accumulate via the exploitation of quantified units in a social space modulated by financial algorithms, securitized environments, and social graphs.[22] The replacement of atomized "creative" individuals by quantified selves perhaps adds another twist to literary theorist Walter Benjamin's 1930s assessment of fascism as masses encouraged to express themselves in lieu of exercising their rights.[23] It also adds a complication to

22   See Stefano Harney and Fred Moten, *The Undercommons: Fugitive Planning & Black Study* (Brooklyn, NY: Autonomedia, 2013).
23   Walter Benjamin, "The Work of Art in the Age of its Technological Reproducibility: Second Version," in *The Work of Art in the Age of Its Technological Reproducibility, and Other Writings on Media*, Michael W. Jennings, Brigid Doherty, and Thomas Y. Levin, eds., Edmund Jephcott, et al., trans., (Cambridge, MA: Harvard University Press, 2008), p. 41.

the "obstinacy" of labor that refuses imperatives of work as well as expression mentioned before. It is difficult to counterpoise "obstinacy" to creativity as a mode of refusal of work when an agential term such as refusal, apart from the often individualized and romanticized valence carried by the term, has less critical purchase in a phase when subjectivity no longer plays an important role in the regulation of labor.[24] The turn to a colonial architecture of power in the "first world" as it transitions to being governed by brutal austerity regimes and financialized population management internally and externally highlights the important turn von Osten herself made in the mid- and late 2000s to examining the scope of built and published modernity in the colonial space, as if making a parallel turn to an elsewhere in time and space wherein subjectivity could still (collectively) act as a radical basis or a counterpower and provide a less frequented global archive for today.

It is now evident that von Osten was all along pursuing a specific type of infrastructural critique—kaleidoscopic, sophisticated, transversal, yet also provisional and delaminated from the subjective and critical authority wielded by most artist-as-curator practices. This is not to argue that the early 2000s projects on which I am focusing were isolated—art historian Helmut Draxler and Fraser's project *Services* (1994–1997) could likewise be noted as an approach to a worker's inquiry without a workplace, albeit with a passion for the institution von Osten and her cohort could never muster. I call this a "specific type" because of course there were and are so many—the radically open-ended nature of von Osten's methodology is what makes it distinctive, a paradoxically fierce commitment to research as permanent

24 This is also a conviction gaining ground in contemporary debates that are shifting away from the focus on subjectivity central to the post-operaist discourse in order to analyze infrastructures such as logistics, finance, and management, as well as "non-human" ecological dimensions.

incompletion, without exemptions, up to and including authorship and institutional positioning, which, most avowedly, radical
practices moving between modes and subjects of enunciation
are a bar hard put to reach. This is perhaps then the point at
which institutional critique has been jettisoned in the span of
work under examination, and we return to where we began.
If the project of critique always ends up affirming its subject—
the institution of art—in its valorization of both the affective
subject and its critical capacity, this can inflate the artist as
critical subject beyond all reason, much like how philosopher
Theodor W. Adorno deems art a grotesque, inflated "absolute
commodity" with no use value in place to stop it from expanding
to whatever the market will bear.[25] Only labor can check the
infinite expansion of the "automatic subject"[26] of capitalist value
in art as elsewhere. Such acts of emancipatory, feminist defla-
tion occur repeatedly in the von Osten archive, and they can be
models if we recognize them.

25 Theodor W. Adorno, *Aesthetic Theory*,
trans. Robert Hullot-Kentor (London:
Continuum, 2007), p. 28.

26 Karl Marx, *Capital*, vol. 1, trans. Ben
Fowkes (New York: Vintage Books, 1976),
p. 255.

Lotte Arndt, Mihaela Gherghescu, Fanny Gillet-Ouhenia, Olivier Hadouchi, Marion von Osten, Pascale Ratovonony, and Cedric Vincent, *Action! Painting/Publishing*, 2011–2012, research and exhibition project, research room, Les Laboratoirs des Aubervilliers, Aubervilliers, photo: © Ouidade Soussi-Chiadmi

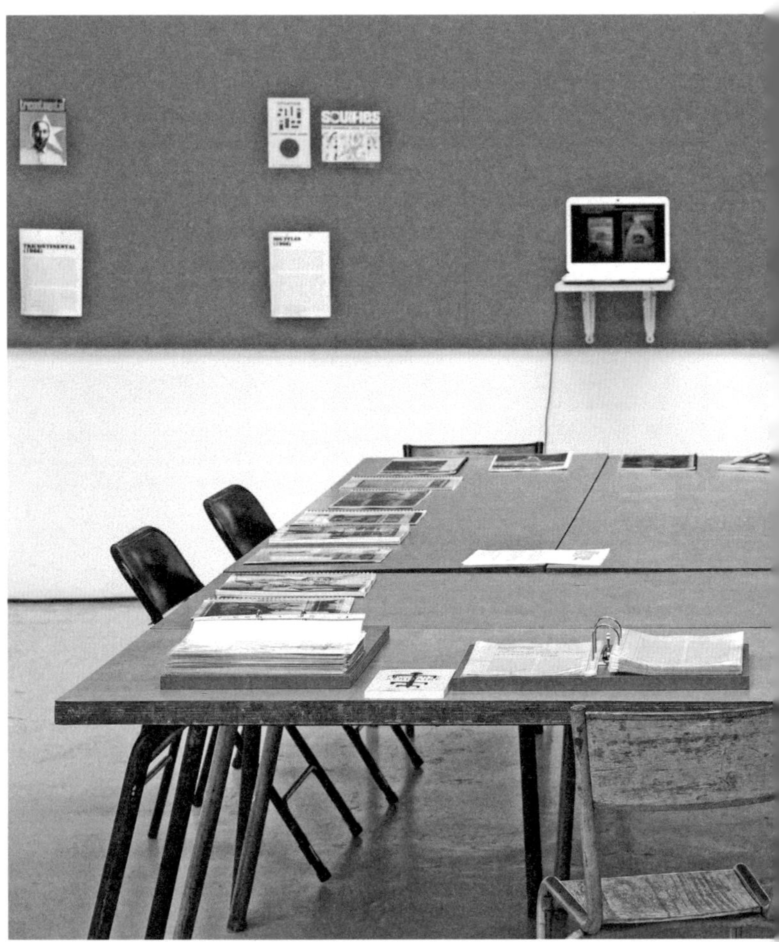

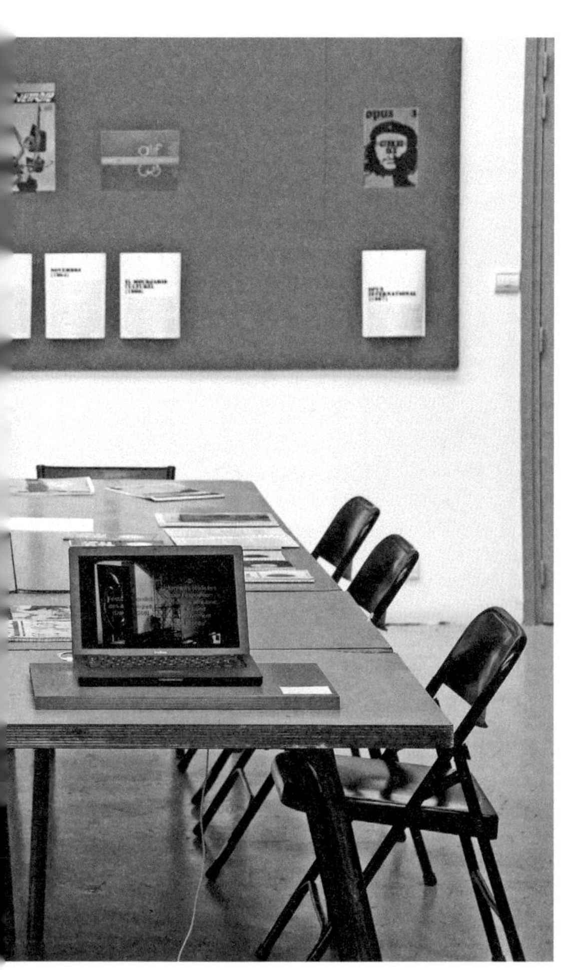

Tirdad Zolghadr
The Transversal Imperative

A friend of mine recently remarked that many solo shows look like group exhibitions, a comment that haunts me as I write this text. What said friend, who of course happens to be an artist, is implying is that if your exhibition winds up looking like a group show, it "fails" as a solo. Now, usually the overarching discourse, the market pressures, and the proverbial magic of the white cube, not to mention the presence of the artist herself, will successfully conspire to produce a more or less seamless producer persona. The irony, however, is that contemporary art now greets the prosthetic, artificial, constructed nature of the author, the solo-as-group with increasing enthusiasm, perhaps even a touch of *Schadenfreude*.

Thus the most convincing biography is presently the one that consistently draws attention to its inconsistencies. And a solo-as-group will at worst be "failing" (as opposed to genuinely Failing) in that it actually comes across as the more transparent and reflexive, and thus more contemporary approach. In discursive terms, there seems to be no big difference, in this regard, between a BAK reader aiming for "critical mapping" and a big old coffee-table monograph, with those glossy pictures that pop; even when one is a 12x16 cm simpatico paperback while the other is the kind of book you weigh in both hands as you quietly ponder how you can kill a man with the thing. Both will shy away from a rhetoric of the comprehensive to highlight instead the violence of cropping. Both will mourn the dark backdrop of silenced matter that allows the single name to shine brightly.

Surely enough, my own cutting room floor is awash with fantastic material, cropped and discarded. I would have enjoyed discussing the Hildegardis high school, for example, that Marion von Osten visited in Bochum; her own private educational complex, which so wonderfully embodies the mainstream middlebrow modernism of deep *Westdeutschland*. Not to mention the work von Osten did as an art student in Karlsruhe. Or her time as the keyboarder/songwriter of the Swiss-German goth-pop band *Xanadu*. But also, thinking of von Osten's interest in the fashion industry, as labor force and ideological cipher alike, I would have enjoyed discussing her impeccable sense of fashion. I could go on. Instead I will, rather conventionally, zoom in on a collaboration within the frame of the *Lapdogs of the Bourgeoisie* exhibition project (2006–2008), although I will also dwell on moments before and after.

It would be strange to deny or obfuscate the impact von Osten has had on my own trajectory. One might go so far as to blame her—among a few others—for my landing in contemporary art. As a comparative literature student in Geneva, I was often dragged by eager friends all the way to Shedhalle Zürich, in Zurich, where von Osten was curator between 1996–1998, only to frown at things I only partially appreciated, even as I was marked by them indelibly. It's hard to tell what I would think of those shows today; as I revisit the documentation, the view is obstructed by so many sentimental blasts from the past. But the fact that her projects attracted even comp. lit. nerds, utterly clueless in the idiom of art, and blew their stubborn minds with lasting effect confirms the oomph of the work in question. You cannot offer this kind of verve if you are some kind of walking rhizome.

Indeed, if we genuinely mistrust the solo signature so deeply, then why "Marion von Osten" to begin with? Why not "Marion Schmidt"—the birth name she often uses? Or "X," or maybe "the transversal vector formerly known as Marion"? The answer being that at the end of the day, the unique selling point of a solo is that it sticks its neck out for someone in particular. Compare a group setup, where the sheer entropy of materials, projects, and bodies, the quasi-comprehensive scope, combined with all the disclaimers of art as we know it will let you get away with murder. The presence of a single artist, meanwhile, highlights the fact that a selection is inevitably an arbitrary, ideological one. I belabor this point because it is key to doing justice to von Osten's work. Her oeuvre, and I use that term with conscious, nervous circumspection, does not offer the usual paraconceptual escape hatches of contemporary art. The political hypotheses are clear, the intellectual accountability is obvious, and the aesthetics are driven by historical and structural considerations that are rarely taken lightly.

This is what makes the work distinctively vulnerable, even without resorting to vulnerabilities of an intimate, voyeuristic, personalized variety. Indeed, what I wish to argue is that the work conveys the kind of signature that need not, and does not, engage in any liturgy of individualism. If anything, one unmistakable feature of the work in question is how persistently depersonalized it is. There is no quirk, taste, or penmanship that is instantly recognizable as such. I myself, having followed her itinerary for nearly two decades, can probably recognize the pitch. A bit like a lapdog hears a dog whistle. But I'm not sure others would.

After all, a number of artworks are explicitly structured as group efforts from the outset, whether in terms of conceptualization, production, execution, or all of the above. Even the projects she has individually crafted over the last decade or so—several of which are discussed below—are as unfussy in content as they are poker-faced in tenor. The curating is somewhat more humorous and flamboyant, but just as marked by an ethos of disciplinary outreach, activist momentum, and professional teamwork. And even when von Osten teaches and lectures, she avoids the rhetorical registers her many professional registers would allow for; the *Narrenfreiheit* of artists, the escape hatches employed by curators, the charismatic scholarship.

Instead, the tone reflects a contagious sense of urgency, while the content is informed by a didactic desire to propose and persuade. All of which is equally palpable in her essays, in which the writing is often torn between the temptation of detail and the will to hypothesize; this on occasions when many of her colleagues would simply revel in free-associative artistic innuendo.

Said desire to propose and persuade is what forges a common ground between teaching, curating, producing, and so on. Consider the pedagogical brunt of von Osten's exhibitions, for example, in which the teaching and the curating are hardly two skill sets that can be neatly subdivided, like two different sections of a CV or résumé. The two are viscerally enmeshed, so as to mobilize the discourse, the data, the political argument just as much as the design, the atmosphere, and the physical material, to make an overarching point, however circuitously. The resulting shows are as theoretically ambitious as they are hyper-somatic, semi-subliminal, pleasure-seeking introductions to complex sets of knowledge. Knowledge taken in with haunting, lingering effect.

Some may take offense at the idea of thematically driven shows being "introductions" to a given debate. But whether the issue is Marx, postcolonialism, or the idea of Europe, what is usually on offer in contemporary curating as we know it is indeed a refined form of vulgarization. This isn't an accusation so much as a compliment based on empirical fact, for an effective introduction is no small feat. I am forever grateful for being introduced, for example, to basic notions of the "creative imperative" by von Osten and her collaborators, just as she and I are to be thanked for basic pointers regarding the art-world-as-class.

Admittedly, when it comes to von Osten's work on the creative industries, it seems as if the more the subject matter overlaps intimately and immediately with the concerns of art and culture, the more precise and potentially groundbreaking the discussion becomes. Thereby venturing beyond the layman's 101 initiation somewhat. The show *Be Creative! The Creative Imperative* at the Museum für Gestaltung in Zurich in 2002–2003 pursued several aims simultaneously, but what it did most effectively was instantiate a notion of agency, a firm sense of co-responsibility regarding the field of art in particular. Instead of typically portraying the art world as some melancholic cog within a cultural-industrial machinery, it was portrayed, instead, as a proactive, cutting-edge contributor to the update of late-capitalist ideology as we know it. More than a decade on, these ideas have gained widely in traction, but at the time they added up to a rather exotic proposition.

In 2003, I had just started out in contemporary art. What I remember most vividly was that first, creepy glimpse of the professional persona that was expected of me within my new-found milieu, a persona I was being trained to expect of others in turn. Namely, a persona to whom a layoff is not the opposite of employment, but part and parcel of any job; to whom "servile virtuosity"[1] isn't a regrettable mindfuck, but a healthy coping strategy within a feast-or-famine economy. It is in light of these emerging working conditions that *Be Creative!* helped us reread the recent legacy of cultural studies—that of British scholar Angela McRobbie first and foremost—even as it laid the ground for sociologist Luc Boltanski and economist Ève Chiapello to shortly thereafter make their uproarious entrance into the Euro-American art world with *Le nouvel esprit du capitalism* (The New Spirit of Capitalism).[2]

The show equally underlined the role exhibition design has played within von Osten's practice. *Be Creative!* was ambitious in terms of self-reflexivity, but also scenographic punch in equal measure. The show was installed in the design department of a local academy—a rather charged locus within the design bastion of Zurich—which in turn shared a wing of the building with the administration. The resulting setup was as instructively polemical as it was evocatively, exquisitely weird. The visual complexity was also the result of a complicated relationship with the exhibition designers, who, in this case, were preordained by the school, and with whom compromises needed to be negotiated on a daily basis.

Whenever possible, however, von Osten took the display and executed it with and as a team, preferably as a member of the Labor k3000 collective, which she co-founded back in the late 1990s. Visual kicks aside, the advantage of this claiming of ownership of the design process lies in a modest reshuffling of the usual division of labor, with micro-economic repercussions that are in themselves linked to the post-Fordist pressures mentioned above. More often than not, the budget for exhibition design is accorded to outsourced service providers. Pooling the resources into one single labor force lends more artistic leeway to von Osten and her collaborators, but also leads to situations that are economically less exploitative.

It bears mentioning that von Osten's notion of exhibition design includes the verbal mediation of a project within its scope. Even in an exhibitionary setting, von Osten will resort to language with liberal generosity, often perilously so; whether as a polemical pointer, a theoretical harangue, an informational deluge, a lyrical pun, or otherwise. (Which might prompt the impression that her projects will find their most natural habitat within a logocentric setting such as this very reader.) But her methods only sporadically allow language to call the shots. In the best of cases, language is mobilized to the benefit of what was once alluded to as the "theatricalization of knowledge."[3] As one tool among many, it is submitted to the same editorial, chromatic, architectural strictures as a museum vitrine, a cardboard maquette, a modular panel, a Persian carpet, a fast food stand, or a sculptural ensemble obliquely cross-referencing the Russian Constructivists.

All of which points back once again to the aforementioned pedagogical ambitions to propose and persuade. A tight choreographic ensemble marks a welcome contrast to the now widespread (and somewhat lazy) individualization of the exhibition experience. Rather than a vaguely liberating sense of "nobody-sees-everything"—which means I may as well choose my own adventure—the viewer is invited to take in a particular, politico-aesthetic argument. Through which, the viewer's subject position is quite dramatically revamped.

Before turning to *Lapdogs of the Bourgeoisie*, allow me to also mention the slow-burn, long-term efficiency of shows of this bent, which hinge, in turn, on a slow-burn, long-term investment in the processes preceding them. By and large, many of von Osten's endeavors correspond to the project exhibition, a term for comparatively collaborative, research-driven, discursively ambitious queries, transdisciplinary as well as transinstitutional in outlook. What is peculiar about said model is not only the material upshot, but also the discrepancy that often emerges between the project and the audience, or the backstage and the limelight. To organizers and participants, pursuing these extensive investigations offers an incomparably rich, inspiring, seminal experience—with knowledge production

3   Karin Rebbert, 6th Werkleitz Biennale   werkleitz.de/html_en/index_e.html.
website, online at: http://biennale2004.

progressing very much in sync with the planning, discussing, producing, and installing, but also, of course, the processes of reconsidering, regretting, waking up at night screaming, revisiting, re-discussing, etc. Such is the rare advantage of building on things over time—as opposed to working up to a singular Big Bang moment on stage—and indulging in trial and error, feedback, and fine-tuning.

A process of this kind is rather difficult to convey to a public by means of the kaleidoscopic, semi-tangible thing that is a show. Of course you can edit, summarize, publish, and ensure a certain quality of installation shots and so on. But the particular cognitive surplus that makes these long-term endeavors important is not possible to circulate in an unadulterated fashion. The potential forte of any exhibition, after all, is the movement of bodies in a room and the resulting memories that linger. And the more background data, anecdotes, sources, and side effects that you attempt to cram into the space, the less the bewildered audience will grasp the gist of it all—and the less you will be making use of said forte.

Lapdogs of the Bourgeoisie was not a project exhibition by von Osten's methodological benchmarks precisely, yet in terms of our relationship to the audience, the four-year collaboration with curator Nav Haq that investigated class structures that constituted the art world—and that are perpetuated by the art world—is worth dwelling on. During the initial years, we two curators did intend to eventually translate all the backstage developments into some publicly accessible form. Over the years, however, it dawned on us that this visualization would present an entirely different effort, a whole new mission altogether. Which is why the resulting publication, for example, ultimately strived to be more of a sourcebook than documentation.

The project was premised on elaborating upon five different exhibitions in five venues—Arnolfini (Bristol), Tensta konsthall (Stockholm), Townhouse Gallery (Cairo), Platform Garanti Contemporary Art Center (Istanbul), and Gasworks (London)—over a span of four years, alongside occasional meetings in Berlin and elsewhere. A core of four or five artists—including von Osten, Annika Eriksson, Chris Evans, San Keller, and Hassan Khan—were intermittently joined by four or five others—including Neil Cummings, Liam Gillick, and Natascha Sadr Haghighian—and a handful of scholars who joined the fray every now and then—Suhail Malik of Goldsmiths, University of London chiefly among them. Given the working conditions at play, the commissioned work was as ambitious as it could possibly be, while the collaboration was increasingly heartfelt and increasingly rewarding over time.

Somewhat ironically, however, in a typical case of art world leniency, the show became what it beheld. What started as a critical examination of the role of class in the art world became a de facto micro-embodiment of the precariat. (Imagine investigating whether lapdogs can talk, only to find yourself also becoming a lapdog and thus incapable of answering your own question, as it was posed in a language you no longer master.) In other words, the project was as cosmopolitan, versatile, self-reflexive, self-critical, and politically sincere as it was utterly self-exploitative; traveling and working the usual long hours for nearly no remuneration. In a telling twist, the one setting where we hoped for decent compensation was Tensta konsthall, but the institution was embroiled in a scandal involving the embezzlement of government funds. So there was barely cash for production, let alone anything else; this in a public venue in Stockholm. (What is the world coming to?)

Among von Osten's contributions to the project, three stand out. To begin with, *I Am Like That Anyway* (2006–2008), this piece is where she turned to an Hennes & Mauritz (H&M) campaign that was overbearingly prominent at the time, featuring Madonna and her crew represented as a nonhierarchical community, very much reminiscent of art-canonical posses like Warhol's Factory. The posters were helpful in that they raised painful questions about access and accessibility, hierarchy, and intellectual ownership, again not unlike Warhol's Factory itself. Engaging with the staff of both Gasworks and Platform Garanti, von Osten used Madonna's campaign as a conversation piece for touching on the aesthetics of success, the projected glamor of creative labor, and more. All of this was documented by means of an audio recording of this conversation that took place in London and a tableau vivant reconstruction of the H&M poster with members of the Platform Garanti team.

What came to light was not only the shrugging, naturalized nonchalance with which precariousness is widely handled nowadays. What was even more revealing was the actual difficulty, or perhaps impossibility, of institutional representation, of displaying working realities within the cultural factory any more accurately (or any less inaccurately, rather) than Warhol once did. Moreover, as the exhibition unfolded over the years, von Osten's research helped reveal the unrelenting class bias of the structures we were dealing with. For example, among the three Gasworks interns who participated in 2006, two could rely on middle-class backgrounds for support during their internships, while one could not. The latter intern had to work multiple jobs alongside the underpaid Gasworks gig just to make rent. And while the two other interns soon moved on to work in commercial galleries, the latter dropped out of the arts altogether.

A second contribution to *Lapdogs of the Bourgeoisie* culminated in *The Glory of the Garden* (2009), a video work tracing the recent economic history of the United Kingdom and its impact on cultural institutions. The title references Rudyard Kipling's poem about the merits of honest labor within the singular garden body that is England (its glory "glorifieth every one," so "seek your job with thankfulness and work till further orders").[4] Importantly, the poem addresses not only divisions of labor but also the division between walk and talk: "Our England is a garden, and gardens are not made/by singing 'oh how beautiful' and sitting in the shade."[5] Kipling goes on to praise manual laborers, in particular, by besinging them, ironically which, of course, is what you tend to "do" as an artist in general and a poet in particular. This irony was not lost on Kipling—who liked to be coquettish even when besinging imperialism—but it is not an irony von Osten would enjoy dabbling in, even if she is not free of it entirely.

As a video, *The Glory of the Garden* is an example of showing-as-doing, of mimesis and/as identification. Instead of moderating a conversation with the staff, as she did in London and Istanbul, von Osten drew them into a group exercise involving Froebel blocks. These were originally designed as an improvisational children's toy, and are now widely used in job interviews and team building stints. For this project, a small group of Arnolfini staff were invited to use the blocks to visualize structural relaunches of the venue's past and present. By way of preparation, the participants engaged in archival research about key stages in the institution's genealogy, from its foundation to its (ever ongoing) reorganization. Their hand movements as they used the Froebel blocks to visualize this institutional memory were captured by a ceiling-mounted camera, their brightly-lit hands standing out in stark contrast to a pitch-black tabletop.

[4] Rudyard Kipling, "Glory of the Garden"   [5] Ibid.
(New York: Gilliss, 1923).

As you follow the video, the story of the institution, reduced to an assortment of wooden chunks, becomes somewhat abstract and hard to follow, and is gradually outshined by the physical movements of the four sets of hands and fingertips. Hands, a stock synecdoche of ("manual") labor, become not only physical means of arranging and rearranging narrational objects, but also metonymies of consensus-building and persuasion in and of themselves. The shovels digging the ditches of Kipling's garden, in other words, consist of a whole immaterial grammar of gestures, pointing and waving, and what looks like one, big, melodic melee at the outset becomes rather more structured at second glance. The grammar of gender, for example, becomes plain to see, as one rare voice is emitted by a woman who needs to lean over to reach the blocks on the table. Thanks to the bird's-eye perspective of the camera, we notice that the Froebel blocks persistently wind up in a position asymmetrically further away from her. As she repeatedly reaches across the table-as-stage, she becomes the one staff member whose features become the most distinct, recognizable, embodied.

The third and last contribution to *Lapdogs of the Bourgeoisie* that I will briefly mention here is von Osten's selection and presentation of films by the late Swiss filmmaker Daniel Schmid, particularly *Thut alles im Finstern, eurem Herrn das Licht zu ersparen* (Do Everything in the Dark in Order to Save Thy Lord the Light) (1970) and *Heute nacht oder nie* (Tonight or Never) (1972). Both are searing, satirical takes on age-old class relations and on our failures to fundamentally challenge them, let alone do away with them. "In the end," von Osten has laconically commented, "nothing changes other than the different classes getting to know each other better."[6] A third Schmid feature, the documentary film *Il bacio di Tosca* (Tosca's Kiss) (1984),

6   Personal correspondence.

touches on conditions of production in a more literal, but also more poignant fashion by depicting the Casa Verdi, Giuseppe Verdi's home for old artists who wind up destitute even after dazzlingly glamorous careers. Schmid's work became a cinematic, sensuous component within an exhibitionary context that was at times just a little too stilted for its own good. Von Osten took responsibility for these screenings with signature persistence, even with loud and angry fervor when necessary. I remember one curatorial attempt of mine to embed a Schmid feature within a willfully overbearing, artist-designed screening contraption. It was the only time I saw von Osten blow her top. It wasn't funny.

In other words, her engagement with Schmid not only under-lined political and cinematic interests, but also that willingness to take on professional roles and categories without reserva-tion. Curatorial responsibilities are assumed with the same no-nonsense commitment as artistic or academic ones. I have been insisting on the term "curator" here even though, as some readers may already guess, von Osten will probably object, preferring, as she does, the moniker *Ausstellungsmacherin.* The overarching, *Gesamtkonzept* flair of the term "exhibition maker" does more elegantly convey the collectivist spirit I have repeatedly evoked here.

But the advantage of terms as ghastly as "curator," "oeuvre," or "signature" is that they insist on the still-unresolved matter of answerability in the field of art, within which I am stubbornly situating von Osten's practice. Given that the defining, trans-versal ethos of contemporary art is one of persistently speaking truth to power, and persistently disidentifying with power in the process, the orthodox gesture is to challenge predominant categories, and instead of offering new categories of its own, to leave the last word to the viewer, who creatively completes the work. Such is precisely the "creative imperative" that translates post-Fordist ideology into exhibitionary experience. Hence my insistence on von Osten's eagerness to position and persuade beyond mere "questions" and "subversions."

Which in turn implies that a transparency of categories is the only way to account for that dogged sense of accountability that runs through von Osten's own practice-at-large, as thematic focus and working premise alike. It is a temperament I have been peddling as a kind of signature style here.

At the end of the day, which contemporary artist, writer, or curator wouldn't prefer to subscribe to "escaping easy categorization," or "challenging confinements," or "being transversal"? It's not that these phrasings are nonspecific. Many phrasings are. But they generate an armor of indeterminacy. And through the chinks of this armor, we see the authorial function peering through, with those beady little eyes twinkling, as safe and happy as ever before. So the question is not whether von Osten's work becomes a cohesive thing, a human snapshot in the pages of this reader. Avoiding that snapshot is an aim that is not only tedious, but deeply uninteresting. Why frame the transversal factor in von Osten's work as some kind of escapist complication when it can be a rock-hard, geometric axis in its own right? A temperament of push and pull that is just as forceful, bullish, and cohesive as all other contenders at play? Such is the difference between a tropography of open horizons, and an exercise in pedagogy and persuasion. In other words, if we cannot avoid discussing von Osten's work as though it were a body of its own, magically coherent and articulate, we may as well do so unapologetically and in all vulnerability, very much in the spirit of the body of work we're discussing here.

Marion von Osten, *The Glory of the Garden*,
2009, video still

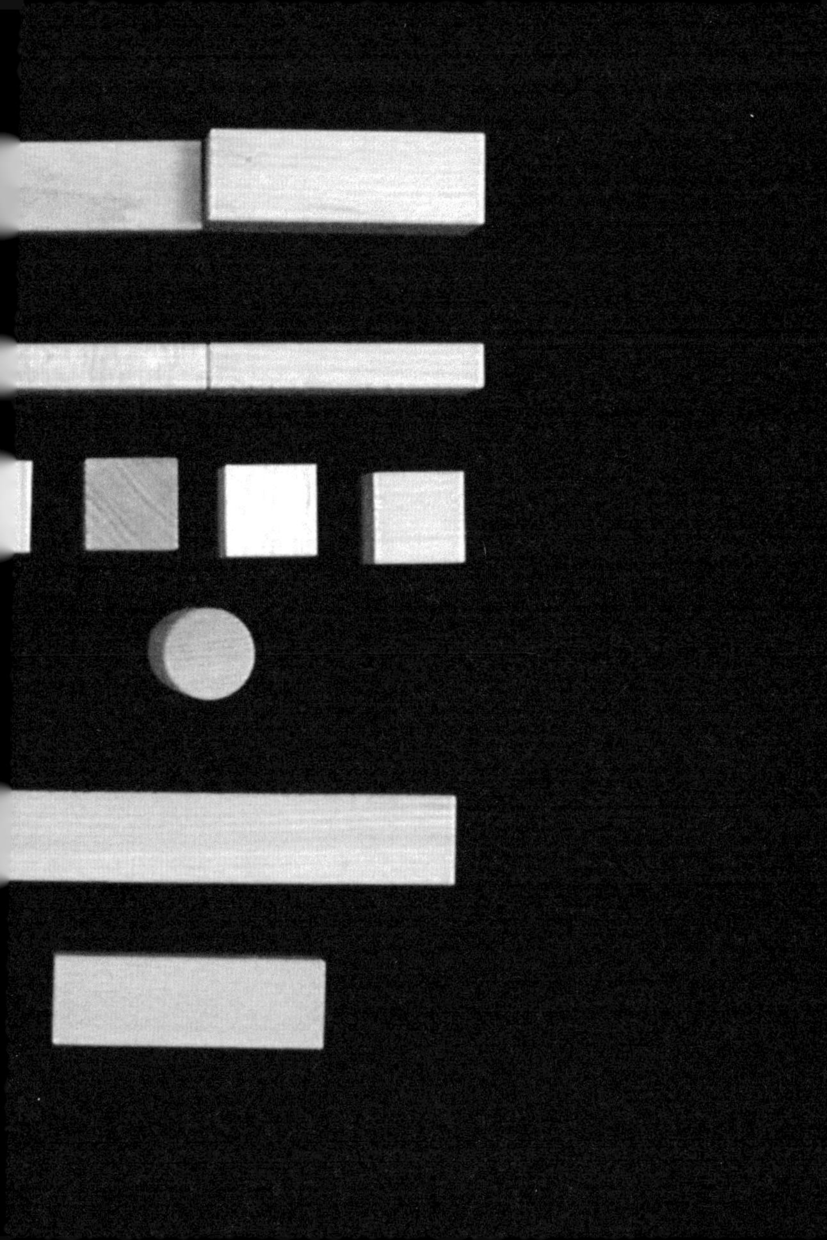

Marion von Osten, *The Glory of the Garden*, 2009, video still

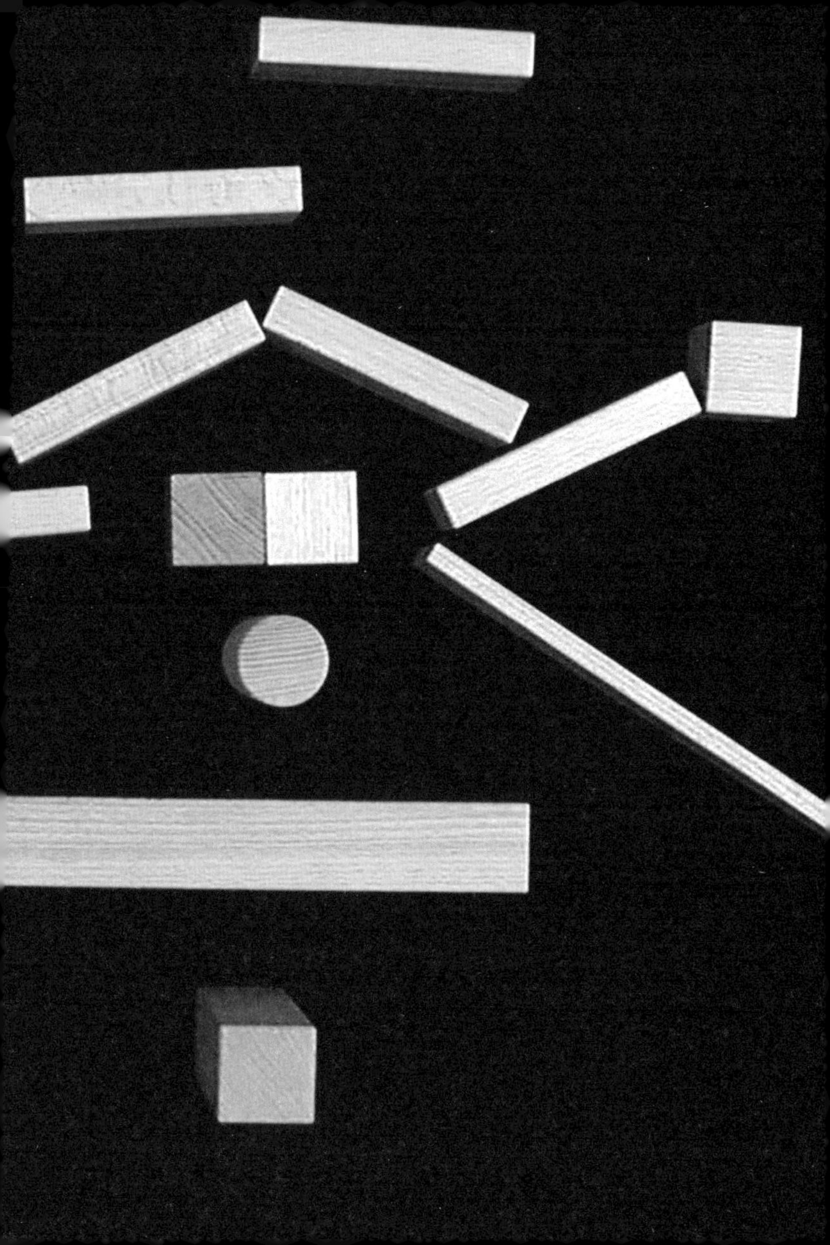

Annotated List of Productions

<u>Action! Painting/Publishing</u>, 2011–2012, research and project exhibition, Les Laboratoires d'Aubervilliers, Aubervilliers

Concept by: Marion von Osten
Closing events and exhibition with: Lotte Arndt, Mihaela Gherghescu, Fanny Gillet-Ouhenia, Olivier Hadouchi, Pascale Ratovonony, and Cédric Vincent
Produced by: Khiasma, Les Lilas; and Les Laboratoires d'Aubervilliers, Aubervilliers in collaboration with L'École des hautes études en sciences sociales, Paris; and research program "l'Art et la mondialisation," Institut national de l'histoire de l'art, Paris; with support from the Goethe-Institut Paris, Paris

Action! Painting/Publishing was a collaborative research project on anti-colonial magazines from Algeria, Cuba, France, Morocco, Nigeria, Tunisia, and Uganda produced in 1930–1970. Cultural magazines such as *Alif*, *Black Orpheus*, *Transition*, and *Légitime Défense* served as case studies showing ways in which anti-colonial movements have trans-formed western epistemologies, informed radical aesthetics in print culture, and helped usher in the decolonization of culture and knowledge. The closing exhibition included a research room that showcased the studied volumes alongside issues of magazines the project had not examined, including *Presence Africaine, Souffles, Tricontinental*, and *Partisans Magazine*. Visitors were welcome to browse the volumes, thus continuing the research in new formations.

Image(s): 236–237; References in text(s): 225

<u>Architecture Without Architects—
Another Anarchist Approach</u>
Marion von Osten, "Architecture
Without Architects—Another
Anarchist Approach," *e-flux
journal*, no. 6 (May 2009), online
at: http://www.e-flux.com/
journal/06/61401/architecture-
without-architects-another-
anarchist-approach/

This text—its title referring to the
1964 MoMA, New York exhibition
Architecture Without Architects
and architect and anarchist Colin
Ward's famous book *Housing: An
Anarchist Approach* (1976)—
offers "some open-ended
thoughts" related to von Osten's
research on modernist housing
projects implemented both in
formerly colonized cities and on
the outskirts of European cities.
Primary examples in this text are
the *cité verticale* and the (Michel)
Écochard grid, both realized in
Casablanca in 1951. The text
reflects on the research trips and
conversations that led to the
exhibition *In the Desert of
Modernity: Colonial Planning and
After*, Haus der Kulturen der Welt,
Berlin, 2008 and La Fabrique
Culturelle des Anciens Abattoirs
de Casablanca, Casablanca,
2009, and the publication
*Colonial Modern: Aesthetics of
the Past, Rebellions for the Future*,
edited by Tom Avermaete, Serhat

Karakayali, and Marion von Osten,
2010.

References in text(s): 24–25, 42,
109

<u>Atelier Europa</u>, 2003–2004,
research and exhibition project,
Kunstverein München, Munich

Image(s): cover, 181; References
in text(s): 107–108, 150, 160n,
183, 210, 225, 229

Produced by: Søren Grammel and
Kunstverein München, Munich
Concept by: Marion von Osten in
collaboration with Pauline Boudry,
Søren Grammel, Brigitta Kuster,
Maria Lind, Isabell Lorey, Angela
McRobbie, and Katja Reichard

Atelier Europa created a
transnational network of artists,
activists, and researchers
that surveyed the social and
production conditions of cultural
producers in Austria, France,
Germany, Spain, Switzerland, and
the United Kingdom in order to
deduct the commonalities of their
individual experiences of precarity.
The project comprised a research
period leading up to an exhibition
—subtitled *A Small Post-Fordist
Drama*—performances, film
productions, and two conferences
in 2004 that explored ways of
working that opposed the idea
of the artist as a role model for
neoliberal politics. The project
marked the foundation of
the working group kleines
postfordistisches Drama (small
post-Fordist Drama, kpD), which
conducted research on fashion
designers in Berlin and London,
led by feminist cultural theorist
Angela McRobbie.

Bauordnungslehre, 1995, mixed media installation consisting of drawings, a desk, architecture plans, and found photographs, Kunst-Werke, Berlin

The installation *Bauordnungslehre* (The Principle of Building Codes), part of the exhibition *when tekkno turns to sound of poetry: Technologie, Feminismus, Konzept-Kunst & Politik* (Technology, Feminism, Conceptual Art & Politics) (1995) at Kunst-Werke, Berlin, consisted of a windowless room with a desk, to scale to the *petit atelier* by architect Le Corbusier. Le Corbusier's designs for the *petit atelier* were shown on the walls along with his floor plans for the Couvent Sainte-Marie de La Tourette, Éveux. These were juxtaposed with photographs taken by the resident of a 45 m² apartment in what was at the time West Germany. The photos were taken for relatives in the German Democratic Republic. On the desk, drawn portraits of modernist architects, accompanied by handwritten quotes, were displayed.

Image(s): 105; References in text(s): 97, 100–101, 104–107, 108

Be Creative! The Creative Imperative (with Labor k3000, Zurich), 2002–2003, exhibition and conference, Museum für Gestaltung, Zurich

Concept by: Marion von Osten in collaboration with Peter Spillmann Co-produced by: D/O/C/K department of the Academy of Fine Arts, Leipzig; Institut für Theorie der Gestaltung und Kunst, Zurich; Labor k3000, Zurich; and Museum für Gestaltung, Zurich

Be Creative! The Creative Imperative was an exhibition and public program dedicated to thinking about how creativity has been increasingly considered a professional and productive asset (or requirement), alongside self-organizing abilities and flexibility. Through four public group discussions, the exhibition investigated the implications of this for the living, learning, and working models and the experiences of local artists and designers, each discussion focusing on a specific geographical/sectoral case.

Conference contributors: Beatrice von Bismarck, Ulrich Bröckling, Sabeth Buchmann, Helmut Draxler, and Tom Holert

Website: http://www.k3000.ch/
labor/becreative

Image(s): 93; References in
text(s): 17, 70, 95, 106, 115,
209–210, 231, 243–244

Colonial Modern: Aesthetics of
the Past, Rebellions for the Future
Tom Avermaete, Serhat
Karakayali, and Marion von Osten,
eds., *Colonial Modern: Aesthetics
of the Past, Rebellions for the
Future* (London: Black Dog
Publishing, 2010)

This 320-page publication
followed the project *In the Desert
of Modernity: Colonial Planning
and After* (2008–2009) and
provided an interdisciplinary body
of texts on the interrelated
histories of urban planning in
French-colonial northern Africa
and the resulting European
architecture and governing
discourses.

Contributors: Mogniss H.
Abdallah/Agence IM'media,
Nezar AlSayyad, Kader Attia, Tom
Avermaete, Madeleine Bernstorff,
Mark Crinson, Hassan Darsi,
Kahina Amal Djiar, Monique Eleb,
Serhat Karakayali, Christian
Kravagna, Brigitta Kuster, Labor
k3000, André Loeckx, Kobena
Mercer, Valentin Mudimbe,
Françoise Navez-Bouchanine,
Alona Nitzan-Shiftan, Marion von
Osten, Bernd M. Scherer, Horia
Serhane, Sven-Olov Wallenstein,
and Daniel Weiss

References in text(s): 70, 91, 137

<u>Das Erziehungsbild: Zur visuellen Kultur des Pädagogischen</u>
Tom Holert and Marion von Osten, eds., *Das Erziehungsbild: Zur visuellen Kultur des Pädagogischen* (Vienna: Schlebrügge.Editor, 2010)

Das Erziehungsbild: Zur visuellen Kultur des Pädagogischen (The Education Image: On Pedagogy's Visual Culture) is an inter-disciplinary collection of essays on different forms of knowledge production. It includes both artistic and educational practices, the tensions between them, and the use of images in education. The volume questions whether and how artistic-theoretical discourses intervene in pedagogical cultures.

References in text(s): 60–61, 70, 96

<u>Das Phantom sucht seinen Mörder: Ein Reader zur Kulturalisierung der Ökonomie</u>
Justin Hoffmann and Marion von Osten, eds., *Das Phantom sucht seinen Mörder: Ein Reader zur Kulturalisierung der Ökonomie* (Berlin: b_books, 1999)

Das Phantom sucht seinen Mörder: Ein Reader zur Kulturalisierung der Ökonomie (The Phantom in Search of Its Murderer: A Reader on the Culturalization of the Economy) is closely related to the exhibition projects of the 1998 Shedhalle Zürich, Zurich program (*SUPERmarkt: money, market, gender politics*; *There Is No Business Like Business*; and *MoneyNations*) curated by Justin Hoffmann, Marion von Osten, and Yvonne Volkart. The publication includes texts on art, popular culture, fashion, and the economy.

Contributors: PoYin Auyong, Martin Beck, Roderich Fabian, Stuart Hall, Justin Hoffmann, Schorsch Kamerun, Gülsün Karamustafa with Maurizio Lazzarato, Angela McRobbie, Ayşe Öncü, Elisabeth Stiefel with Marion von Osten, Res Strehle, Yvonne Volckart, and Anna Wessely

References in text(s): 70, 74

Die aktuelle Wirtschaftswoche (with Sylvia Kafehsy, Brigitta Kuster, Mascha Madörin, Marcus Maeder, and Res Strehle), 1997, exhibition and workshops, Kombirama, Zurich

The exhibition and series of events of *Die aktuelle Wirtschaftswoche* (The Current Economic Week), which took place at the artist-run space Kombirama, were set to critically comment on neoliberalism. *Die aktuelle Wirtschaftswoche* investigated the social omnipresence of neoliberalism by focusing on its structuring rituals present in everyday life, its visual representation, its capacity to enforce these rituals (through advertising, for example), and the ways in which it transforms cultural and artistic practices.

References in text(s): 191

EuroVision2000 by Labor k3000 (Marion von Osten, Susanna Perin, and Peter Spillmann), 2000–2001, events and local television project, Centrum Brussel 2000, Brussels; Roxy, Prague; and Villa Serena, Bologna

Co-produced by: Cafe9.net, international and Labor k3000, Zurich, with support from APEXchanges, European Cultural Foundation, Amsterdam; Austrian Cultural Forum, Prague; Canadian Embassy, Prague; Open Society Foundation, New York; and Pro Helvetia, Zurich

EuroVision2000 took place between 2000 and 2001 with installments in different cities. It featured lectures, film screenings, and discussions in which nationalism and racism, as well as social, economic, and political transitions within the construction of the Schengen Agreement, the European Union, and the post-1989 European identity, were explored. Videos—some specially produced for the project—were broadcast, with an archive kept on the project's website. The three main locations of the project were Bologna (organized by Susanna Perin), Brussels (organized by von Osten), and Prague (organized by Peter Spillmann).

EuroVision2000 in Brussels entailed a three-day series of screenings, discussions, interviews, and an intervention, done in close collaboration with artist Marion Baruch/Name Diffusion, social and economic researchers like Yann Moulier-Boutang, and nongovernmental organizations like Sans Papiers Antwerp. The pivotal topic was the struggle of undocumented immigrants in Belgium and France, which extended to interconnected issues of labor conditions, legislative equality, and cultural production. Works of various artists were screened, including collaborations by Labor k3000, such as *Fashion is Work* (1999), and von Osten's *Nordreise – Südreise* (2000), which deals with the struggles of undocumented postcolonial migrants in Belgium.

Website: http://www. eurovision2000.net

References in text(s): 203–207, 210–213

<u>Fashion is Work</u> (with Gülsün Karamustafa and Peter Spillmann), 1999, three-channel video (VHS), 30 min.

In this three-channel video, situations involving both formal and informal economic activities in the textile and fashion industry are shown: 1. documentary accounts of market places in Istanbul, 2. staged scenes of the daily lives of freelance visual image makers in Zurich, and 3. a composite treatise on contemporary labor conditions, deploying citations from fashion discourses and fragments of interviews with a globalization sociologist and a union representative of the Swiss textile industry. By stringing these accounts together, *Fashion is Work* elucidates the shared levels of (in)formality, exploitation, and precarity present in divergent industries.

References in text(s): 196, 209

The Glory of the Garden, 2009,
video, 14 min.

The Glory of the Garden shows
variously sized, wooden children's
blocks—now commonly used in
team-building exercises—on top
of a dark surface, placed and
replaced by several sets of hands
in a continuous flow of
constellations. The moves are
prompted by staff members of an
art institution in the United
Kingdom who analyze how their
art space has been transformed
over the last thirty-odd years.
The enacted pseudodidactic
play charts the institution's
transformations in spatial
arrangement, language, and
managerial structures and
strategies, spurred by
conservative policies and
the wider corporate move
for organizations to become
market-fit, competition-driven,
profit-oriented players with
corresponding programming,
services, and fundraising policies.
The video gives insight into how
these transformations have
affected language, behavior, and
the work ethos of cultural workers
inside the institution.

Image(s): 254–257; References in
text(s): 249

How Do You Shipwreck in the
Harbor?, 2013, board-mounted
posters, Göteborg International
Biennial for Contemporary Art,
Gothenburg

Poster design by: Labor k3000,
Zurich

During the 2013 Göteborg
International Biennial for
Contemporary Art, visitors
strolling along the harbors near
Gothenburg's city center would
encounter posters dispersed
along the *Drömmarnas kaj* (Quay
of Broken Dreams), named for its
ships in various states of
dilapidation. The boldly lettered
posters posed the question: "How
do you shipwreck in the harbor?"
and included an alphabetical list
of direct and indirect answers,
such as "accident,"
"authorization," "fire," "fraud,"
"sabotage," "Schengen," and
"speculation." Hinting at the
biennial's sub-exhibition title, *Art
Crime. Legally on the Edge. A
Forensic Exhibition*, the posters
presented both an inquiry into
and a poem about averages
and losses; or, alternatively, an
incentivizing list of strategies.

Image(s): 122; References in
text(s): 119–120

<u>Human Genome Project</u>,
1994–1995, mixed media
installation including a fax station,
fax prints, mounted text and
reproductions, projection, and
folder, Shedhalle Zürich, Zurich
and Kunst-Werke, Berlin

The installation *Human Genome
Project*—in the exhibition *when
tekkno turns to sound of poetry:
Technologie, Feminismus,
Konzept-Kunst & Politik*
(Technology, Feminism,
Conceptual Art & Politics)—
included faxed statements about
a fake cloning case in the United
States. In the entry hall of
Shedhalle Zürich, a fax machine
was set to receive with a wall of
reproductions of pictures of
architect Le Corbusier's *Unité
d'habitation*, titled with his
biopolitical assumptions, installed
as a background. In the second
installation, von Osten overlapped
visuals from the project's
namesake, the international
scientific research project on
human DNA, and artist Alighiero
Boetti's embroidered maps, which
were created by female labor in
Afghanistan. This created a
speculative and tactile relation
between body and space,
conceptual art and biotechnology.

Image(s): 64, 76–77; References
in text(s): 67–68, 108

<u>I Am Like That Anyway</u>, 2006–
2008, plinths, audio recordings,
video, and camera, Arnolfini,
Bristol; Gasworks, London;
Platform Garanti Contemporary
Art Center, Istanbul; Tensta
konsthall, Stockholm; and
Townhouse Gallery, Cairo

In 2006, a campaign of global
fashion retailer Hennes & Mauritz
(H&M) featured an advertisement
with pop star Madonna pictured
amidst 17 of her tour dancers and
crew members. The image, shot
by videographer and fashion
photographer (John) Rankin
(Waddel), shows the crew
standing, sitting, and leaning on
and between variously sized
white plinths—reminiscent of
omnipresent exhibition space
furniture—in a brightly lit studio. At
Gasworks and Platform Garanti
Contemporary Art Center, von
Osten reviewed the image and its
sociopolitical and art historical
implications with the institutions'
staff members. The recorded
discussions put forth analogies
with the cultural industry, hence
transposing questions of
nonhierarchical representation
vis-à-vis hierarchies, class, and
gender inequality, and of
precarious working conditions of/
within the institution itself. Seated
on similar plinths in the gallery
space, visitors could listen to the

recordings while watching a video of staff members reenacting the original picture. At Townhouse Gallery in 2008, these conversations were interpreted and performed by young actors on a stage.

References in text(s): 248

<u>In the Desert of Modernity: Colonial Planning and After</u>, 2008–2009, exhibition and conference, Haus der Kulturen der Welt, Berlin and La Fabrique Culturelle des Anciens Abattoirs de Casablanca, Casablanca

Curated and artistic direction by: Marion von Osten
Co-curated by: Tom Avermaete and Serhat Karakayali
Exhibition design by: Jesko Fezer, Andreas Müller, and Anna Voswinckel
Co-produced by: Center for Post-Colonial Knowledge and Culture, Berlin; Haus der Kulturen der Welt, Berlin; and La Fabrique Culturelle des Anciens Abattoirs de Casablanca, Casablanca with support from Academy of Fine Arts Vienna, Vienna; Casamémoire, Casablanca; Delft University of Technology, Delft; and École Supérieure d'Architecture de Casablanca, Casablanca

In the Desert of Modernity: Colonial Planning and After was an extensive research and exhibition project comprising collaborative research and a series of live events, screenings, and a conference. It was dedicated to the interrelated histories of European modernist architecture and (experimental) urban planning projects in colonial northern Africa that were based on essentialist notions of living habits and marked by universalist claims, exemplified by those instituted in Casablanca. The project's closing exhibition included the online video platform *This Was Tomorrow!* (2008) and culminated in the book *Colonial Modern: Aesthetics of the Past, Rebellions for the Future* (2010).

Contributors to the exhibition and events: Mogniss H. Abdallah, Lázaro Abreu, Nezar AlSayyad, Luis Álvarez, An Architektur, Arsac A., Ascoral des Jeunes, Atelier Archives Audiovisuelles BDIC, Kader Attia, Élie Azagury, Wafae Belarbi, Jacques Belin, Claude Beraud, Madeleine Bernstorff, Vladimir Bodiansky, Georges Candilis, Giancarlo De Carlo, Henri Cartier-Bresson, Casamémoire Casablanca, Talal Chaïbia, Jean-Louis Cohen, Hassan Darsi, Robert Doisneau, Michel Écochard, Monique Eleb, Pierre-André Emery, Aldo van Eyck, Patrick Forest, Jesús Forjans, Gérard-Aimé, Georges Godefroy, Faïza Guéne, Marcel Gut, Jean Hentsch, Monique Hervo, Bernhard Hoesli, Jyoti Hosagrahar, François Issaverdens, Romain Jeannot, Alexis Josic, Kanak Attak, Bernard Kennedy, Christian Kravagna, Brigitta Kuster, Labor k3000, J. Lambert, Yasmeen Lari, L'Association les Engraineurs, Le Corbusier, Guy Le Querrec, Jean de Maisonseul, Mario Marret, Pierre Mas, Kobena Mercer, Louis Miquel, Valentin Y. Mudimbe, Joe Nasar, Janine Niépce, Peter Osborne, L. Ouhayoun, Henri Piot, Fernand Pouillon, Remember Resistance, Bernard Richard, Willy Ronis, Alfrédo Rostgaard, Bernard Rudofsky, Moshe Safdie, Elsa de Seynes, Roland Simounet, Wit Sklias, Alison Smithson and Peter Smithson, André M. Studer, L. Tamborini, Marcelle Vallet, Jean Vidal, Sven-Olov Wallenstein, J. Wattez, Daniel Weiss, and Shadrach Woods

Image(s): 30–31, 53; References in text(s): 22, 33, 108, 116–118, 134, 137, 182

<u>In Search of the Postcapitalist Self</u>
Marion von Osten, "In Search of the Postcapitalist Self," *e-flux journal*, no. 17 (June 2010), online at: http://www.e-flux.com/journal/17/67350/editorial-in-search-of-the-postcapitalist-self/

e-flux journal no. 17 was guest-edited by von Osten as her contribution to the 6th Berlin Biennale, Berlin, 2010. Rather than following the exhausted master narratives of capitalism and crisis, this issue of *e-flux journal* investigates how cultural producers are already in the process of creating and reflecting new discourses and practices in the current climate of "zombie neoliberalism." It formulates possible answers to the questions of what is disclosed and what changes if cultural production can be imagined precisely from the vantage point of postcapitalist politics.

References in text(s): 149, 184n

<u>Insert 1-4: Common Property</u>, 2004, installation, *Common Property*, 6th Werkleitz Biennale, Halle

Concept by: Simone Hain, Marion von Osten, Christiane Post, Karin Rebbert, Katja Reichard, Peter Spillmann, and Axel John Wieder
Produced in collaboration with: Andrea Börner, Oliver Clemens, Sabine Horlitz, and Robert Schnitz-Michels

Insert 1-4: Common Property consisted of four intervening installations, situated within Halle's Volkspark, the exhibition venue of the 6th Werkleitz Biennale. The installations were partly reconstructions of displays and architectural settings by Laszlo Moholy-Nagy, Alexander Rodchenko, and Vladimir Tatlin—architects and artists known for their statements on the social roles of fine arts, theater, and architecture. These references framed the theme of the biennale, *Common Property*, which raised questions about the cultural and social production of knowledge and the ways in which it is distributed.

Image(s): 145, 146–147

Irene ist Viele (with Rachel Mader), 1996, film program, discussions, and exhibition, Shedhalle Zürich, Zurich

Program by: Rachel Mader and Marion von Osten
Produced by: Shedhalle Zürich, Zurich

Irene ist Viele (Irene Is Many) was a film program organized by von Osten and art historian Rachel Mader as part of the *FrauenFilmTage Schweiz* (Swiss Women Film Days) (1996), dedicated to feminist films from Germany and Switzerland. The program's title was derived from the film *Eine Prämie für Irene* (A Bonus for Irene) (1971) directed by Helke Sander, which presents the interconnections of the private and public work spheres. Together with invited filmmakers, the films were reviewed and discussed, drawing parallels between and discerning differences in their approaches.

Image(s): 84–85; References in text(s): 66

Irene ist Viele! Or What We Call Productive Forces
Marion von Osten, "Irene ist Viele! Or What We Call Productive Forces," *e-flux journal*, no. 8 (September 2009), online at: http://www.e-flux.com/journal/08/61381/irene-ist-viele-or-what-we-call-productive-forces/

In this essay, von Osten discusses questions around the permeation and mutual conditionings of the social, cultural, and economic domains; a reality that especially marks the living and working conditions of cultural producers. Von Osten takes the film *Die allseitig reduzierte Persönlichkeit—Redupers* (The All-Around Reduced Personality—Redupers) (1978), directed by Helke Sander, as a starting point for "the debate over forces of production, precarity, and critical potential [because of its] illustrating that, even in the upheaval of changes in the capitalist as well as gender o! from Fordism to post-Fordism, many networked and self-organizing production conditions . . . were already present—and were being analyzed by feminists."

References in text(s): 79–80, 231–232

<u>Kamera läuft!</u> (with kpD), 2004, video, 32 min.

Actors: Ludwig Böttger, Silke Geertz, Catriona Guggenbühl, Sylvester von Hösslin, Kathrin Irion, Krishan Krone, Mona Kuschel, Dorothee Müggler, Marion von Osten, Josef Ostendorf, Katja Reichard, Peter Spillmann, and Joey Zimmermann
Directed by: Mona Kuschel, Brigitta Kuster, Marion von Osten, and Katja Reichard
Camera: Annette Amberg, Martina Fischbacher, Stefanie Hablützel, Brigitta Kuster, Irene Ledermann, Ulrich Schaffner, Pia Siegrist, and Lena Thüring
Costumes by: Mona Kuschel and Katja Reichard
Edited by: Brigitta Kuster, Isabell Lorey, Katja Reichard, Peter Spillmann, and Marion von Osten
Produced by: Marion von Osten and Peter Spillmann at Labor k3000, Zurich

Kamera läuft! (Rolling!) is a video based on dramaturgically reworked interviews with Berlin's cultural producers, conducted by kleines postfordisches Drama (kpD). Interview questions such as "How would you describe your work life?," "What is a good life?," and "What do you do when it all becomes too much?" prompted conversations about precarious working and living conditions and desires for change. The interview material was transformed into a script that was performed on a nondescript film production set.

Image(s): 162–163; References in text(s): 107–108, 160–161, 210

<u>MigMap</u>, 2005, online project and digital print on paper

Produced by: Labor k3000, Zurich, Peter Spillmann with Helmut Dietrich, Matthew Gaskins, Sophie Goltz, Nana Heidenreich, Sabine Hess, Sylvia Kafhesy, Serhat Karakayali, Astrid Kusser, Maureen Müller, Marion von Osten, Efthimia Panagiotidis, Susanna Perin, Vassilis Tsianos, and Michael Vögeli, with support from Aargauer Kuratorium, Aarau; the German Federal Cultural Foundation, Halle; and Pro Helvetia, Zurich

MigMap is a virtual cartography of European migration policies developed in the framework of Transit Migration and featured as an artistic contribution to *Projekt Migration* (2002–2006). The website presents a navigable overview of public and private actors, institutions, debates, and events that are important for understanding Europe's border regime. Through four map-charts— "key players," "discourses," "Europeanisation," and "places and practices"—the information from the Transit Migration research can be accessed.

Website: http://www. transitmigration.org/migmap/

Image(s): 214–217; References in text(s): 201

<u>MoneyNations</u>, 1997–2001, project exhibition, Shedhalle Zürich, Zurich and Kunsthalle Exnergasse, Vienna

Concept by: Marion von Osten with Nathalie Seitz and Peter Spillmann (Zurich), and Jochen Becker, Rike Frank, Gabriele Marth, Jo Schmeiser, and Michael Zinganel (Vienna)
Co-produced by: Labor k3000, Zurich and Shedhalle Zürich, Zurich, and Kunsthalle Exnergasse, Vienna with support from the German Federal Cultural Foundation, Halle

MoneyNations started by establishing a network of artists, filmmakers, activists, researchers, and theorists. Rather than merely attributing the intensification of European Union border policies to capitalist production, the project focused on the roles that post-communist countries played in these formations, the significance that racism and sexism have had for the productive forces of late capitalism, and the contradictions, instabilities, and resistances that can be derived from the post-1989 transformations. The transnational exchange of perspectives led to various cultural productions, videos, online radio projects, congresses, and screenings, as well as the exhibitions *MoneyNations@access* at Shedhalle Zürich (1998) and *MoneyNations II: For People on Their Way in Europe* at Kunsthalle Exnergasse (2000), both accompanied by three-day conferences.

Website: http://www. moneynations.net

Image(s): 186–187, 199, 200; References in text(s): 110–111, 115, 190, 195–198, 203–204, 206, 213, 225–226

MoneyNations: Constructing the Border – Constructing East-West

Marion von Osten and Peter Spillmann, eds., *MoneyNations: Constructing the Border – Constructing East-West* (Vienna: edition selene, 2003)

Contributors: Mogniss H. Abdallah, Dragan Ambrozic, Edit András, Zeigam Azizov, Marion Baruch/Name Diffusion, Jochen Becker, Luchezar Boyadjiev, Dani Busic, Axel Claes and Mark Saunders, Deportation Class, Helmut Dietrich, Dana Diminescu, Sabine Hess and Ramona Lenz, Brian Holmes, Bertha Jottar-Palenzuela, Kanak Attak, Gülsün Karamustafa, Anna Kowalska, Martin Krenn and Simone Bader, Labor k3000 (Marion von Osten, Susanna Perin, and Peter Spillmann), Djonia Oliveira-Mendes, Marion von Osten, Dan Perjovschi, Lia Perjovschi, Peter Riedlinger and Pascal Petignat, Encarnación Guttiérrez Rodríguez, Jo Schmeiser and Gabrielle Marth, Peter Spillmann, Shirley Tate, Universal Embassy, Tristan Wibault, and Anna Wessely

This 256-page publication asserts the relevance of the debates, approaches, and methods employed in the project *MoneyNations* (1997–2001) —which took place through videos, photography, installations, texts, meetings, as well as two exhibitions and several conferences—providing visual documentation of, as well as theoretical and artistic contributions to the project.

References in text(s): 110n

Norm der Abweichung

Marion von Osten, ed., *Norm der Abweichung* (Vienna and Zurich: Springer and Edition Voldemeer, 2003)

Norm der Abweichung (Norm of Deviation) departs from this hypothetical question: What happens when "anti-order" becomes the new norm? When, for example, the labor economy demands social mobility and flexibility? The emergences of subcultures, cultural and political avant-gardes, and everyday subversive micropolitics show that (patriarchal) governing apparatuses cannot fully absorb the will of subjects. The book's contributions speculate on what happens when norm and deviation are in such close relationship; when dissidence, critique, and subversion become driving forces of modernization and the global economy.

Contributors: Beatrice von Bismarck, Luc Boltanski, Ulrich Bröckling, Ève Chiapello, Helmut Draxler, Karen Lisa Goldschmidt Salamon, Michael Hardt, Tom Holert, Angela McRobbie, Yann Moulier-Boutang, Keith Negus, and Faith Wilding

References in text(s): 70, 88–89

Oblomov's Corner, 2000–2002,

lecture-performance and mixed media installation including display of videos (VHS), round bed, textiles, and viewing station

Co-produced by: Kunsthaus Dresden, Dresden; plug.in, Basel; and Swiss Institute, New York

Oblomov's Corner—which refers to Ivan Goncharov's 1859 novel about the apathetic, indecisive, and bedbound namesake protagonist Ilja Oblomov—consisted of a *vidéothèque*-like display of VHS video tapes filled with feature films depicting United States-American labor struggles. The shelved cases were situated around a circular bed near the gallery's reception desk, allowing gallery staff and visitors to watch videos of their choosing. At plug.in and Kunsthaus Dresden, it was activated with a lecture performance by von Osten who, dressed in a sequin dress, discussed Hollywood's studios, its low budget films, and its representation of labor.

Image(s): 121; References in text(s): 119

<u>Projekt Migration</u> (with Kathrin Rhomberg), 2002–2006, project exhibition, various locations in Cologne

Artistic direction by: Marion von Osten and Kathrin Rhomberg
Curated by: Aytaç Eryılmaz, Marion von Osten, Martin Rapp, Kathrin Rhomberg, and Regina Römhild
Co-produced by: Kölnischer Kunstverein and the Documentation Center and Museum of Migration in Germany, Cologne, in co-llaboration with Goethe-University, Frankfurt; Institute for Cultural Anthropology and European Ethnology, Berlin; and Institute for Critical Theory at Zurich University of the Arts, Zurich, initiated and supported by the German Federal Cultural Foundation, Halle

Projekt Migration (Project Migration) was an extensive research and exhibition project that sought to investigate and represent past and current labor migration, specifically involving Germany, as well as migration's social and cultural potentials. The exhibitions in 2005 and 2006—at the Kölnischer Kunstverein and several other venues in Cologne— marked the 50th anniversary of the bilateral recruitment agreement between Germany and Italy, the first of a range of similar agreements with Mediterranean and later Eastern European countries that formed the basis of the "guest worker" regime. The project's outcomes consisted of exhibition artworks, conferences, and screenings, followed by a large publication called *Projekt Migration* (2005), which offers an overview of the artistic and theoretical contributions to the project.

Image(s): 2–5, 114; References in text(s): 19, 21, 73, 112–113, 115–116, 201

<reformpause>, 2006,
installation, poster, and intervention, Kunstraum, Leuphana
Univerisity of Lüneburg, Lüneburg

Poster design and installations by:
Marion von Osten
Authors of *Plakat* newspaper:
Christiane Autsch, Kristina
Geertz, Ludmila Gerasimov,
Julia Hammer, Rahel-Katharina
Hermann, Katharina Looks,
Jenny Nachtigall, Maria Petersen,
Kathrin Roes, Stephanie
Schneider, Frauke Schnoor,
Stephanie Seidel, Valentina
Seidel, Nike Thurn, and Anna Till
Produced by: Leuphana University
of Lüneburg with support from the
Culture 2000 Programme of the
European Commission

Together with students and
lecturers of the Art and Visual
Studies program at the Leuphana
University of Lüneburg, von Osten
conducted research on the history
of education reforms in Germany
and those that were at play at the
time. Concerned with an ominous
crisis of education due to
economization and the possible
re-hierarchization of knowledge,
workshops and seminars explored
potential alliances and coalitions
amongst students and lecturers
as being alternative spaces of
knowledge. These led to the
publication of a student

newspaper called *Plakat*, a series
of film screenings on education,
and a concluding exhibition. The
central installation filling the
Kunstraum exhibition space
consisted of scale models of the
campus buildings of the Ruhr-
Universität Bochum, which were
built in 1965, made in order to be
used as benches during
gatherings.

Image(s): 125, 126–127;
References in text(s): 120, 123

Schöneggstrasse 5 (with Labor
k3000, Zurich), 2002, installation,
three channel video, eight
interviews, each 7 min., Museum
für Gestaltung, Zurich

Directed by: Marion von Osten
Post-production by: Bernd
Schurer and Michael Vögeli

For *Schöneggstrasse 5*, artist
collective Labor k3000's
production space was set up
so as to record video and still
images of conversations and (self)
representations of the graphic
and web designers, electronic
musicians, and cultural producers
with whom von Osten, Rachel
Maeder, Susan Perin, Bernd
Schurer, Peter Spillmann, and
Michael Vögeli (members of Labor
k3000) shared their studio and
office building. For the exhibition
piece, two screens showed the
protagonists talking about their
days of self-organizing and their
strategies for survival in the
cultural and IT industries. The
third screen presented visual
culture affiliated with each
producer's pop and subcultural
contexts.

References in text(s): 209

Sex & Space: Space. Gender.
Economy (with Pauline Boudry,
Rachel Mader, and Michael
Zinganel), 1996–1997, exhibition,
film studio, and workshops,
Shedhalle Zürich, Zurich and
Forum Stadtpark, Graz

In *Sex & Space*, artists, architects,
and theorists deconstructed
gendered principles that structure
the private and public spheres.
Sex & Space was the site of public
workshops and discussions with
feminist architects and urban
planners, and hosted a series of
artist presentations on the theme
of sex and space, along with its
representations in imaginative
counter-spaces of visual culture.
A second installment took place
at Forum Stadtpark during the
steirischer herbst festival, and
focused on city marketing and
feminist perspectives on globalization and migration.

Website: http://k3000.ch/
sex&space/

Image(s): 170, 171; References in
text(s): 62, 66, 71, 108

<u>Studio Hellerau</u>, 1995, collaborative residency and film production, Festspielhaus Hellerau, Dresden

Concept by: Marion von Osten with Alice Creischer, Helmut Draxler, Jesko Fezer, Ulrich Heinke, Justin Hoffmann, Anke Kempkes, Pia Lanzinger, Kathrin von Mahlzahn, Ariane Müller, Heike Munder, Katja Reichard, Christoph Schäfer, Cornelia Schmidt-Bleek, Andreas Siekmann, Cathy Skene, Stefan Thiel, Klaus Weber, Axel John Wieder, and Florian Zeyfang

Set in the early twentieth-century *Gartenstadt* (garden city) of Hellerau, Dresden, and initiated by von Osten, members of Labor k3000 lived together in the artist residency of Festspielhaus Hellerau in order to produce a film that reflected on architecture and city planning, as well as on alternative forms of housing and squatting. This included thinking about the utopian models that once informed the architecture of the garden city where *Studio Hellerau* itself took place

References in text(s): 60, 98–99

<u>SUPERmarkt: money, market, gender politics</u>, 1998, exhibition, Shedhalle Zürich, Zurich

Concept by: Marion von Osten with Pauline Boudry, Sylvia Kafhesy, Markus Maeder, and Peter Spillmann
With contributions by: Julie Ault, PoYin Auyong, Pauline Boudry, Alice Creischer, Orshi Drodzik, Freies Fach, Stephan Geene and Judith Hopf, Sylvia Kafehsy, Brigitta Kuster, Rachel Mader, Mascha Madörin, Marcus Maeder, Marion von Osten, Alexandra Papadopoulos, Lilian Räber, Nathalie Seitz and Markus Jans, Andreas Siekmann, Peter Spillmann, Franz Stauffenberg and Christopher Roth, Res Strehle, Martin Warnke, and Michael Zinganel

Critiquing the idea that the "free market" naturally regulates the socio-economy, the project *SUPERmarkt* looked at several economic assumptions from a feminist and cultural studies perspective. *SUPERmarkt* discussed the "free market" as a cultural construction in which subjectivities, influences, and the prevailing notions of value and professionalism are part of symbolic and ritual practices.

References in text(s): 191

This Was Tomorrow! (with Peter
Spillmann and Michael Vögeli),
2008, online project

Concept, research, and design
by: Marion von Osten, Peter
Spillmann, and Michael Vögeli
(Labor k3000, Zurich) with
support from the Center for
Post-Colonial Knowledge and
Culture, Berlin; Haus der Kulturen
der Welt, Berlin; MACBA (Museu
d'Art Contemporani de Barcelona),
Barcelona; and Museum of Modern
Art in Warsaw, Warsaw

This was Tomorrow! contains an
archive of over 100 video and film
clips that were made by residents
of 1950–1980s housing projects
across Europe and northern
Africa and contributed by the
makers to the project. Visitors
navigate through a schematic grid
of cities and districts to which the
locations of the submitted videos
correspond. Through varied
approaches, the videos portray
neighborhoods, residents, and
their activities inside and around
the vast housing structures.
Website: http://www.this-was-
tomorrow.net

References in text(s): 207

Transcultural Modernisms
Model House Research Group,
ed., *Transcultural Modernisms*
(Berlin: Sternberg Press, 2013)

Contributors: Fahim Amir, Eva
Egermann, Moira Hille, Jakob
Krameritsch, Christian Kravagna,
Christina Linortner, Marion von
Osten, and Peter Spillmann

Transcultural Modernisms
harvests the findings of the
Model House Research Group,
an interdisciplinary research
project group that investigated
the networks of transnational
encounters, exchanges, and
influences at play in the circulation
of architectural modernity. The
book departs from three case
studies examining housing projects
realized in eras of decolonization,
and includes analyses of housing
projects in India, Israel, Morocco,
and China. Unlike the well-
distributed narrative of modernism
moving from the global north to the
south, and from the west to the
rest of the world, *Transcultural
Modernisms* attests that
"modernity" is a circulatory
concept constantly subject to
renegotiation.

References in text(s): 60, 70

<u>Transit Migration</u> (with Regina Römhild), 2002–2006, transnational research group and project exhibition

Artistic direction by: Marion von Osten and Regina Römhild with Sophie Goltz and Sabine Hess Research by: Rutvica Andrijasevic, Manuela Bojadzijev, Serhat Karakayali, Efthimia Panagiotidis, and Vassilis Tsianos Artists: Al Abdani, Gülsün Karamustafa, Brigitta Kuster, TeleNovela, and Želimir Žilnik Co-produced by: Institute of Cultural Anthropology/European Ethnology, Goethe University, Frankfurt am Main; Institute for Theory of Design and Art at the Institute for Cultural Studies, Zurich University of the Arts, Zurich; and Labor k3000, Zurich with support from the German Federal Cultural Foundation, Halle

Transit Migration developed new research and production methods on the basis of collaborative, transdisciplinary cooperation between sociologists, political theorists, anthropologists, media activists, and artists. Set in the emergence of the European border regime, movements of transnational migration beyond its borders, and the governing actors within its border zones, the group studied representations and the representability of these realities in academic discourses, the media, and the arts. It resulted in a number of cultural productions, such as *MigMap* (2005), texts and analyses, workshops, publications, and international symposia (Crete, 2004 and Cologne, 2005). Since 2007, part of the group is organized as an independent association based in Berlin under the name Transit e.V./ Center for Post-Colonial Knowledge and Culture.

Website: http://www. transitmigration.org

References in text(s): 201, 225

Utopia, 1995, installation
consisting of lounge furniture,
plants, and botanic descriptions,
Department of Art History,
Bonn University, Bonn and
Lothringer13, Munich

The installation *Utopia* combined
research on historical imperial
overseas travel by Europeans and
plant "discoveries" claimed during
these missions with data on plant
breeding techniques, such as
genetic manipulation. Staged
in a lounge-chair environment
modeled after the entry halls of
many company offices, plants
were placed as office greenery.

References in text(s): 119

Viet Nam Discourse Stockholm
(with Center for Post-Colonial
Knowledge and Culture, Berlin),
2016, research and exhibition
project, Tensta konsthall,
Stockholm

Concept by: Marion von Osten
and Peter Spillmann (Center for
Post-Colonial Knowledge and
Culture, Berlin)
Co-produced by: Center for
Post-Colonial Knowledge and
Culture, Berlin; Tensta konsthall,
Stockholm; and University of
Dance and Circus, Stockholm
with support from the Creative
Europe Programme of the
European Union

As part of Tensta konsthall's
project *The Eros Effect: Art,
Solidarity Movements and the
Struggle for Social Justice*, von
Osten and Peter Spillmann
revisited the complex production
and cultural-political context of
the play *Viet Nam Diskurs* (1968),
written by artist and filmmaker
Peter Weiss. Dedicated to
Vietnamese liberation history and
movement, the play served as the
project's pivotal case study for
examining the interrelations
between international solidarity
movements of the 1960s and
1970s and the arts. Through a

variety of private archival material, testimonies—among others, that of stage designer Gunilla Palmstierna-Weiss—and a program of film screenings, the project investigated and activated the play's political potential.

·Image(s): 316–319

Walk and Talk (with Judith Hopf et al.), 1998, group performance, Hamburg

Written and performed by: Mercedes Bunz, Lukas Duwenhögger, Martin Ebner, Julian Göthe, Judith Hopf, Ariane Müller, Marion von Osten, Gunter Reski, Alexander Schröder, and Katharina Wulff

Walk and Talk was a series of performances within the larger project of *Park Fiction* (1994–ongoing), part of the Right to the City Network Hamburg, a network created in opposition to the urban building developments in the St. Pauli district. In the intervention, the group played well-known artists and writers (as well as sculptures and plants) who discussed "landmark" sculptural projects that intervened in public spaces. The audience was guided by the characters, such as novelist (Sidonie-Gabrielle) Colette who posthumously discussed with artist Daniel Buren his *Les Deux Plateaux* (1985) in Paris, and the commissioner, from the United States General Services Administration's Art in Architecture Program, of *Tilted Arc* in New York, who spoke with artist Richard Serra, played by von Osten, about a fictive

protest-intervention on the work,
which in reality had been removed
after public protests.

Image(s): 75; References in
text(s): 58–60

Many of these productions have
been realized over time, through
multiple iterations, and with several
contributors. The titles of these
productions are frequently used
in primary source documents in
variation. Eds.

Biography Marion von Osten

Marion von Osten is an artist, exhibition maker, researcher, and writer, as well as an editor, organizer-facilitator, and teacher. Her body of cultural practice is comprised of curatorial, artistic, and theoretical endeavors that are often distinctively collaborative, transnational, and transdisciplinary in their aims and approaches. Her exhibitions and research projects involve artists, scholars, activists, researchers, and (multi-media) designers, and include various media or formats—from installations, videos, netzines, texts, and publications, to exhibitions, screenings, conferences, and reading groups—functioning as discursive sites of knowledge production and exchange.

As they regularly originate from a feminist perspective and often both substantively and chronologically overlap, von Osten's projects and (written) works are closely interlinked. Several recurring topics include the legacy of modernism and its entanglement with anti-colonial struggles, the decolonizing of culture, and the autonomy of migration versus Europe's "border regime," its concurrent xenophobia, and its hostility. Other projects have involved continuous investigations into the labor and living conditions that mark precarious lives—those of cultural workers in particular—a topic that, through commonalities, is extended to various other issues, from wage labor in the fashion industry to the precarity of cultural institutions and universities, all prompted into reforms by neoliberalism's omnipresence.

Von Osten has co-initiated several long-term collaborations, such as: the Center for Post-Colonial Knowledge and Culture, Berlin (founded in 2007); the collective kleines postfordistisches Drama (kpD, 2003–2006); and Labor k3000, Zurich (founded in 1999), a transnational platform of artists, activists, and multimedia designers, which she founded with Peter Spillmann and has worked with extensively; as well as the artist collective MetaAusStelLung (MetaExhibition) (1987–1990).

Research and exhibition projects include: *Viet Nam Discourse Stockholm* (with Peter Spillmann), Tensta konsthall, Stockholm, 2016; *Tricontinentale.net*, Center for Post-Colonial Knowledge and Culture, Berlin, 2015; *Architectures de la Décolonisation*, Les Laboratoires d'Aubervilliers, Aubervilliers, 2012; *The American Home*, Hessel Museum, CCS Bard Center for Curatorial Studies and Hessel Museum of Art, Annandale-on-Hudson, 2011; *In the Desert of Modernity: Colonial Planning and After* (with Tom Avermaete and Serhat Karakayali), Haus der Kulturen der Welt, Berlin, 2008 and La Fabrique Culturelle des Anciens Abattoirs de Casablanca, Casablanca, 2009; <reformpause>, Kunstraum, Leuphana University of Lüneburg, Lüneburg, 2006; *Projekt Migration* (with Kathrin Rhomberg), various locations, initiated by Kunststiftung des Bundes, Halle, 2002–2006; *transnational europe I* (with Transit Migration), University of Crete, Rethymnon, 2004; *Be Creative! The Creative Imperative* (with Labor k3000), Museum für Gestaltung, Zurich, 2002–2003; *Atelier Europa* (with Angela McRobbie), Kunstverein München, Munich, 2003–2004; *Never Look Back*, Shedhalle Zürich, Zurich, 2001; *Utopian Spaces*, Labor k3000, Zurich, 1999; *MoneyNations II: For People on Their Way in Europe*, Kunsthalle Exnergasse, Vienna, 1999; *Public Utility*, Kombirama, Zurich, 1997; and *Sex & Space II, Space. Gender. Economy*, steirischer herbst festival Graz, 1997. As a curator at Shedhalle Zürich, Zurich, she organized and curated: *MoneyNations@access* (with Labor k3000), 1998;

SUPERmarkt: money, market, gender politics (with Pauline Boudry, Sylvia Kafhesy, Markus Maeder, and Peter Spillmann), 1998; *Alt.Use.Media*, 1997; *Netz. Punkt.Media* (with Radio LoRa), 1997; *The Funky Sight of Zürich*, 1996; *Irene ist Viele* (with Rachel Mader), 1996; and *Sex & Space: Space. Gender. Economy* (with Martine Anderfuhren, Rachel Mader, and Peter Spillmann), 1996. Others include: *Studio Hellerau*, Förderverein Hellerau e.V., Dresden, 1995; and *Connecting Things*, The Kitchen, New York, 1990.

Von Osten participated in exhibitions such as (selection): *The Eros Effect: Art, Solidarity Movements and the Struggle for Social Justices*, Tensta konsthall, Stockholm, 2015; *Sights and Sounds: Poland*, Jewish Museum, New York, 2014; *Der Ungeduld der Freiheit Gestalt zu geben*, Württembergischer Kunstverein, Stuttgart, 2013–2014; *Offside Effect*, 1st Tbilisi Triennial, Tbilisi, 2013; *Former West: Notes from Berlin*, BAK, basis voor actuele kunst, Utrecht, 2013; *Joyful Wisdom*, Rezan Has Museum, Kadir Has University, Istanbul, 2013; *Living as Form*, Creative Time, New York, 2011; *What is Waiting Out There*, 6th Berlin Biennale for Contemporary Art,

Berlin, 2010; and *Modernologies: Contemporary Artists Researching Modernity and Modernism*, Museum of Modern Art in Warsaw, Warsaw and MACBA (Museu d'Art Contemporani de Barcelona), Barcelona, 2009.

She has contributed to several printed and online publications, and was (co-)editor of the following publications: *Transcultural Modernisms* (with Model House Research Group), Berlin: Sternberg Press, 2013; *Colonial Modern: Aesthetics of the Past, Rebellions for the Future* (with Tom Avermaete and Serhat Karakayali), London: Black Dog Publishing, 2010; *Das Erziehungsbild: Zur visuellen Kultur des Pädagogischen* (with Tom Holert), Vienna: Schlebrügge.Editor, 2010; *MoneyNations: Constructing the Border – Constructing East-West* (with Peter Spillmann), Vienna: edition selene, 2003; *Norm der Abweichung*, Vienna and Zurich: Springer and Edition Voldemeer, 2003; *Das Phantom sucht seinen Mörder: Ein Reader zur Kulturalisierung der Ökonomie* (with Justin Hoffmann), Berlin: b_books, 1999; *MoneyNations@ acccess: The Correspondent*, Zurich: Shedhalle Zürich, 1998; and *Sex & Space II: Space.*

Gender. Economy (with Wolfgang Zinganel), Zurich: Shedhalle Zürich, 1997.

Currently, von Osten is a co-curator of the research and exhibition project *Migrant Bauhaus* (with Grant Watson), various locations, 2017–2019, a guest professor at the Lucerne School of Art and Design, Lucerne, a lecturer at the master's Fine Art program at MaHKU, Utrecht Graduate School of Visual Art and Design, Utrecht, Honorary Professor at the Academy of Fine Arts Vienna, Vienna, and a PhD candidate in Fine Arts at the Malmö Art Academy, Malmö. Von Osten lives and works in Berlin since 1991, and was born as Marion Schmidt in Dortmund in 1963.

Contributors

<u>Kader Attia</u> is an artist who works with installation, photography, and sculpture. His work frequently explores the wide-ranging effects of western cultural hegemony and colonialism on non-western cultures, creating a genealogy of our globalized world through investigating the identity politics of historical and colonial eras. In recent years, Attia has thematically focused on the concept of "repair," considering it a constant on which western modernity and traditional extra-occidental thought have historically had opposing views. His selected exhibitions include: *Sacrifice and Harmony*, MMK Museum für Moderne Kunst, Frankfurt am Main, 2016; *Kader Attia: Injuries Are Here*, Musée Cantonal des Beaux-Arts de Lausanne, Lausanne, 2015; *Contre Nature*, Beirut Art Center, Beirut, 2014; and *Continuum of Repair: The Light of Jacob's Ladder*, Whitechapel Gallery, London, 2013–2014. Attia lives and works in Berlin and Algiers.

<u>Sabeth Buchmann</u> is an art historian and art critic. She is Professor of Modern and Postmodern Art at the Academy of Fine Arts Vienna, Vienna, and a co-editor of *PoLYpeN*, a book series on art criticism and political theory. Buchmann is a co-founder of the artist, theater, and author group *minimal club* (Munich and Berlin, 1983–1999). Recent publications include: *Putting Rehearsals to the Test: Practices of Rehearsal in Fine Arts, Film, Theater, Theory, and Politics* (co-edited with Ilse Lafer and Constanze Ruhm, 2016); *art works: Ästhetik des Postfordismus* (with Netzwerk Kunst & Arbeit, 2015); and *Textile Theorien der Moderne: Alois Riegl in der Kunstkritik* (co-edited with Rike Frank, 2015). Among her recent curatorial projects are: *Putting Rehearsals to the Test* (with Ilse Lafer and Constanze Ruhm), Galerie Leonard & Bina Ellen Art Gallery, Montréal, SBC Gallery of Contemporary Art, Montréal, and VOX—Centre de l'image contemporaine, Montréal, 2016; and *Ready to Sleep*, Galerie Mezzanin, Vienna, 2014. Buchmann lives and works in Berlin and Vienna.

<u>Diedrich Diederichsen</u> is a cultural critic and music journalist whose work explores the intersections of contemporary art and music, with a particular focus on pop culture. He teaches at Merz Akademie, Stuttgart and the Academy of Fine Arts Vienna, Vienna and writes regularly for *Artforum* and *Texte zur Kunst*. He was an editor of the German magazine *SOUNDS* in the early 1980s and the editor in chief of the influential magazine *Spex – Magazin für Popkultur* in the 1990s. Selected publications include: "Art et Non-art," *Revue Incise*, no. 2 (2015); "River of Many Returns," in *Matthew Barney: River of Fundament*, edited by Okwui Enwezor (2014); and "Mourning States and Their Minimalist Citizens: On European Memorial Culture," in *The Way of the Shovel: On the Archaeological Imaginary in Art,* edited by Dieter Roelstraete (2013). Diederichsen lives and works in Vienna.

<u>Tom Holert</u> is an art historian and writer. He recently co-founded the Harun Farocki Institut, Berlin and is currently finishing a book-length study on contemporary art and knowledge politics. An exhibition on writer Carl Einstein and the thresholds of the avant-garde around 1930 is forthcoming at Haus der Kulturen der Welt, Berlin, (with Anselm Franke), 2018, and his recent research on spaces of knowledge and learning has led to the exhibition *Learning Laboratories: Architecture, Instructional Technology, and the Social Production of Pedagogical Space Around 1970*, BAK, basis voor actuele kunst, Utrecht, 2016–2017. Among his books are: *Übergriffe: Zustände und Zuständigkeiten der Gegenwartskunst* (2014); *Regieren im Bildraum* (2008); and *Fliehkraft: Gesellschaft in Bewegung – von Migranten und Touristen* (with Mark Terkessidis, 2006). Holert is a (co-)editor of *Troubling Research: Performing Knowledge in the Arts* (with Carola Dertnig and Diedrich Diederichsen, 2014); *Das Erziehungsbild: Zur visuellen Kultur des Pädagogischen* (with Marion von Osten, 2010); and *Imagineering: Visuelle Kultur und Politik der Sichtbarkeit* (2000). Holert lives and works in Berlin.

Judith Hopf is an artist who works with film, sculpture, installation, and performance. She is Professor of Fine Art at Staatliche Hochschule für Bildende Kunste – Städelschule, Frankfurt am Main. Her work frequently explores themes of normativity and exclusion, often focusing on the ways in which institutionalized roles and behaviors influence the development of individual subjectivities. Selected solo exhibitions include: *UP*, Museion, Bolzano, 2016; *More*, Neue Galerie, Kassel, 2015–2016; and *Testing Time,* Studio Voltaire, London, 2013. Hopf lives and works in Berlin.

Brian Kuan Wood is a writer and editor. He teaches at the master's program in Curatorial Practice at the School of Visual Arts, New York and is an editor of *Tamawuj.org,* the online publishing platform of the Sharjah Biennial 13. In 2008, he co-founded *e-flux journal*. Kuan Wood lives and works in New York.

Isabell Lorey is a political theorist at the European Institute for Progressive Cultural Policies (eipcp) and an editor of *transversal texts*. She is Professor of Political Theory at the University of Kassel, Kassel and has been a guest professor at the Center for Gender Studies at the University of Basel, Basel (2012–2015). From 2001–2007, she held a professorship for Gender and Postcolonial Studies at the Berlin University of the Arts, Berlin and, together with Marion von Osten, was a founding member of kleines postfordistisches Drama (kpD). She has published on the precarization of labor and life in neoliberalism, democracy and representation, and political immunization. Her recent books include: *Immer Ärger mit dem Subjekt. Theoretische und politische Konsequenzen eines juridischen Machtmodells: Judith Butler* (republished 2017); *State of Insecurity: Government of the Precarious* (2015); and *Figuren des Immunen: Elemente einer politischen Theorie (2011)*. Her book on presentist democracy is forthcoming in 2018. Lorey lives and works in Berlin.

Angela McRobbie is a cultural theorist and commentator whose work combines the study of popular culture, contemporary media practices, feminist theory, the global fashion industry, and creative labor and the modern work economy. She is Professor of Communications at the Department of Media and Communications at Goldsmiths, University of London, London. Her recent publications include: *Be Creative: Making a Living in the New Culture Industries* (2015), *Top Girls: Feminismus und der Aufstieg des neoliberalen Geschlechterregimes* (2010), and *The Aftermath of Feminism: Gender, Culture and Social Change* (2009). McRobbie also contributed to the research project *Making a Living as a Visual Artist in 4 European Cities: London, Berlin, Glasgow and Vienna* (with Marion von Osten), Academy of Fine Arts Vienna, Vienna, 2008. McRobbie lives and works in London and Berlin.

Peter Spillmann is an artist, curator, and cultural producer. He currently teaches art and is researching at the Lucerne School of Art and Design, Lucerne. He is a founding member of the art collective Labor k3000, based in Zurich and Berlin, and the Center for Post-colonial Knowledge and Culture, Berlin. His research frequently focuses on artistic techniques of space exploration and mapping, cultural effects of globalization, and postcolonial perspectives. His recent projects include: *Viet Nam Discourse Stockholm* (with Marion von Osten), Tensta konsthall, Stockholm, 2016; and contributions to *Model House— Mapping Transcultural Modernisms* (with Model House Research Group), Academy of Fine Arts Vienna, Vienna, 2010–2013; *In the Desert of Modernity: Colonial Planning and After,* La Fabrique Culturelle des Anciens Abattoirs de Casablanca, Casablanca, 2009; and *Projekt Migration*, Kölnischer Kunstverein, Cologne, 2002–2006. Spillmann lives and works in Zurich and Berlin.

Marina Vishmidt is a writer and lecturer in Culture Industry at Goldsmiths, University of London, London, where she convenes a course on theories and practices of creativity, labor, and precarity. She runs a theory seminar at the Dutch Art Institute, Arnhem and her work has appeared in *South Atlantic Quarterly, ephemera, Afterall, Journal of Cultural Economy, Australian Feminist Studies*, and *Radical Philosophy*, among others, as well as a number of edited volumes. She is a co-author of *Reproducing Autonomy: Work, Money, Crisis and Contemporary Art* (with Kerstin Stakemeier, 2016), and is currently completing a book-length project entitled *Speculation as a Mode of Production* (2017). Vishmidt lives and works in London.

Tirdad Zolghadr is a curator
and writer. He is the director of
Sommerakademie im Zentrum
Paul Klee, Bern, an associate
curator at KW Institute for
Contemporary Art, Berlin, and
teaches at the Dutch Art Institute,
Arnhem. His most recent book is
Traction (2016). His curatorial
work includes biennial settings as
well as numerous long-term,
research-driven projects.

Acknowledgments/ Financial Partners

We thank all participating artists, writers, and other art practitioners involved in the realization of this reader, as well as the individuals listed here, who have contributed generously in a variety of ways to make this publication possible: Lise Hermans and Asja Novak, BAK, basis voor actuele kunst, Utrecht; Silvan Hillmann and Katharina Morawek, Shedhalle Zürich, Zurich; and Dorothee Richter, Zurich University of the Arts, Zurich. Above all, we thank Marion von Osten for her challenging work, remarkable engagement, and generosity throughout our collaboration.

Marion von Osten wishes to thank: the BAK team and especially the editors of the book, Maria Hlavajova and Tom Holert, as well as Lucy Lopez and Hidde van Greuningen, for the strong intent and energy that has made this project possible, as well as all writers for their fantastic contributions: Kader Attia, Sabeth Buchmann, Diedrich Diederichsen, Judith Hopf, Brian Kuan Wood, Isabell Lorey, Angela McRobbie, Peter Spillmann, Marina Vishmidt, and Tirdad Zolghadr. My thanks also go to collaborators, advisors, and friends who have discussed with me over many years, shared ideas and works, as well as made projects finally possible: Fahim Amir, Edit András, Horst Antes, Lotte Arndt, Julie Ault, Tom Avermaete, Marion Baruch, Martin Beck, Jochen Becker, Madeleine Bernstorff, Beatrice von Bismarck, Pauline Boudry, Joanna Burton, Binna Choi, Nelleke Deen, Dana Diminescu, Helmut Draxler, Lukas Duwenhögger, Eva Egermann, Antje Ehmann, Angelika Engberg, Harun Farocki, Jesko Fezer, Benedikt Forster, Rike Frank, Ingrid and Rolf Funk, Sabine Gebhardt Fink, Wolfgang Gopon, Julian Göthe, Søren Grammel, Olivier Hadouchi, Nav Haq, Johanna Henkel, Leo Florus Henkel, Claudia Honecker, Jörg Huber, Serhat Karakayali, Gülsün Karamustafa, Nathalie Koger, Christian Kravagna, Mona Kuschel, Brigitta Kuster, Élisabeth Lebovici, Susanne Leeb, Maria Lind, Thomas Locher, Geert Lovink, Rachel Mader, Marcus Maeder, Sarat Maharaj, Ivana Marjanović, Andreas Müller, Bonaventure Soh Bejeng Ndikung, Doina Petrescu, Nataša Petrešin-Bachelez, Catherine Queloz, Karin Rebbert, Juliane Rebentisch, Katja Reichard, Kathrin Rhomberg, Irit Rogoff, Regina Römhild, Gertrud Sandqvist, Bernd Scherer, Anette Schindler, Helga and Gerd Schmidt, Cornelia Schmidt-Bleek, Andreas Schnelle, Bernd Schurer, Felicity Scott, Nathalie Seitz,

Simon Sheikh, Mischa Sideris,
Vassilis Tsianos, Anna Voswinckel,
Martin Warnke, Joanna Warsza,
Hermann Weber, Daniel Weiss,
Axel John Wieder, Ulf Wuggenig,
Florian Zeyfang, and Želimir Žilnik.
I would also like to thank my
four-legged companion species
for bringing me up and down right
when it was needed. And above all,
I thank my partner, my companion,
and collaborator Peter Spillmann
for his unlimited friendship and
support.

The activities of BAK, basis voor
actuele kunst have been made
possible with financial support
from the Ministry of Education,
Culture and Science, the
Netherlands and City Council,
Utrecht.

Ministerie van Onderwijs, Cultuur en
Wetenschap

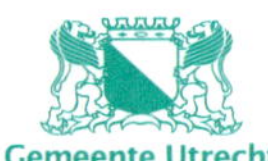

Gemeente Utrecht

Index

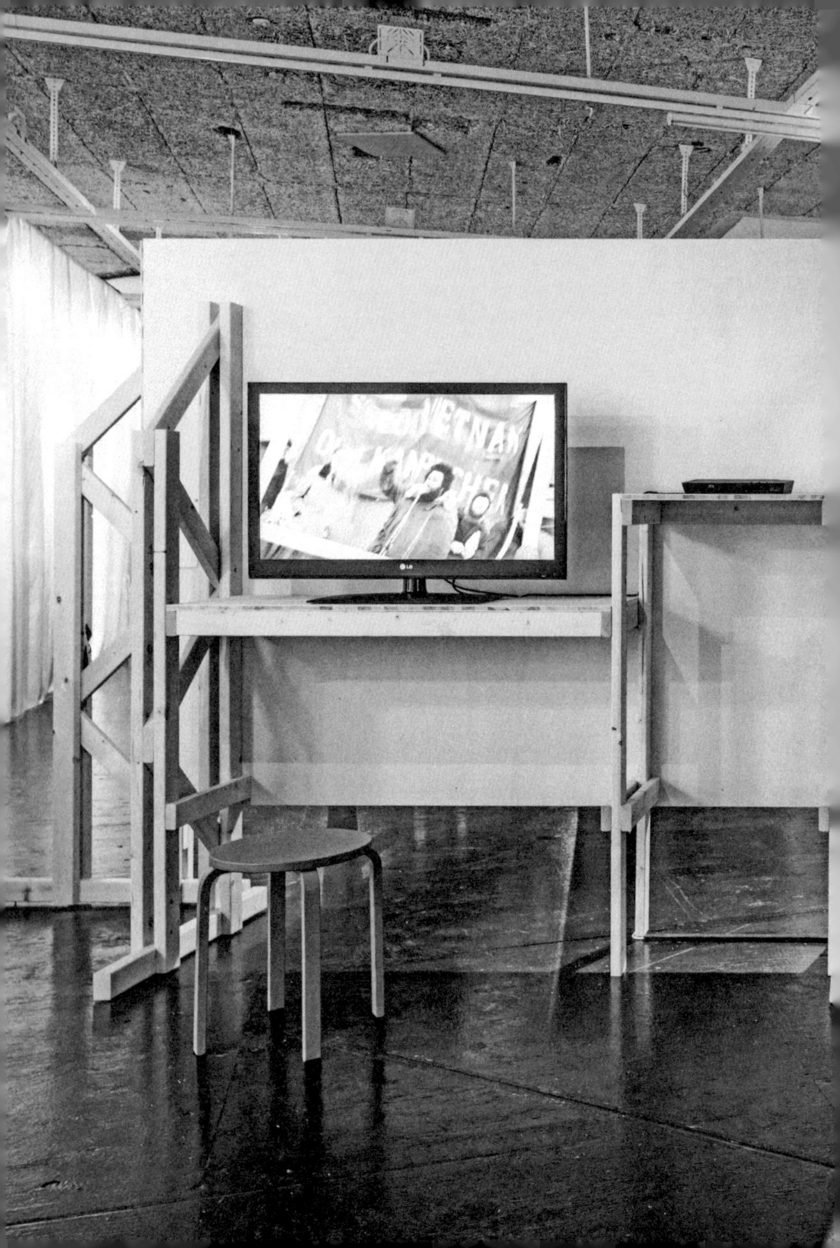
VIETNAM
KAMPUCHEA

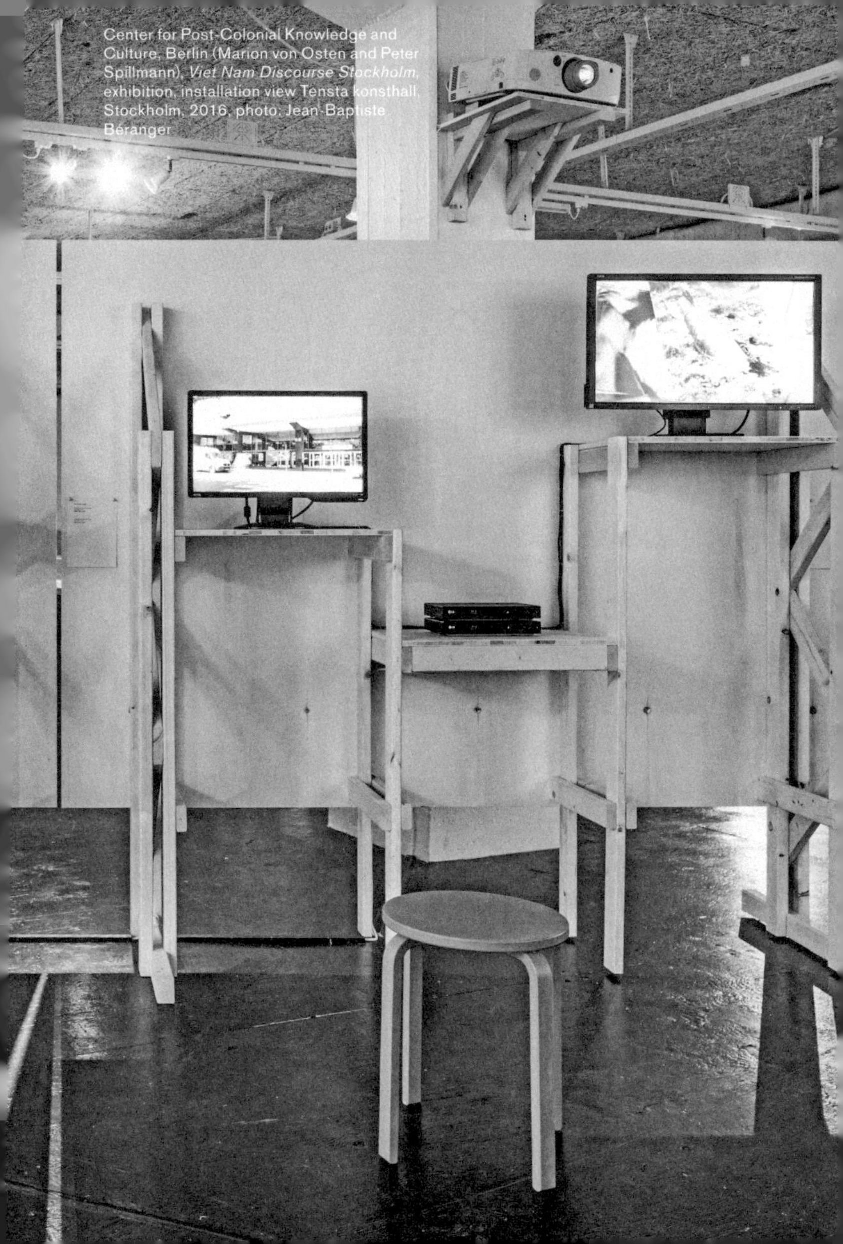

Center for Post-Colonial Knowledge and Culture, Berlin (Marion von Osten and Peter Spillmann), *Viet Nam Discourse Stockholm*, exhibition, installation view Tensta konsthall, Stockholm, 2016, photo: Jean-Baptiste Béranger

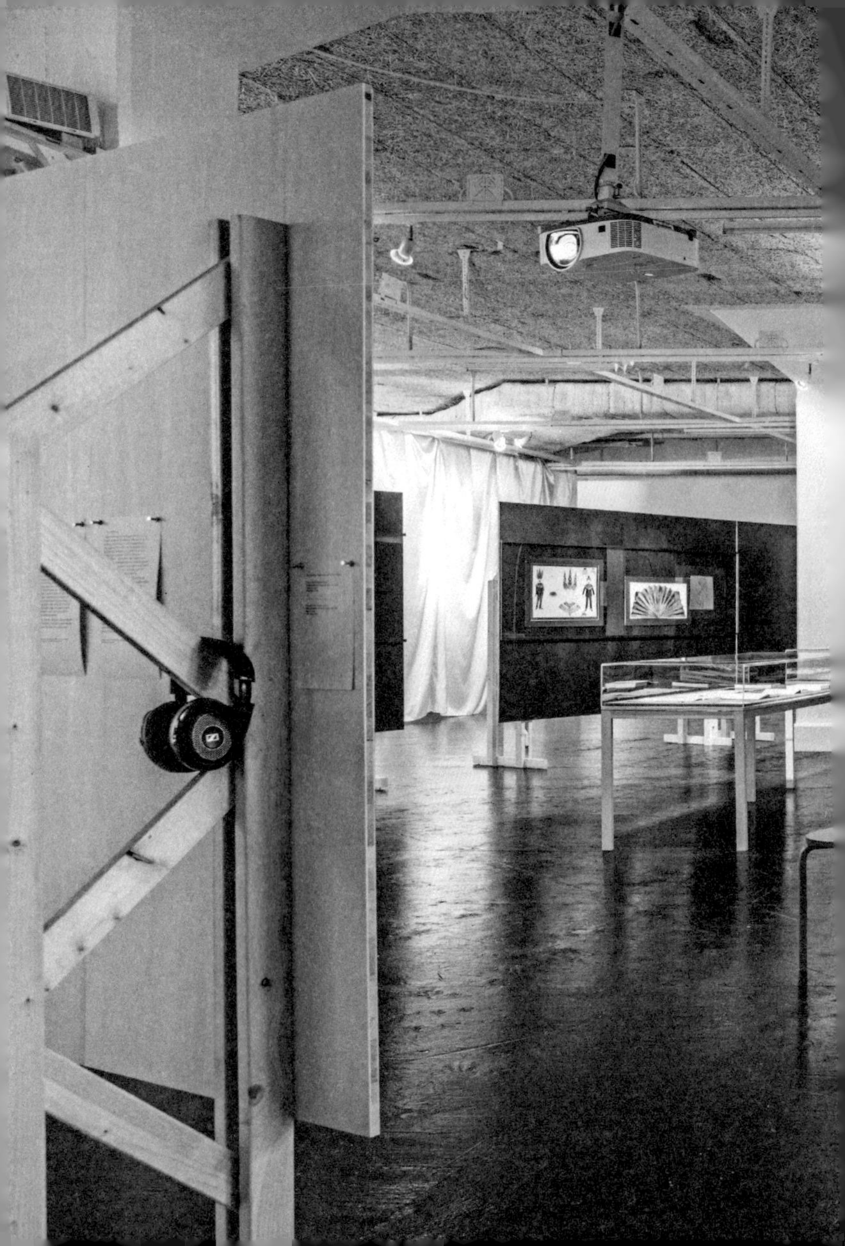

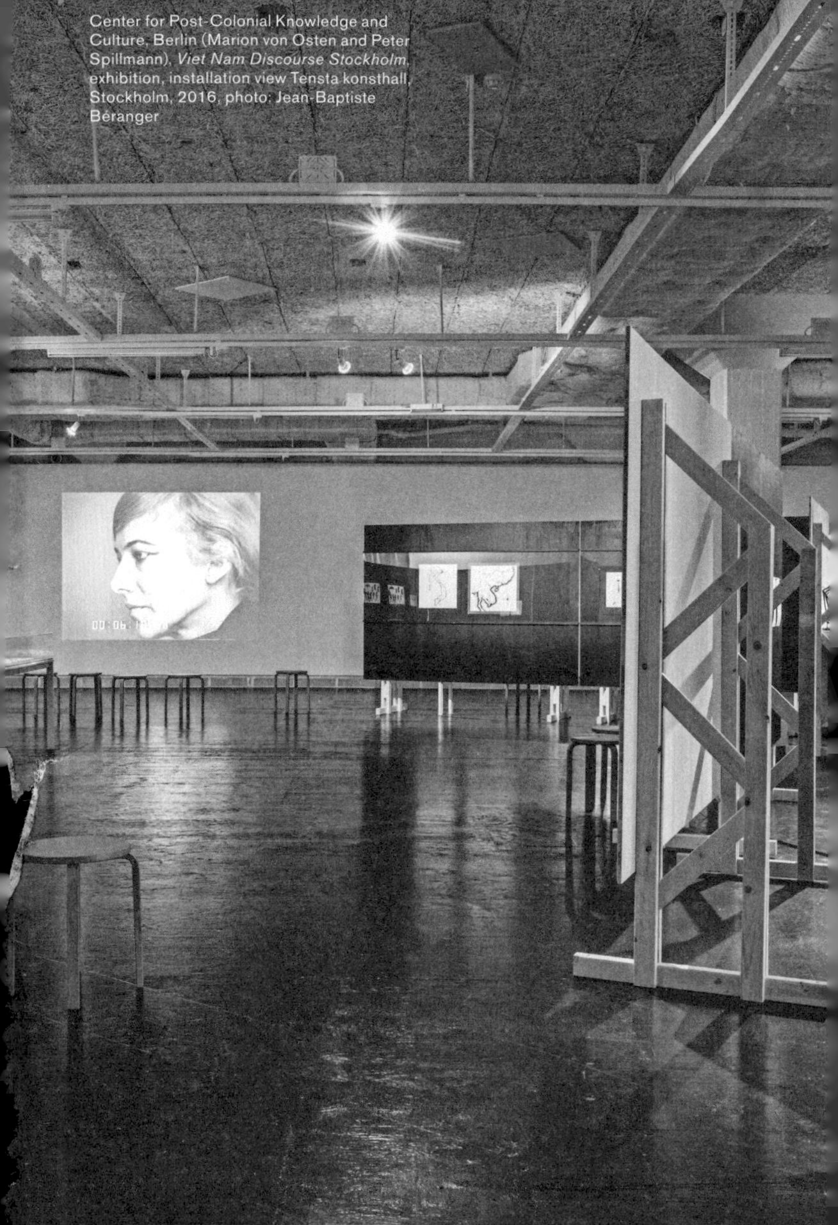

Center for Post-Colonial Knowledge and Culture, Berlin (Marion von Osten and Peter Spillmann), *Viet Nam Discourse Stockholm*, exhibition, installation view Tensta konsthall, Stockholm, 2016, photo: Jean-Baptiste Béranger